TRIGGER HAPPY

Steven Poole was born in London in 1972, and read English at Cambridge. He writes for the *Guardian*, the *Independent* and the *Times Literary Supplement*, and has also worked as a composer for television and short film. In his spare time he saves the planet from zombies and plays chess.

TRIGGER

the inner life of videogames

HAPPY

STEVEN POOLE

FOURTH ESTATE • London

First published in Great Britain in 2000 by
Fourth Estate Limited
6 Salem Road
London W2 4BU
www.4thestate.co.uk

Quote on p. vii from 'Burnt Norton' from Four Quartets in
Collected Poems 1909–1962 by T. S. Eliot published courtesy of
Faber and Faber Ltd. Extracts from *Invasion of the Space Invaders*
(1982) by Martin Amis published courtesy of The Wylie Agency.
Every effort has been made by the author to clear permission on
copyrighted material. Please contact the publishers if any oversight
has been made.

1 3 5 7 9 10 8 6 4 2

A catalogue record for this book is available from the
British Library.

ISBN 1-84115-121-1

Typeset by Rowland Phototypesetting Limited,
Bury St Edmunds, Suffolk
Printed in Great Britain by Clays Ltd, St Ives plc.

TO MY PARENTS

'Man is the plaything of the gods, and that is the best of him; and so we should play the noblest games.'

PLATO

'Human kind cannot bear very much reality.'

T. S. ELIOT

'Aha!'

LARA CROFT

CONTENTS

1

RESISTANCE IS FUTILE

Our virtual history

In the beginning, the planet was dead.

Suddenly, millions of years ago, arcane spontaneous chemical reactions in the primeval ooze resulted, by a freak cosmic chance, in the first appearance of what we now call 'the code of life'. Formed in knotty binary strings, each node representing information by its state of 'on' or 'off' and its place in the series, the code grew adept at replicating in ever more complex structures. Eventually, the organisations of code became so dense that an overarching property emerged which could not be explained by reference to any of the constituent parts. This was 'life' itself.

The first videogame formed in the sludge. It was a simple organism, but a father to us all. Soon enough (in geological terms) videogames crawled out on to the shore, developed rudimentary eyes and legs, and gradually began to conquer Earth.

Biologically speaking, early videogames were, as they are today, radically exogamous – that is to say, they did not replicate by breeding with each other, but with 'humans', a pre-existing carbon-based lifeform whose purpose was, and still is, unknown but seemingly providential. If the videogame managed to impart particularly intense pleasure to a parasitic human during the reproductive act, the chances of its offspring surviving were enhanced. Obviously, videogames were programmed by Nature to be as promiscuous as possible: the more humans impregnated with code, the more likely that some of the next generation would survive to breed in their turn. The work of such genetic programming persists in the primeval substratum even of modern, sophisticated videogame civilisation.

Over this vast meander of time, the pressures of adapting to

15

varied conditions prompted the formation of different genera and species of organism with different habitats, social structures and breeding strategies. The fittest survived.

But nothing could be certain in the great evolutionary game. Some seemingly successful species found it impossible to adapt swiftly enough to catastrophic changes in the environment, and died out. They were the dinosaurs. (By copying their 'code' and letting it gestate under laboratory conditions, however, we can actually bring these fossils to life again, and let them roam happy, if confused, in virtual amusement parks.)

Nor was this evolution a gradual and inexorable expansion of possibilities and types. There seems to be no final goal to the random machinations of Nature. Some species of game, for example, turned at certain points down evolutionary blind alleys and failed to develop, concentrating instead, like the peacock, on attracting partners with ever more lurid visual displays. Other species merged, pooling resources and erasing previous distinctions to become the great games that we know and love.

The narrative of these manifold splittings and fusings, this world-historical struggle of the will encoded in our deepest selves, is not a mere just-so story for the young. For through the noble history of videogame species, with due homage made to the great examples that have paved the way for us, the heroic story unfolds of how we came to be the planet's masters. Remember, humans, it's not how you play the game that counts, it's whether you win or lose.

>*Player 1 Ready*

01011111101010100111110101011111111101010100 11
00111111001010100010000001010101000000011111100101110
10100100001010001111010010101001001010100010110111

Pixel generation

Like millions of people, I love videogames. I also love books, music and chess. That's not unusual. For most of my generation, videogames are just part of the cultural furniture. In particular, videogames, among people all over the world, are a social pleasure. The post-pub PlayStation session is one of the joys of modern British life.

Videogames are in one sense just another entertainment choice – but compared to many, a much more *interesting* one. And yet there seems to be a fear that videogames are somehow nudging out other artforms, and that we're encouraging a generation of screen-glazed androids with no social skills, poetical sensitivity or entrepreneurial ambition. But new forms don't replace the old. Film did not replace theatre. The Internet did not replace the book. Videogames have been around for thirty years, and they're not going away.

When I was ten years old, my parents bought me a home computer. It was a ZX Spectrum, brainchild of the celebrated British inventor Sir Clive Sinclair (this was before he went on to create the savagely unsuccessful electric tricycle called the C5). The entire computer was about half the size of a modern PC keyboard, and it plugged into a normal television. It was black, with little grey squidgy keys and a rainbow stripe over one corner. Tiny blocky characters would move around blocky landscapes lavishly painted in eight colours, while the black box beeped and burped. It was pure witchcraft. But the magic wasn't simply done *to* me; it was a spell I could dive into. I could swim happily in this world, at once mysterious and utterly logical, of insubstantial light.

Doubtless my parents imagined the Spectrum would be educational. In a way it was, for very soon I was an expert at setting exactly the right recording levels on hi-fi equipment to ensure a perfect copy of a hot new game. (In those days, videogames came on cassette, and I would swap copies and hints with my schoolfriends.) For many years, the myriad delights that videogames offered were a reliable evening escape, their names now a peculiarly evocative roll-call of sepia-tinged pleasures: Jet Pac, Ant Attack, Manic Miner, Knight Lore, Way of the Exploding Fist, Dark Star ... Then I decided, at the age of sixteen, to put away childish things. So I bought a guitar and formed a skate-punk heavy-metal band.

While I was away practising my axe heroics, home computers – the ZX Spectrum and Commodore 64, as well as a later, more powerful generation comprising the Atari ST and

Commodore Amiga – were gradually being supplanted by home videogame consoles. These little plastic boxes could not be programmed by the user, and the games came on cartridge rather than on cassette tape. The big players in the late 1980s and early 1990s were two Japanese giants: Nintendo, with its Nintendo Entertainment System (or Famicom) and the more powerful Super NES; and Sega, with its Megadrive. Each company was represented by its own digital mascot: Nintendo had Mario, the world-famous moustachioed plumber, and Sega had Sonic, a cheeky blue hedgehog.

Already by this stage a great number of teenagers were more interested in videogames than in pop music. And Nintendo and Sega inspired fanatical loyalty. They were the Beatles and Stones of the late 1980s and early 1990s. Nintendo was the Beatles: wholesome fun for all the family, with superior artistry but a slightly 'safe' image; Sega, on the other hand, were the snarling, street-smart gang, roughing it up for the hardcore videogame fans.

As videogaming culture grew and the games became ever more complex and adventurous (with ever larger profits to be made), the hardware companies realised that technology had to keep pace with the designers' ambitions. The seemingly unassailable Nintendo, having seen enormous success with the 1989 launch of the handheld Game Boy, decided to soup up the SNES by adding a CD-ROM drive. CD-ROMs hold a lot more information than cartridges, so the games could be even bigger in scope. But Nintendo had no expertise in that area of hardware, so they hooked up with Japanese audio giants Sony, manufacturers of hi-fi and inventors of the Walkman. It seemed like a marriage made in heaven.

But after various behind-the-scenes shenanigans, Nintendo pulled out of the deal. It was to lose them their market pre-eminence, because Sony weren't happy about being messed around by the arrogant Mario machine, and decided to go it alone and muscle in on the videogames business themselves. Thus the Sony PlayStation was born. On its launch in 1995 it blew Sega's new machine, the Saturn, out of the water. Nintendo, meanwhile, didn't have a competitive console out until two years later: the Nintendo 64, which had a handful of brilliant games but was woefully under-supported by most software developers. The landscape of power had irrevocably shifted while my back was turned.

Apart from the odd blast in an arcade, I hadn't thought about videogames again. Then, one summer, I was staying in a friend's Edinburgh flat while watching more or less disastrous pieces of fringe theatre at the rate of three or four a day. The odorous broom-cupboard I was sleeping in had only one particularly interesting piece of furniture: a PlayStation. My friend introduced me to something called WipEout 2097, a fast, futuristic hover-racing game. My jaw dropped.

Over the previous decade, it seemed, videogames had really grown up. This was an amazing, sense-battering, physically thrilling trip. Artistically, it felt superior to anything I had seen on the Fringe. And so, after sacrificing most of my sleep during that Edinburgh stay to improving my lap times, I decided I needed to buy a PlayStation of my own. Perhaps one day, I thought, I might even write something about videogames.

So I bought the console. And then I had to buy a few games. Soul Blade (fighting), WipEout 2097 (racing), Tomb Raider (Lara Croft) – that would do for starters. On second thoughts, better add V-Rally (more racing) and Crash Bandicoot (marsupial wrangling). My research had to be dutifully wide-ranging, didn't it? Soon, I also bought the Nintendo 64, which slotted neatly on to my shelves with Super Mario 64 and 1080° Snowboarding. Now they're joined by a Dreamcast (Sega's re-entry into the market), and a PlayStation2, the dazzling new superconsole from Sony.

It hasn't been cheap. But my experience is one that's shared by millions of people all over the planet. Indeed, this acceleration in videogame evolution would not have been possible otherwise.

Meme machines

Videogames today are monstrously big business. Their present status is largely to do with the shift in demographics, of which I was a part. In the 1980s, videogames were indeed mainly a children's pursuit, but now games cost between £30 and £45 and are targeted at the disposable income of adults. The average age of videogame players is now estimated to be twenty-one; one 1998 survey reported that 63 per cent of all US videogamers are over eighteen, with a full 29 per cent thirty-six years of age or older.* More and more grown-ups choose to play videogames rather than watch TV or go to the cinema. According to the European Leisure Software Publishers' Association, the British videogame market already grosses 60 per cent more than total cinema box-office receipts in this country, and 80 per cent more than video rentals. How did this strange invasion happen? How did this stealthy virus insinuate itself into so many homes?

Well, one company has done more than any other over the last six years to stake out videogames' huge place in adult popular culture: Sony, manufacturers of the PlayStation, the unassuming grey box that reinvigorated my own interest and that of so many others. The last time they counted, Sony had sold five million PlayStations in the UK alone. 'The focus for the brand,' explains Guy Pearce, Sony's UK PR manager, 'is eighteen to twenty-five. That's the age group we aim at, and always have done.'

Sony's initial stroke of marketing brilliance was to release an early game, 1995's WipEout, with a thumping techno soundtrack featuring well-known electronic acts of the calibre of Orbital, Leftfield and the Chemical Brothers. The success of this product had the Prodigy and Underworld clamouring to provide tracks for the sequel. Sony had a PlayStation room built in London superclub the Ministry of Sound, and got its logo on to club flyers all over the country. Soon PlayStation was happily associated with dance culture, with enthusiastic support from early adopters such as the band Massive Attack, who had bought theirs while on tour in Japan. Control of the soundtrack to the third game in the series, 1999's Wip3out, was handed over to superstar DJ Sasha, thus ensuring another

---

* According to figures published in the Interactive Digital Software Association's fourth annual *Video and PC Game Industry Trends Survey*, 1998.

soundtrack cleverly poised between cutting-edge and mass-appeal dance music.

Sony targeted the youth market with intelligent aggression. During the 1995 Glastonbury Festival, they distributed thousands of perforated cards adorned with PlayStation logos, which could be torn up to make convenient roaches for marijuana joints – or, as Sony claimed, to dispose of chewing gum.

And then God created woman. Enter Lara Croft, the pistol-toting, ponytailed, hotpants-and-shades-wearing digital star of a revolutionary 1996 game, Tomb Raider. Much has been written about her. She has been on the cover of *The Face* and the subject of countless Sunday-supplement articles. The publisher of Tomb Raider, Eidos, was named Britain's most successful company in any industry in 1999. It has sold more than sixteen million copies worldwide of the first three games in the series. Add a conservative estimate for sales of the fourth instalment, Tomb Raider: The Last Revelation, and Lara's getting on for being a billion-dollar babe.

Lara is such a recognisable icon that she now advertises other products, appearing, for example, in computer-generated television commercials for Lucozade. *Generation X* author Douglas Coupland contributed to the devotional tome *Lara's Book*; the Germans have a monthly magazine dedicated to her. In the summer of 1999, Lara could be seen hanging from the back of buses all over London. Jeremy Smith, managing director of Lara's birthplace, Core Design, points out what a gift her exploding profile was to the company: 'Who knows how many millions and millions of pounds' worth of free marketing we got from the press, by them putting it in front of people who'd then think, "Well, wow, that looks like a great game." We could *never* have spent that sort of money on the marketing that we got from the media.' And of course, Lara's contribution to the PlayStation brand itself cannot be overestimated. An exclusivity deal with Sony ensured that the next three games appeared only on PlayStation, and a Tomb Raider game will no doubt accelerate sales of PlayStation2.

These days, videogames generate a large spin-off industry of playing cards, posters, strategy guides, clothes and plastic figurines. In the summer of 1999, sales of Bandai's Duke

Nukem action figures soared, with the majority of purchasers being women. (Duke is the testosterone-dripping digital hero of humorous shoot-the-aliens games. He sports a blond crop and mirrored shades and uses arch catchphrases such as, 'It's time to chew gum and kick ass!') Bandai claimed to have received an 'anxious' call from a woman after her local store ran out of Nukem figures. According to their press release, she claimed that 1990s women were turning away from Ann Summers and Tupperware parties in favour of Duke Nukem evenings. Even if this is just a tease, it is illuminating that Bandai feel the potential female audience is large enough for them to make such a claim.

Game companies have also cultivated strong commercial links with the UK's biggest game, football. Videogame companies pay stars like Michael Owen and Alan Shearer to endorse their football games. In 1997, Sony paid £10 million to sponsor the UEFA Champions League. For the 1999/2000 football season, Sega paid to put the Dreamcast logo on the shirts of European football teams Arsenal, Sampdoria and St Etienne. This was just part of a $100 million marketing campaign for the European launch of the new console. In addition, an extra $20 to $30 million was earmarked for each key game.

And videogames have gradually become a marketing medium in their own right. My first experience of the PlayStation, WipEout 2097, featured neon advertisements for Diesel jeans and Red Bull caffeine drinks that flashed by as you sped round its virtual racecourses. Stockholm company Addgames released Mall Maniacs in 1999, a bizarre 'virtual supermarket' game whose entire development costs were covered by retail companies paying to have reconstructed presences in the digital world.

The music industry, too, is slowly waking up to the commercial possibilities of placing an artist's song in a videogame. British rock band Ash are rumoured to have earned around £600,000 in royalties by licensing just one song to the hit driving game Gran Turismo. Gremlin's Actua Ice Hockey 2 has a soundtrack entirely by cult post-rockers Mogwai, whose faces have also been digitised and slapped on to the team members' heads. Trent Reznor, the man behind industrial-techno outfit Nine Inch Nails, composed the soundtrack for Quake. CDs of specially written videogame music now regularly enter the pop charts in Japan, and America's National Academy of Recording Arts and Sciences has confirmed that videogame music will be honoured at the 43rd Grammy Awards in 2001.

Videogames now have such a potent influence on other forms of entertainment that they raise a clutch of questions about what they really have in common with the older forms. For example, David Bowie, well known as a man with an eye for the next big thing, wrote and performed (with guitarist Reeves Gabrels) an entire concept album for the soundtrack to the 1999 videogame Omikron: the Nomad Soul. At the Los Angeles press conference to announce this collaboration, Bowie said he approached the project as he would a film, 'to provide an emotional heart to the game'. And it doesn't stop there: the rock star's involvement extends to being a digitised character in the game itself.

Videogames also extend their silvery tentacles into the worlds of film and books. *Star Wars* director George Lucas has had his own videogames division, the widely respected LucasArts, for many years; Sega put up a chunk of the budget for David Cronenberg's movie *eXistenZ*; and Japanese software giant Square is making an $80 million computer-generated feature film based on its enormously successful Final Fantasy games, with voices provided by Hollywood stars Steve Buscemi, James Woods and Donald Sutherland. Amazingly, videogames now compete directly with the cinema in terms of financial returns. Over the six-week Christmas 1998 period in the US, one videogame, Nintendo's Legend of Zelda: Ocarina of Time, grossed $160 million, well outpacing the most popular film, Disney's *A Bug's Life*.

Meanwhile, thriller novelist Tom Clancy now writes scenarios for videogames produced by his own company, Red Storm, so that eventually his paper-based products may be demoted to the status of videogame tie-ins. Michael Crichton is also setting up his own videogame development studio. And in 1998 Douglas Adams – who had had a hand in the first videogame based on his sci-fi comedy *The Hitch-hiker's Guide to the Galaxy*, a text adventure game published by Infocom in 1985 – scripted the adventure videogame Starship Titanic before the appearance of the tie-in novel, which he didn't even write himself. These guys aren't stupid; they know which way the wind is blowing.

The major videogame console manufacturers, meanwhile, have epic ambitions for their little lumps of extruded plastic. Consoles aim to be not just gaming machines but the one-stop entertainment centre in the homes of millions. One Sony insider has been overheard saying that the company's aim with PlayStation2 is to 'own the living-room'.

You can already play audio CDs on a PlayStation, but that's small beer. Sega's Dreamcast comes with a modem for Internet access. With a plug-in keyboard it is currently by far the cheapest way to enjoy basic email and web-surfing facilities – a quarter of the price of an iMac or an entry-level PC. Sony's next-generation PlayStation2, meanwhile, plays movies through your television on the new consumer film format DVD (digital versatile disc), and through various interface ports allows the connection of digital video cameras for editing home movies, printers, scanners, storage devices and much else besides.

Can anything stop this fun-juggernaut? Research from US analysts Datamonitor suggests that sales of games consoles and software in Europe and the US will generate over $17 *billion* worth of business a year by 2003. The conventional media – Hollywood, music, even books – are scared. Who can blame them?

The shock of the new

Videogames are not going to go away. You can't hide under the stairs. Resistance is futile. Any industry with such a vast amount of money sloshing around in it is by that token alone worthy of investigation.

Videogames are powerful, but they are nothing without humans to play them. So the inner life of videogames – how they work – is bound up with the inner life of the player. And the player's response to a well-designed videogame is in part the same sort of response he or she has to a film, or to a painting: it is an *aesthetic* one.

Alain and Frédéric Le Diberder, authors of an excellent French book on videogames called *L'Univers des Jeux Vidéo*, welcome this idea with open arms. They already declare that the videogame is the 'tenth art'.* Most people are not yet so progressive. But videogames clearly have the potential to become an artform, even if they are not there yet.

Here's why. A videogame is put together by highly talented artists and graphic designers, as well as programmers, virtual architects and sonic engineers. Increasingly, first-class graduates in computer science from Cambridge are moving into videogames rather than academic research; there is also a large flow of animation talent from traditional cartoons into videogame development. Musicians who might once have become television or film composers are now writing videogame soundtracks, and there is even such a beast as the professional videogame scriptwriter. There's a huge amount of thought and creativity encoded on to that little silver disc. And aesthetics, by which I mean in the most general terms the systematic study of why we like one painting or one film more than another, cannot ignore this bizarre digital hybrid.

The original Greek meaning of 'aesthetics' refers to things that are perceived by the senses. Modern videogames – dynamic and interactive fusions of colourful graphic representation, sound effects, music, speed and movement – are unquestionably a fabulously sensual form; furthermore, the simple fact is that some videogames are better than others, yet so far no serious attempt has been made to understand why. Videogames are an increasingly pervasive part of the modern cultural landscape, but we have no way of speaking critically

---

* Tradition (since the Athenian Greeks and Confucian Chinese) has held that there are six distinct arts: music, poetry, architecture, painting, dance and sculpture. The Le Diberders add TV, cinema and *bandes dessinées* (graphic novels) to the list, and then declare the videogame the tenth.

about them. The noisy lightshows competing for attention in living-rooms around the globe appear as some kind of weird, hermetic monolith: mysteriously exciting to the initiated, baffling to the non-player. But both kinds of people are affected by videogames in one way or another. Even if you've never played Tomb Raider, you can't escape the clutches of Lara Croft.

People are always loath to admit that something new can approach the status of art. Take this rather aggressive ejaculation: 'A pastime of illiterate, wretched creatures who are stupefied by their daily jobs, a machine of mindlessness and dissolution.' Such high moral bile is typical of the attacks on videogames today.

But this sentence wasn't written about videogames; it was written seventy years ago by French novelist Georges Duhamel, about the cinema. Yet today, few people would argue that film-making is not an artform. An artform that is dependent on new technology always makes some people uneasy. The German philosopher and musicologist Theodor Adorno expressed his wariness of jazz (dependent on a recently invented instrument, the saxophone, as well as emerging recording technologies) in similar terms during his correspondence with philosopher and critic Walter Benjamin.

Videogames today find themselves in the position that cinema and jazz occupied before the Second World War: popular but despised, thought to be beneath serious evaluation. Yet today there is a huge critical literature that has expanded our understanding and appreciation of films and jazz music. In half a century, I don't doubt that this will also be true for videogames.

I'm not trying to argue that there's going to be a revolution. Like it or not, the revolution has already happened. Videogames are an enormous entertainment business. The numbers, as we've seen, are huge.

When people talk about videogames, they tend to compare them with forms they already know and love: film, painting, literature and so on. But there's one critical difference that we need to bear in mind, and it throws a huge spanner in the works of any easy equation between videogames and traditional artforms. It's this. What do you do with a videogame? You *play* it.

In his *Laws*, Plato defined 'play' like this: 'That which has neither utility nor truth nor likeness, nor yet, in its effects, is harmful, can best be judged by the criterion of the charm that is in it, and by the pleasure it affords. Such pleasure, entailing as it does no appreciable good or ill, is play.' It looks as if today's graphically astonishing videogames *do* have something like 'truth' or 'likeness'. A casual observer would certainly note the vast improvements in graphical style and detail every year and conclude that videogames are increasingly realistic. Those cars look pretty real; those trees at the side of the racetrack, waving gently in the wind, look satisfyingly (arbo)real.

This turns out to be the subject of a fundamental tension in videogames, one which will appear in many guises throughout this book. It's a version of a very old question about art, concerning what Plato called mimesis ('representation'). Is it real or not? How can videogames claim to be 'realistic' at all? But the peculiar nature of videogames gives the old question several intriguing and novel digital spins. The problem of mimesis in this context – the virtual representation of 'realities' – informs the inner life of nearly every videogame.

Plato allows something to be a game as long as it is not 'harmful' and has no 'utility'. There is an increasingly vocal charge from some sections of society that videogames are in fact morally harmful. But do they have positive effects – do they have 'utility'? Squabbles between psychologists as to whether videogames enhance visuo-spatial and motor skills are largely unresolved. The only thing that everyone agrees on is that playing videogames makes you better at playing videogames. Their effects on our inner lives can only be investigated once we have a more rounded view of what videogames actually are.

What does this novel sensual fusion really have in common with films, with storytelling, or with painting? Where do videogames fit in the development of leisure technologies, of perspectival representation, of the narrative arts? Where do videogames fit in the history of play?

Playing videogames may or may not be 'useful'. That's beside the point. This book is about their *charm*: the life in them, and their life in us. Videogames are fun, but just what kind of fun is it?

What does it mean to be Trigger Happy?

2

THE ORIGIN OF SPECIES

Beginnings

It all started at the Massachusetts Institute of Technology, one night in 1962. The first Soviet Sputnik spacecraft had been launched five years previously, and John F. Kennedy had just promised that America would get to the moon within the decade. Six months earlier, Digital Equipment Corporation had delivered a hulking new mainframe computer, a model PDP-1, to MIT's electrical engineering lab. An innovative, massively expensive tool for serious scientific research. And by happy chance, there was a revolutionary achievement with that machine: the invention of the world's first videogame.

Well, that's how the story usually goes.* But beginnings are slippery things. Actually, the world's first videogame was created four years earlier, at a US government nuclear-research facility, the Brookhaven National Laboratory. William A. Higinbotham, an engineer who had designed timing devices for the Manhattan Project's atomic bomb and helped in the first developments of radar, worked at Brookhaven in charge of instrumentation design. He was trying to dream up an entertaining exhibit for visiting members of the public, and he hacked together a

---

* Both J. C. Herz (in *Joystick Nation*) and Le Diberder & Le Diberder (*L'Univers des Jeux Vidéo*) give this erroneous starting point. A thorough history is provided by Leonard Herman's excellent *Phoenix: the Fall and Rise of Videogames* (2nd edn, 1997), to which I am indebted in this section.

rudimentary two-player tennis game. An analogue computer showed the trajectories of bouncing balls drawn as ghostly blips on an oscilloscope, controlled by a button and a knob. It was a smash hit with the visitors for two years.

But owing to this lone pioneer's modesty – he didn't think he had created anything earth-shatteringly novel – the game never left the confines of the facility. 'I considered the whole idea so obvious that it never occurred to me to think about a patent,' Higinbotham said wryly, years later. Luckily for the future of games, in fact, because the owner of any patent on oscilloscope tennis would have been the United States government. And so – as if, aeons ago in the primordial soup, one helix of a DNA molecule had winked into existence without the other, and therefore didn't catch on – the videogame spark fizzled and went out. If that oscilloscope could have spoken, it might have said: 'There is one who comes after me.'

And so there was. Three years later a big package arrived at MIT. Until this point, computers had mostly been tedious, mute hulks that usually had to be programmed with ticker-tape or punchcards, and were strictly for esoteric mathematical applications. But the new-fangled circular, dedicated VDU screen and keyboard of the PDP-1 tempted programmer Steve Russell and his friends* to indulge in a little creative slacking. They began to fiddle around with the interface, writing little bits of code that caused the display to respond in real-time to physical input. A virtual typewriter and calculator. A model of the night sky. And then . . . Spacewar.

The name's melodrama, of course, grew out of the geopolitical tensions of the time. But despite the lurid sci-fi connotations, the game itself, which you can still play on the Internet,† was serene, austere, a thing of alien beauty. Two

---

* I refer only to Russell by name for reasons of ease and fluency. These are the full credits. Conception: Martin Graetz, Stephen Russell and Wayne Wiitanen. Programming: Stephen Russell, Peter Samson, Dan Edwards and Martin Graetz, together with Alan Kotok, Steve Piner and Robert A. Saunders.

† Java-capable browsers can just point themselves at http://lcs.www. media.mit.edu/groups/el/projects/spacewar/

duelling spaceships in a *pas de deux* against an electronic star-field, firing lazy torpedoes at each other in the silence of space, avoiding all the while the lethal gravitational pull of a central sun.

A leap of faith had been made. What these coffee-guzzling student pioneers realised was that new technology made possible a new sort of experience. The photons fizzing from the screen were conceived as manipulable packets of pleasure in themselves, rather than simply a fancy way for the computer to tell its user the result of a calculation via a dull string of numbers. Russell and his friends designed – or redesigned independently, to give Willy Higinbotham his due – the first symbolic visual interface. That is why, along with the work done by Xerox-Parc in the 1970s, you use word-processors and other software based around 'windows' and 'icons' rather than text. (Playing videogames, though, is generally acknowledged to be more fun than using Microsoft products.)

Spacewar sprang so fully formed into the microcosmos that it took a very long time for other games to catch up. Its structure offered many of the virtues that are still essential features of videogames: simple rules with innumerable combinational possibilities; the competitive urge to destroy your opponent's spaceship; the pleasure of mastery over a well-defined, consistent system; the challenge of reacting instantly to craft governed by inertial physics; and the sensual buzz of playing with animated patterns of light. The game is remarkably similar to Asteroids, an arcade machine that appeared some seventeen years later.

Having briefly considered trying to sell this curio, Russell and his team decided that no one would want to buy it, so they gave away the source code to anyone who was interested. Within a few years it was everywhere, a benign virus, an unstoppable meme, eating up time all over the world on government, military and scientific mainframes. And if you can't beat them, join them: in the end, Digital Equipment Corporation used the game as a centrepiece for commercial demonstrations of their computer. In the same pivotal decade that saw the global war of the space race and the tectonic cultural shifts of pop music, videogames had launched a successful initial blitzkrieg on the digital plains.

The lessons of the PDP-1's unwitting involvement in game history are twofold. First: give a man a tool, and he will play with it. Second: pretty soon, everyone will want one. Spacewar, however, never became a mainstream entertainment, because so few people had access to computers at the time.* The videogame concept was there, but it had to wait ten years for cheap computer-chip technology to make possible its wider distribution.

Meanwhile, throughout the 1960s, the small community of mainframe programmers produced other highly influential game templates in tiny programs. Lunar Lander was a turn-based game with a text interface that required the player to administer rocket-thruster firing without running out of fuel before meeting the surface. Hammurabi was the first God game, requiring the user to manage a feudal kingdom by planting grain and assessing tax rates each year – a direct ancestor of Civilisation. And later, the advent of ADVENT (1972). Short for Adventure, this was the first of a lost genre of game that was hugely popular on personal computers right up until the late 1980s. It was the first computerised version of 'interactive narrative': the computer described a location and the user typed in commands – 'north', 'look', 'kill snake', 'use torch' – to move around the virtual world, use objects and solve fiendish puzzles. But the world at large remained ignorant of the myriad charms of these proto-videogames. It was a closed community, a priesthood without a parish.

Most people assume that coin-operated arcade games preceded home videogame technology. In fact, in terms of conception rather than commercial distribution, the reverse is the case, for by 1967 Ralph Baer, the consumer-products manager of a military electronics company, Sanders Associates, had invented a TV-based home-tennis game and more complex 'hockey' simulations. Unfortunately it took him several years to persuade

---

* DEC sold about fifty PDP-1s in total. Even by 1971, there was only a total of about 50,000 computers in the world (*The Economist*, 28 September 1996). By the end of 1993, there were more than 173 million computers in use, not counting videogame consoles.

other manufacturers of the commercial possibilities. At last, at the turn of the decade, Intel got their act together and invented the microprocessor. Videogames could now be just as clever with much smaller, cheaper brains.

Back in 1965, an engineering student at the University of Utah called Nolan Bushnell had Spacewar on his computer, and like the other techies Bushnell played it obsessively. He began to wonder whether people might actually pay to play videogames in an amusement park, but given the size and expense of computers, it was a mere pipe dream at the time. By 1970, however, thanks to the microchip, the project had become commercially feasible, and Bushnell joined pinball company Nutting Associates to develop a mass-market version of Spacewar. In 1971, 1,500 units of Computer Space, the first arcade game, were produced. The project bombed.

So much for the future of entertainment. Computer Space was just too complicated for the videogame virgins of the general public. What the hell was it *for*? Pinball, fine – it's immediately obvious what to do: there's two flipper buttons, you light a cigarette and get on with it. But this intimidating machine, with its reams of instructions and its bizarre, bulbous casing, like something out of *Barbarella* – it was just weird. Bushnell learned the lesson. He would have to make a videogame that anyone could just walk up to and play, without having to learn it first. He left Nutting, determined to go it alone.

And so Pong was born. 'Avoid missing ball for high score' ran the only line of instructions on Pong's cabinet. It was a very simple version of tennis. A square dot of light represented the ball, and two vertical lines at each side of the screen were the bats. Players only had to use one hand to rotate the paddle control, thus facilitating simultaneous beer consumption. The first Pong machine, hand-built in Bushnell's apartment, was set up in Andy Capp's tavern, a California pool bar. It was soon collecting $300 a week in quarters – six times as much as the neighbouring pinball machine.

Amazed at the game's success, Bushnell founded his own company, the now-legendary Atari (named after a term used in the Japanese chess-like game 'Go'), which was staffed by young, Led Zeppelin-loving, herb-smoking hippies. Atari released the first commercial Pong in November 1972. It was a huge success, and altogether ten thousand of the machines were manufactured. Four years later, Nolan Bushnell sold Atari to Warner for $28 million, staying on as chairman himself. Silicon entrepreneurialism, it seemed, was the new rock'n'roll.

But it was not all plain sailing. When Pong first came out, Atari was immediately sued. Ralph Baer's home-tennis game had finally been taken up by Magnavox. The first home console, the Magnavox Odyssey, had been released six months before Atari's debut. And it was to all intents and purposes a home Pong *avant la lettre*. It lacked the hypnotic sonar-blip soundtrack of the arcade game, but there was no doubt that it had got there first, and Atari were forced to pay Magnavox a licence fee on every game sold.

Of course, all these Pong-style games were direct descendants of the lost oscilloscope program by Willy Higinbotham, who never made a penny. Rip-offs of home tennis and multiplayer arcade versions of 'tennis' or 'hockey', as well as the first simplistic shooting and driving games, flourished over the next few years. But, as if punished by the Fates for not honouring its ancestor, the booming videogame industry was soon brought to its knees – and the reason was the very multiplicity of Pongs. By 1977, there were so many rival home machines that shops began dumping them at knockdown prices, and many manufacturers went bust. It looked as if videogames had been a mere fad, a fad which had now burnt itself out. The industry was on the verge of total meltdown.

And then a little-known Japanese Pachinko manufacturer called Taito rode in to the rescue. Their extraordinary new arcade game was the seed of the modern era. Within a few months of its 1978 release in Japan, the game had caused a nationwide shortage of the coin required to play it. Twenty thousand cabinets were sold the next year in America, and over its lifetime the game grossed $500 million. It was called Space Invaders.

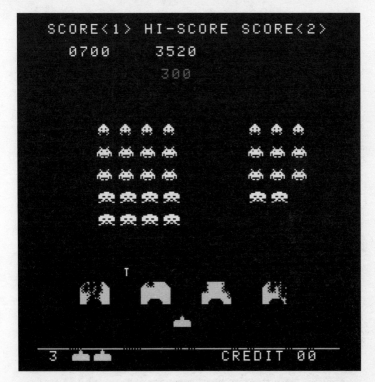

Fig. 1. Space Invaders: time to get trigger happy (© 1978 Taito Corp.)

Art types

Videogames today are a broad church. I'm using the term 'videogames' to encompass arcade games, home-console games, and computer games. The bewildering array of different forms and styles could lead a casual observer to think that the only thing all these games have in common is a microprocessor. In fact, all such games share crucial low-level qualities.

As with any form, videogame genres mutate and shift over history. If they never exactly die, they can sleep for a long time, while other, newer types spring up to take their place. Furthermore, few modern videogames slot neatly into very discrete categories. But I'll start mapping out this confusing terrain by identifying certain families of videogame.

Happiness is a warm gun

Perhaps the purest, most elemental videogame pleasure is the heathen joy of destruction. You've got your finger hovering over the trigger, you line up an enemy and you fire. Such is the task presented by that venerable videogame genre, the shoot-'em-up. Space Invaders (see fig. 1) was not the first shoot-'em-up (Atari's Tank preceded it in 1974, and of course Spacewar itself involved torpedo firing), but it was revolutionary all the same. You control a laser turret that can move from side to side at the bottom of the screen. Further up, a phalanx of fifty-five evil aliens tramps across the screen in a smug dance of death. When they reach one side of the screen, they all descend one space and go back the other way. Your task is simple: fire at will, and wipe them out.

Not so simple, though, because they are raining bombs on you. You must dodge the bombs, or let your four shields soak up the firepower. The shields, however, crumble with every blast and are soon shot through with holes, offering as much protection from the merciless army above as a white handkerchief. As you shoot off the invaders, their colleagues do not panic, they do not break formation; in their infinite, ego-less confidence they just move a little faster, and faster still. They must not reach the bottom of the screen. You might manage to blast the entire division away, but then another reappears in its place, lower down and more bomb-happy. The eerie bass thumping of the invaders' progress increases in tempo, along with your heartbeat. Just how long will you last, soldier?

Space Invaders was the first game to feature animated characters. The serried ranks of aliens waggled their brutish tentacles across the screen; the movement, for the time, was so realistically ugly that it was all the more pleasurable to blast the critters away. Space Invaders was also the first game to feature a 'high score' facility. The current highest score was constantly displayed on your game screen, sneering at your puny efforts, or encouraging you to develop your own strategies to ever greater heights. (Later games would enable you to enter your initials and remember them along with your high score. As Martin Amis put it in an early and engagingly enthusiastic book on videogames, *Invasion of the Space Invaders*: 'To appear on the Great Score sheet is a powerful incentive in space-game praxis – a yearning perhaps connected with schooldays and the honour or notoriety of having your name chalked up on the board, white on black.')

Space Invaders was also the first 'endless' game. Previously, videogames had stopped when a certain score was reached, or restarted; Taito's classic, on the other hand, just kept getting harder and harder, the aliens becoming a terrifying blur as they whipped across the screen raining bombs and hurtled ever closer to ground zero. Therein lies the game's special tension: it is unwinnable. The player's task is to fight a heroically doomed rearguard action, to stave off defeat for as long as possible, but the war can never be won. Earth *will* be invaded. And, of course, it was – by the explosion of videogames that followed in Taito's trailblazing footsteps.

The late 1970s and early 1980s were the golden age of classic shoot-'em-ups, with Asteroids, Robotron, Defender, Galaxian, Scramble, Tempest et al pushing the tension envelope of this most fiery, physically draining of videogame genres. Indeed, the extreme simplicity of the basic concept – destroying things with guns – is the reason why, for a few years, the shoot-'em-up expanded the possibilities of videogame action more than any other type of game. Throughout the 1980s, shoot-'em-ups boasted ever more dazzling lightshows and huge varieties of offensive weapons, while gradually replacing the static Space Invaders arena with larger, roamable spaces. Examples such as the Commodore 64 and Spectrum classic Uridium (easily as compelling as any arcade shooter of the time) required not just shooting accuracy but high-speed inertial negotiation of solid obstacles in two-and-a-half degrees of freedom (the extra fraction granted by virtue of the player's ability to flip his craft on to its side and zip through narrow spaces).

As processing power increased in the 1990s, the genre

definitively broke the bounds of flat-plane representations with the emergence of the 'first-person shooter', exemplified by Doom and its multifarious clones. Doom casts the player as a marine on Mars, tramping around an invaded base from the hero's point of view and, with the aid of a comically powerful arsenal, blasting demons back into the bloody hell from which they have erupted. This, a sub-genre that traces its roots back to Atari's 3D tank game Battlezone (1980), ousted its two-dimensional counterparts as king of the hill, at the same time adding rudimentary quest and object-manipulation require-ments which – especially as environments and programmed enemy cunning became more complex, as in the extraordinary Half-Life (1998) – edged it into the grey zone between shoot-'em-up, exploration and puzzle games.

The pure shooter, however, persists in the form of lightgun games: Virtua Cop, House of the Dead or the viscerally thrilling Time Crisis. This game has one of the simplest, most intuitive human-computer interfaces ever conceived: the player uses a moulded plastic handgun (with properly aligned sights and a force-feedback mechanism to simulate recoil) to shoot directly at the enemies on screen, and works a footpedal to reload the gun (after every six bullets) and duck behind objects to avoid enemy fire. Each section must be completed before the clock runs out. Though the games could hardly look more dissimilar, it is Time Crisis which is the true modern descendant of Space Invaders. Where the old enemies were alien spacecraft in two-dimensional formations, the enemies in Time Crisis are human terrorists scurrying about in virtual arenas; where you used to be Earth's last hope, you are now a member of a US govern-ment SWAT team protecting the interests of national security. But the purism and simplicity of the gameplay shows that the games are brothers under the skin. Time Crisis even manages to increase the sweating tension, because at your back you always hear Time's winged chariot. But relax into your task and revel in the challenge, for the blissfully simple rules are still the same. Kill them all.

The Origin Of Species

In my mind and in my car

Gamers of a certain age often argue that the oldies were the best, in much the same way as the pop records of one's own youth seem so much better than the rubbish the kids listen to today. But we can't rewind; we've gone too far.* True, I have a certain fondness for Vanguard, a game I could happily clock as a nine-year-old on a family holiday in Wales (you could shoot in four directions and the beepy tunes were evil mind-limpets). Clearly, however, Goldeneye, a first-person shooter for the Nintendo 64 console which lets you play the role of James Bond, is a much better game.

One genre that certainly refutes this nostalgia-tinged argument is the racing game. In most sorts of videogame, 'feel' is at base more important than fancy graphics or speed for its own sake. But in the racing game, graphics and speed are part of the 'feel'. Every increase in technological power enhances the genre's unique pleasure: the feeling of hurling a vehicle around a realistic environment at suicidal velocities. Conversely, because of this intimate relationship between hardware base and software superstructure, a racing game has very often been used as a seductive showcase for new technology: the Sony PlayStation was the mouth-watering machine of the future on its release, just because of the unprecedented speed and solidity of one of its first releases, Ridge Racer. That series of games continued to evolve until 1999's Ridge Racer Type 4, which ran on the same hardware but looked many times slicker (see fig. 2).

Early two-dimensional racing games, with a flat road scrolling up the screen, were little more than simple dodge games or, with gun-equipped cars, variations on the shoot-'em-up (Spy Hunter). The first, crude attempt at driver's-eye-view perspective was Atari's Night Driver, but the genre truly

---

* 'Video Killed The Radio Star' (1979) by Buggles, a deathless master-piece of popular song, the *Kindertötenlied* that on the one hand revels in modernist sonic synthesis but on the other mourns the passing of the 1970s and of youth itself.

RANK ❌❌
5|8

RECORD
F:1'25"768
1:1'25"768
2:0'30"563
3:_'__"___

TIMELIMIT0 7'58"

X1000rpm

153 km/h

Fig. 2. Ridge Racer Type 4: prettier, faster, better (© 1999 Namco Ltd; all rights reserved)

blossomed with Namco's arcade Pole Position (1982), whose steering wheel and pedals controlled a bright, colourful approximation of track driving. Ever since, racing games have become better and better at true perspective, while added textures on the tarmac and solid passing landmarks enhance the feeling of speed. One of the best examples at the time of writing is Gran Turismo, with tracks modelled on Japanese suburbs, superbly atmospheric lighting effects and (crucially) wonderfully throaty engine roars. As in most racing games, players must learn to throw their cars into powerslides with abandon and not to worry too much about hitting other competitors; these vehicles might look like racing cars but they act like dodgems.

This is not true, however, of a more serious kind of racer, usually modelled on Formula One cars and real Grand Prix circuits, and in spirit more of a simulation than a pure videogame. Cars suffer real damage and braking technique is vital. Simulation, distinct from the role-playing game, is arguably not a genre in itself; rather, it promotes in certain genres (driving, flight games) the primacy of supposed 'realism' over instant fun. A true videogame deliberately simplifies any given situation (imaginary or real) down to its essential, kinetic parts; a simulation is loath to simplify and only does so when available CPU power is already maxed out. The problem is, as we shall see, that videogame 'realism' is always a fix anyway. Furthermore, simulations stomp roughshod all over one *raison d'être* of certain types of videogame, which is to let the player perform amusingly dangerous and unlikely manoeuvres in perfect safety. If playing an arcade-style racing game is like being a car stuntman in *The French Connection* or *Ronin*, playing a simulation is a much more earnest business. Martin Amis again: 'It sounds rather like *driving*, doesn't it?'

Unlike Space Invaders et al, racing games offer the perfect opportunity for competitive two-person action, either with two arcade cabinets linked together or with one home console splitting the television screen into two separate viewpoints for each player. And you need not be satisfied with racing mere cars against a friend. The racing-game genre splits into driving games (what we have seen so far) and the rest, which encompass cartoon go-kart competitions (the superb Super Mario Kart), snowboard piste challenges (1080° Snowboarding), tiny cars speeding over a kitchen table (Micro Machines) or futuristic hoverplanes thundering around a sci-fi rollercoaster of a course (WipEout).

Racing games not based on traditional cars are usually distinguished by the appearance of power-ups: weapons scattered along the course that can be picked up by a player and used to blow his opponents off the track. But in all categories of racer, the aim is the same: get to the finish line first. If the destructive orgy of the shoot-'em-up captures the essence of human-versus-machine competition, the racing game is the purest expression of machine-mediated human-versus-human competition. There can be no arguments about who won and who lost. You were just too slow.

Might as well jump

Around 1981, a young Nintendo apprentice designer, Shigeru Miyamoto, was asked to write something to replace the innards of Radarscope, a tedious shooter Nintendo's American arm had unwisely stocked up on to the tune of two thousand unsellable cabinets. Miyamoto quickly, if somewhat unpredictably, designed a game featuring a fat moustachioed carpenter and a giant monkey. The carpenter, under the player's direction, had to begin at the bottom of the screen and, jumping to avoid barrels thrown by the infuriated simian, climb ladders and move across platforms to reach the top, where he could defeat the monkey and rescue a princess. It was a far cry from the alien-themed shoot-'em-ups that were popular at the time. But Miyamoto's first game, called Donkey Kong (see fig. 3), became an enormous hit, and invented a new genre: the platform game.*

The carpenter, known cratylically as Jumpman (for it was his nature, uniquely at the time, to jump) in the first game, was transformed by its sequel into a plumber called Mario, who soon became the most recognised videogame 'character' of all, and most of the innovations in the platform-game genre have been made in games starring Mario, and written by Miyamoto himself. Mario Bros. (1983) introduced the plumber's brother, Luigi, along with another paradigm of platform gaming that stuck for years: enemies are destroyed, not by means of projectile weapons, but by the cartoonish method of jumping into platforms underneath them to knock them over, then climbing up and kicking them off the screen while they are still dazed. Super Mario Bros. (1985) turned the platform genre into a sideways-scrolling quest through a world many times the size of one screen, and added power-ups (by eating a mushroom, Mario increased in size and could withstand one hit

---

* In platform games, women are literally on pedestals, with men constantly striving to attain their level. It is an interesting example of plinth ideology; see, for the concept's application in cognitive science, the rather eccentric Tabrizifar, *The Transparent Head*, pp. 332–5.

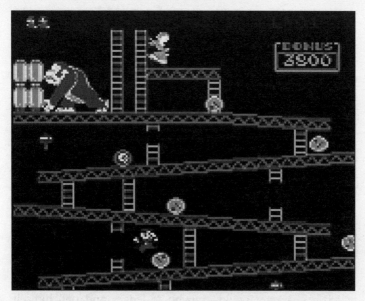

Fig. 3. Donkey Kong: get him over a barrel (© 1981 Nintendo)

from an enemy), a system whereby an extra life could be won after collecting a hundred gold coins, and a regular 'boss' battle at the end of every level.

Throughout its history the platform game has built the most purely fantastical sort of gameworlds. In the Mario universe, baby dinosaurs coexist with masked birds and solid clouds, potent fungi and magical crotchets hanging in the air. In an early platform hit on the Sinclair ZX Spectrum, Manic Miner (1983), the player controls a miner who must negotiate conveyor belts and killer spikes while avoiding robots, malign jellies and the game's hideously deformed author himself* to collect keys before his air supply runs out. In the most popular current platform game, and the closest approach yet to a true interactive cartoon, Crash Bandicoot 3, the eponymous orange

---

* The legendary videogame *auteur* Mathew Smith, following a period of mythical wandering, has now reappeared: see http://www.the-goodstuff.freeserve.co.uk.

marsupial rides on the back of a speeding tiger across the Great Wall of China or does battle with giant glassy-eyed men wielding sledgehammers.

But now the very term 'platform game' is somewhat out-dated; perhaps more appropriate is 'exploration game', which has been the defining point of platformers since Super Mario Bros. This is partly because such games have quite recently made a transition to three-dimensional rather than flat-plane representation – most effectively in the astonishing Super Mario 64 (1996) – and in the process the gameplay has necessarily changed. The old, simple lines denoting 'platforms' are now solid ledges or columns made of brick, wood, earth or steel, and while essential features of the platformer are retained, such as the problem of figuring out a series of jumps to get from 'here' to 'up there', there are hybrid factors from a number of other game types. The first Tomb Raider game, for example, was clearly a development of ideas in the classic 2D platformer Prince of Persia (the first game in which a character could grab on to ledges and pull himself up), yet it is also a three-dimensional block-moving puzzle game with added combat elements. And Crash Bandicoot 3 is not really a platform game at all, even though it requires you very traditionally to jump on enemies' heads and collect fruit. Apart from in the two-dimensional bonus levels, there are very few platforms. Its major influence is in fact the racing game with a dynamic obstacle course: rather than figure out complicated routes in a vertically oriented environment, you must run at full tilt 'into' (or sometimes 'out of') the depth of the screen. It qualifies partly as an 'exploration game' because of the player's simple desire to see what surreal beauties the designers have hidden around the next corner.

The old 'platform game' is no longer a discrete game-type in itself, but denotes an aspect of gameplay that may occur in many different genres. Even first-person shooters like Turok (1997) cravenly require the player to negotiate platform elements, even though current 3D engines make such a task infuriatingly random rather than pleasurably challenging. What is left of the platform game, then, is just the defining physical ability that Shigeru Miyamoto gave to his original monkey-battling woodworker. Go ahead, jump.

Sometimes you kick

Ah, how good it feels to boot a friend in the head several times before applying an armlock and hurling him to the ground. Especially if he's bigger than you. Fighting games allow players to battle each other's characters on screen with an array of absurdly exaggerated martial arts moves; with fists and feet or with swords and flame. Of all the videogame genres, the fighting game, or beat-'em-up, is one where the solo, or player-against-computer, mode is most pointless. It's a two-player genre.

Early beat-'em-ups were particularly popular on the home computers of the day; Way of the Exploding Fist or Yie Ar Kung Fu (both 1985) took, as did most early fighting titles, a relatively sober approach to martial-arts gameplay, with a possible sixteen different moves.* As videogame consoles and arcade machines became more technically accomplished, however, the temptation was to show off the graphical power with ever more visually appealing displays, and never mind the realism. Street Fighter II (1991), the first of the really modern breed of fighting games,† featured enormous blue light trails from swishing limbs and fireball attacks, while Mortal Kombat (1992) attracted vituperative noises from the American Senate and the British Parliament for its terrifically gory 'death moves', where a victorious character would rip out his opponent's spine and hold it bloodily aloft.

One of the attractions of modern beat-'em-ups is the player's

---

* With exceptions such as Barbarian, in which your friend could be graphically decapitated with a broadsword. There was media criticism of this game – not, however, for the violence, but for the fact that it featured a semi-clad Page Three model in its advertising.

† In terms of visual excess, that is. Street Fighter's legacy otherwise continues in a cult sub-genre of the fighting game that eschews three-dimensional, 'solid'-looking characters in favour of a flat-plane, comic-book style with characteristically jerky animation.

Fig. 4. Ready 2 Rumble Boxing: Croatian tank Boris Knokimov (left) takes on cuddly Hawaiian Salua Tua. Rumble bumble ... (© 1999 Midway)

ability to choose to play as any one of numerous different characters, each with his or her own strengths and weaknesses but all lusciously pictured and animated. Do you want to be a blonde, sandal-wearing Greek woman in a miniskirt, or a supernatural pirate with two enormous broadswords (Soul Edge)? A Croatian behemoth or a Hawaiian Sumo wrestler (Ready 2 Rumble Boxing [see fig. 4])? Bruce Lee in a gold lamé leotard, a pogo-happy alien cyborg or a tiny, annoying dragon (Tekken 3)? Black, Asian or Caucasian; male, female or indeterminate xenomorph? Beat-'em-ups are nothing if not politically inclusive; it is much more common for European men to play as women or as Korean ju-jitsu experts than as digital avatars of their own ethnic origins. It doesn't matter who you are in real life; here, the idea of play as experimentation extends to your own genes.

Since fighting games broke into 3D with Virtua Fighter, the physical contact of these lightbeam warriors has grown ever more convincingly thudding and solid. The stunningly graceful animations, meanwhile, are developed with a technique which films real martial artists and digitises the results as movement code that can be applied to the imaginary game characters. This is known as 'motion capture'.

But herein lies a problem. Beat-'em-ups boast ever more complex control methods, with at least three buttons beside the joystick, and baffling combinations of button hits and circular shapes made with the stick unleashing ever more spectacular and lethal activity on screen. These preset special moves, also known as 'combos', actually require the player to memorise a string of ten button-presses; there might be hundreds of such strings in a game. This is the Achilles' heel of the genre, for you cannot design on the fly your own strings of moves which have the same speed and fluidity as the preset combos. You must learn the sequences the programmers have built in to the game – and, okay, there are hundreds of them, but that does not constitute freedom.

Not only is it (understandably) impossible to perform a move for which there is no animation, but motion-capture techniques mean that once an animation has started, it *must* finish before the next one can start. You can't change tactics mid-move. That rules out true feints, which are critical in real fighting sports such as fencing. Oddly, beat-'em-ups such as the Tekken series have extremely complex input methods, but threaten to offer the player far less creative freedom than almost any other kind of game with a much simpler interface. Robotron gives you two joysticks: one to move, one to fire. Simple. But with those tools, there is a huge tactical potential of feints, misdirections and apocalyptic vengeance.

The excessively deterministic, combinatorial template, however, seems to be happily on the wane, overtaken by newer versions such as Power Stone for the Sega Dreamcast (1999), where the controls are very simple and the tactical gameplay is transferred to use of objects (benches, lamp-posts) and hilariously magical power-ups (guided missiles and the like) in the fighting arena itself; or Ready 2 Rumble Boxing, which mixes pleasingly simple controls with beautifully judged tactics. The fighting game, like fighting itself, will always be popular.

Heaven in here

Oh yes, the computer can make us divine. Should you want to build a city from scratch, construct a substructure of water pipes, sewers, power lines and underground trains, populate it with citizens, determine tax levels, build museums, parks, houses and office blocks, and then destroy the whole imaginary metropolis by calling an earthquake on their heads – sure, you can do that. It's called SimCity. Or perhaps you want to operate on a larger scale: create a neolithic tribe and over the course of thousands of years send them out to colonise the land, discover ironwork, sailing and electricity. Play Civilisation. Compete against other gods in a polytheistic mythology? Populous. There are similar 'God games' for the fields of global industry, railroad building and even rollercoaster parks.

There are two basic attractions of games like SimCity. The first is that the virtual city itself, with its apparently autonomous population, functions as a pet. If neglected, it will pine and eventually die; if nurtured, it will flourish. A player might form some sort of emotional attachment to the gameworld. This is the principle abstracted and miniaturised with such extraordinary success by the Japanese company Bandai, with their keyring digital pet, Tamagotchi. Notice, however, that a SimCity or Civilisation pet panders to a peculiarly narcissistic instinct in the player: if he or she does well, monuments will be erected and museums named in honour of the masterful deity. It's a kind of fame.

The second potential pleasure of a God game is a function of the very artificiality of the *soi-disant* 'simulation'. Now, of course, God-game variables are 'kludged' – simplified and imprecise – and their reality is laughably clean compared to the infinitely chaotic and messy real world. As J. C. Herz tartly observes in *Joystick Nation*: 'You can build something that looks like Detroit without building in racial tension.' But what they do offer by virtue of their machine habitat, and what makes them slightly different from what they would be otherwise – complex boardgames – is the modelling of dynamic processes. Time can be sped up or slowed down at will, and interactions of data over time can be readily visualised. In this way, for instance, fiddling with the fiscal and monetary operators of SimCity for a couple of minutes and observing the results for the next accounting period provides a remarkably intuitive way to understand the fundamentals of balancing a budget in a capitalist state.

Now, I have conscientiously played these games in the interests of research, and I find them exceptionally tedious. Even so, God games are highly successful. Many people who aren't at all interested in any other sort of videogame – such as the high-speed, colourful action experiences of racers or exploration games – will often confess a sneaky addiction to Civilisation or Age of Empires. Some people simply prefer the challenge of fiddling relaxedly with a process to that of a high-speed test of reactions.

It seems, anyway, from the method by which God games model dynamic processes that they are not primarily about cities or tribes or any of the putative content. They are process toys. Time is transformed from prison to Play-Doh. Perhaps the fantasy appeal is really about a chance to observe the world over a longer, more sober chronological span than that of a single human life. But if the classic shoot-'em-up or platform game is triumphantly individualistic – one hero against the hordes – the God game is quite the opposite. The individual doesn't matter. He may as well be an ant (in SimAnt, the individual actually *is* an ant). The gameplayer doesn't count as an individual: he is, after all, God. What matters is the inexorable march of the corporate machine. There seems to be a pernicious subterranean motive here: such games offer you a position of infinite power in order to whisper the argument that, as an individual in the world, you have none at all.

Two tribes

Armchair generals are well catered for by the God game's sibling genre, the real-time strategy game. Its natural milieu is that of war. Again in a godlike position (singlehandedly overseeing all military operations), the player is briefed by advisers (actors in video clips), and must then carry out certain missions by issuing commands to numerous small troop units on the battlefield. The player clicks on a certain unit and, for instance, tells it to move somewhere, to attack another unit, to defend itself or to scatter. The stupendously successful Command and Conquer series of games offers with every sequel more lovingly recreated 'theatres of war' and conflict situations drawn from twentieth-century history, yet at the same time litters the battlefield with increasingly fantastic depositories of hi-tech weaponry for your troops to pick up and bash the Axis with.

Real-time strategy games are, at base, congruent with the traditional class of wargame played on a large table at the weekend by men pushing little figures around with brooms – only now the computer allows the precise calculation of thousands of variables. This swamp of numbers, terrains and troop typologies effectively disguises the complementary fact that, as videogames, their formal root is Atari's panic-inducing arcade game Missile Command (1980), which originally grew out of a military simulation to see how many nuclear warheads a human radar operator could track before overload set in. As we noted of simulation, though, as games become ever more complex and hybridised, the essential elements of real-time strategy – control of multiple game pieces and tactical calculus – may crop up in several other genres.

Real-time strategy games do not provide the instant control and feedback of the more visceral videogame genres, yet nor are they such leisurely affairs as God games. Decisions about the disposition of troops and units must be made in 'real time': if you don't react quickly enough, you'll be overrun by the enemy. A certain pleasurable level of sweating tension is thereby induced. This median level of response requirement makes strategy games perfect for the burgeoning field of online play.

Owing to different modem connection speeds, it is often difficult to play a satisfying game of Quake over the Internet against someone on the other side of the world, because that game is a very rapid-response shoot-'em-up. But a real-time strategy game such as the amusing alien wargame Starcraft

(1998) is the perfect vehicle for such global connections, and moreover can handle far more than merely two players at a time. Starcraft's American server, at one point on its 1998 launch weekend, had thirty thousand players connected simultaneously. Earth is truly humming, as you are reading this, with the smoke and crackle of imaginary warfare.

The cognitive demands made on the player of real-time strategy games are among the most complex any videogame offers, and the attraction of logical, combinatorial thinking allied to often beautiful graphics (such as in the extraordinary Commandos 2) makes for a powerful experience. Wargames, too, are the most complex and satisfying example of the videogame pleasure of control: you are in charge not just of one tank or aeroplane, but of an entire army. You are not to be messed with.

Running up that hill

Perhaps the most perverse-looking class of videogame on first inspection is the sports game. After all, videogames are supposedly played in darkened rooms by people who never get any real physical exercise. But in their hovels they can be tennis demons, baseball stars or gifted golfers, or control a whole football or basketball team to world victory.

In its own sweetly abstract way, Pong, of course, was the first sports game. Subsequent refinements of the Pong engine claimed to simulate football with four paddles and two sets of goalposts, but the games were unconvincing. Chris Crawford understandably claimed in 1984: 'I suspect sports games will not attract a great deal of design attention in the future'* – just before higher-resolution graphics on home computers saw a new wave of sports games become highly successful. Konami's Track and Field, Epyx's Summer Games and Winter Games, and Ocean's Daley Thompson's Decathlon were all early hits on machines such as the Spectrum and Commodore 64, multi-event games which required the player to control tiny but

----
* *The Art of Computer Game Design*, p. 28.

well-animated pixel humans in approximations of sprinting, shot-putting, ice-skating, ski-jumping and the like.

Variations on tennis, football (classic examples were Match Day and Sensible Soccer), ice hockey and baseball followed; graphics became more detailed, control methods more complex, and environments more colourful and detailed. The promising sub-genre of 'futuristic sports', where designers, freed from the limitations of having to reproduce a messy, real sport, could attempt to create the perfect physical game, threw up a few fine moments – most notably the wonderful Speedball, a violent, sci-fi kind of tag-hockey which is still considered by many to be the best sports game ever made. But the unbeatable advantage of 'real' football, basketball and hockey games is that the rules are given and everyone knows them: you don't have to spend precious time studying a manual to learn how to win.

When videogames cracked 3D representation in the mid-1990s, sports games flourished as never before. Today the world's largest software publisher is the one that has the most impressive stable of sports games: Electronic Arts, which for the financial year 1998/9 broke the billion-dollar turnover mark. The football game is one of the most popular videogame genres of all, with one of the best being Konami's ISS Pro Evolution (see fig. 5). In EA's Euro 2000, not only are real players licensed, their faces digitally mapped on to computer figures, but the actual stadia are lovingly rebuilt on the screen. Hoardings around the virtual pitch carry real advertisements; hours of football commentary are recorded by real TV commentators, with suitable comments retrieved from the disc to suit onscreen events; and slow-motion replays from multiple angles allow the repeated savouring of a goal.

Sports games have grown up, but in the process they have almost defected to another medium. Of course football videogames are in one sense continuing the heritage of mechanical games like Subbuteo, but now solid-looking players can run smoothly around the football pitch or the hockey rink and be viewed from different camera angles, just like on TV. The modern sports game is no longer a recreation of an actual sport so much as it is a recreation of viewing that sport on television.

Fig. 5. ISS Pro Evolution: the beautiful game (© 1999 Konami)

With a little more involvement than simply shouting at the players over your six-pack.

It's a kind of magic

Dungeons, dragons, elves and wizards, treasure, trolls and spells. Yes, it's the role-playing game (RPG), the synthesis of classic text-based games like ADVENT and the 1970s teenage-male leisure phenomenon, Dungeons & Dragons fantasy board-games. The computer becomes the dungeon master and rolls all the polyhedral dice to determine the outcomes of incantatory duels.

They are very popular, especially since, as with wargames, their relatively slow pace ensures popularity on the Internet. In April 1999, a player's 'character' in Ultima Online, with impressive quantities of treasure and magic amassed over a period of six months, was sold at auction for hundreds of dollars in real money. If you can't be bothered to construct a new identity for yourself, you can always buy one.

We can see immediately an instructive contrast between the appeal of traditional RPGs and that of God games. If God games hold out the opportunity of transcending one's individuality, RPGs offer the player a chance to be fully individual in a world where an individual has real power, where the inexplicable is no longer actually supernatural but domesticated and quantifiable (magic, assessed numerically, is stripped of all its magicality), and where actions always have deterministic consequences for character or events. It is a seductive simplicity. But what RPGs really have going for them is the sense (or perhaps the illusion) of being involved in an epic, mythical story, however clichéd its details might be. In this way they also have roots in the *Fighting Fantasy* gamebooks written by Steve Jackson and Ian Livingstone (the latter is now head of videogame publishers Eidos) in the 1980s.

Modern, complex RPGs owe their shared paradigms to one game series in particular: Final Fantasy, the first game of which was released in 1987. It had detailed, colourful two-dimensional graphics, and a traditional storyline involving an ancient evil once again on the loose, with rapacious pirates on the oceans and demons in the bowels of the earth; the player was required to choose four people to make up a team of Light Warriors to save the world. The systems of magic and fighting grew more and more complex with each sequel, until Final Fantasy VII (1997) not only offered sumptuous cinematic scenes to advance the plot, but updated the milieu to one of magic futurism. Yet it is still based on a remarkably old-hat 'turn-based' system of combat, with roots clearly in the dice-throwing game played by unsocialised boys.

In essence, however, an RPG need not inhabit exclusively such puerile, sub-Tolkien milieux. The basis of any RPG is that the player 'becomes' a character in the fictional world. On a basic level, nearly every videogame ever made is a role-playing game. You play the role of a missile turret defending Earth from the space invaders; you play the role of a ravenous yellow disc being chased by ghosts. In generic RPGs, however, character is not merely a pretext to the gameplay, but part of it. Character is defined by talents, strength, cunning and even certain psychological traits, measured strictly quantitatively in points. Whereas the player is constantly getting killed in shoot-'em-ups, the survival and growth of an RPG character, the acquisition of new skills, are paramount. (Because of this emphasis on character, the RPG is the nexus of developments in what is called 'interactive storytelling', of which more later.)

Donkey Kong designer Shigeru Miyamoto's Zelda games are all RPGs. Even his phenomenal Legend of Zelda: Ocarina of Time (1998) is one, although on the surface it is a seminal 3D exploration game, because the character the player controls learns more about his past and acquires numerous new skills according to his success in the gameworld. One of the most revolutionary home-computer games of the 1980s, Elite, is usually thought of as an early 3D space game. But it is just as much an RPG too, in that success depends on carving out a career, over a period of several real-world weeks or months, as an intergalactic trader in minerals or narcotics. RPGs are the single most popular genre of videogame in Japan, and encompass a far wider and more creative range of subjects, from gardening to schoolday romance.

Role-playing elements are creeping crabwise into any number of other genres, as a way of bolting on a framework of narrative drive to the old repetitive game style. Even arcade-style driving game *par excellence*, Ridge Racer: Type 4 (1999), is an RPG, in that the player is required to complete a full Grand Prix set of races with a particular team manager, who comments on your performance and reveals his or her own fictional preoccupations. And ever more complex role-playing games will be possible with the increased storage and visual capacities of future hardware. Sega's fabulously ambitious Shenmue (2000), which chooses the 1980s as a historical period so that the characters wear leather blousons and ice-washed blue jeans, points the way forward. And Japanese software giant Namco has set up a whole department dedicated to producing RPGs for the PlayStation2. From the genre's trollish beginnings, wonderful things may yet emerge.

We can work it out

While playing videogames may not constitute an intellectual pursuit, they do challenge the mind in a more primitive, kinetic way – in much the same way, in fact, as playing sport. Yet the closest thing to sport in videogames is not necessarily a sports game. Reflexes, speedy pattern recognition, spatial imagination – these are what videogames demand. This is perhaps their fundamental virtue. If so, the king of videogame genres is arguably the most abstract, the least representational, the most nakedly challenging: the puzzle game.

At the most basic level, a videogame puzzle presents the player with a required action that cannot be performed directly. You must therefore find the intermediate steps and execute them in the right order. Puzzle elements abound in all sorts of game genres. As we mentioned earlier, Tomb Raider is in one sense a puzzle game, in that it requires manipulation of blocks in 3D space to unlock certain passages or secrets. Object-manipulation or switch-tripping puzzles abound in classic platformers like the early Mario games. Even a shoot-'em-up like Defender in one sense poses very high-speed puzzles measured in fractions of a second.

But a great puzzle game in its own right requires a combination of perfect simplicity (both in terms of rules and gameplay) and lasting challenge. Classics of this particular genre are therefore thin on the ground. The 1980s curio Sentinel was an intriguing attempt at a sort of three-dimensional, simplified chess: the player had to negotiate a chequered landscape, avoiding the immolating gaze of the sentinel, until he occupied the higher ground, at which point the sentinel could be defeated by having its energy sucked out. A superb, and much simpler, concept is that of Bust-A-Move (also known as Puzzle Bobble). Brightly coloured bubbles hang from the top of the screen; new ones are slowly added. Your job is to fire bubbles at them in such a way that three of the same colour meet; they then burst, and take any others that they were supporting with them.

But really, to understand puzzle games you only need one

word: Tetris. Created by a Soviet mathematician, Alexei Pajitnov, Tetris became the subject of a fascinating intercontinental copyright war (detailed in David Sheff's excellent *Game Over*), and Nintendo's acquisition of the handheld rights to the game helped to sell thirty-two million Game Boys in one year, 1992.

The game itself is viciously simple. It's raining blocks. Some are square, some sticky-outy, some long and thin, some infuriatingly L-shaped. In some unreal universe of fractional gravity, they float down the screen and must be rotated and laterally shifted so that they all fit together at the bottom. When they do, the horizontal line that they complete vanishes, and you have a bit more breathing space. Your job is to clear all the blocks away for as long as you can. Simple, but one of the purest, most addictive videogame designs in history. Where are you in the game? Nowhere. You are pure mind, engaged in a purely symbolic struggle. As in Space Invaders, you know that you can never win, that eventually the blocks will descend so quickly that the screen will be filled with a hideous jumble. Still you try, for maybe this time you will do just a bit better. Herein lies the demonic power, stripped naked of graphical tinsel and storylined misdirection, of every videogame there is.

Family fortunes

This scoot around videogame genres is not meant to be utterly exhaustive. But it's a working sketch, a snapshot. There isn't room here for many videogames through the years that defy easy genre categorisation, such as Deus Ex Machina, Parappa the Rapper, Skool Daze, Nights or Ecco the Dolphin.

But one useful lesson is that the videogame ecology is one rife with inter-species breeding: the lines between genres are gradually being erased. Just as *Hamlet*'s Polonius happily burbles through the permutational possibilities of dramatic genre – 'tragedy, comedy, history, pastoral, pastoral-comical, historical-pastoral, tragical-historical, tragical-comic-historical-pastoral . . .' – so at the beginning of the twenty-first century we are offered driving-RPG games, RPG-exploration games, puzzle-exploration-shoot-'em-up games and more. And increasingly, large-scale exploration games in particular are incorporating 'sub-games' of different styles within them, as a reward for completing certain sections. Sonic Adventure (1999) lets you play pinball or go snowboarding; Ape Escape (1999) has a mini-boxing game locked away inside.

But despite the myriad cosmetic and formal differences, all videogames in fact share similar concerns under the bonnet. When talking about racing games, I mentioned a particular type which seemed very serious and detailed: the simulation. Now, the concept of 'simulation' is actually rather pervasive in all sorts of videogames. After all, God games and real-time strategy games seem to present recognisable, real-life phenomena like cities and armies, while exploration games model seemingly realistic human beings wandering through recognisable environments built of stone or wood.

But how closely can certain videogames ever hope to recreate something from the real world; and how does another sort of videogame, one that is built around a purely fantastic world, persuade us that it is in some sense real?

How can you simulate what doesn't exist?

3

UNREAL CITIES

Let's get physical

You are playing a flashy, modern 3D videogame whose theme is space combat. As your craft spins and yaws around the fighting in response to frantic thumb-presses and stick-yankings, the view from your cockpit shows gorgeously rendered models of battlecruisers with scarred grey hulls, detailed planet surfaces with moving weather systems, accurately mapped constellations and galactic dust-clouds floating serenely by in the distant void. This must be the closest it is possible to get to experiencing actual interstellar dogfighting. You feel almost airsick, but exhilarated. Tracking, homing, rolling, diving, firing, cackling in triumph. It's pretty *real*, isn't it?

Actually, no. Consider this. You fight to get an enemy craft in your sights, you fire off your lasers, but – damn! – you didn't aim far enough ahead of the fighter. By the time your lazy laser bolts reach their destination, he's sailed past. Videogames have nearly always displayed lasers in this way, from the simple fire-ahead of Space Invaders or Asteroids to the rainbow-hued pyrotechnics of Omega Boost (1999). But it's wrong. Firing laser beams is not like skeet shooting, because lasers are made of light,* and light travels very, very fast, at 300 million metres per second. At the sort of distances modelled by videogames, where fighting spacecraft are never more than a few kilometres apart, lasers will take about a millionth of a second or less to hit home. It has been demonstrated that the human mind cannot

---

* Light amplification by stimulated emission of radiation, to be precise.

perceive as separate events things that occur less than roughly three thousandths of a second apart, so you will never have to wait and watch for your lasers to hit home because, to you, they will do so immediately.

But what of your enemy? Say he's a nippy little xenomorph, flying at ten thousand metres per second. That's about twelve times faster than Concorde. Unfortunately, even if he's three kilometres away, and flying directly across your sights (perpendicular to your line of aim) at that high speed, he will have moved a pathetic total of ten centimetres sideways in the time it takes your laser beam to travel from your guns to his hull. So unless he is very small, he is still very blown up. Eat dust, little green man.

But perhaps our alien has very, very quick reactions. Maybe he can spot your lasers firing, and immediately engage some sort of warp drive to get him the hell out of there in time. No, again. Because he cannot see your lasers coming until some light from your firing guns has travelled to his eyes. Unfortunately, your lasers arrive at precisely the same time. As soon as he sees you fire, he's dead.* And thanks to Einstein's theory of special relativity, one of whose principles is that light appears to travel at a constant speed regardless of the speed and direction of travel of any observer, the alien is still fried the moment he sees you fire even if he is running away in the opposite direction as close to the speed of light as his little fusion engines can manage.

That's not all. Most of the time the lasers in this epic space battle should be completely invisible. The multi-hued rain of laser fire all around, a paradigm whose early apotheosis was defined by the beautifully chaotic red and green laser bolt choreography in the film *Star Wars* (1977) – that's wrong too. A laser is a very tightly concentrated ray of photons that have been lined up so they are all travelling in exactly the same direction (unlike a normal light source, which scatters all over the place). Like any sort of light, a laser is only visible if it reflects off something. At a club, for instance, the low-powered

---

* This example is modified from one given in Lawrence M. Krauss, *The Physics of Star Trek*, p. 165.

circling laser beams are visible because they are reflecting off small particles in the intermingled clouds of dry ice and cigarette smoke. However, anyone who tried to smoke a cigarette in the interstellar void would have his brains sucked out through his face (in fact, he wouldn't be able to light the cigarette in the first place, owing to the lack of oxygen). There is no dry ice, either – space is, more or less, a vacuum. Which means there is nothing that light can reflect off on its way to the target. Hence, lasers are invisible, unless they are coming straight at you, in which case you are dead.

One corollary of this, of course, is that if the cunning enemy aliens were to build their craft with perfectly mirrored hulls, they would be impervious to laser attack, because the light would just bounce off them. You'd have thought they'd have worked that one out in all the time they've had since Space Invaders, getting thoroughly vaporised time and time again.

Why, then, do videogames get it so wrong? The answer is they get it wrong deliberately, because with 'real' laser behaviour it wouldn't be much of a game. It would be far too easy to blow things up. The challenge of accounting for an enemy craft's direction and speed, of aiming appropriately off-target, and the concomitant satisfaction of scoring a fiery hit, are artefacts of this unrealism. Generally, the world-building philosophy of videogames is one in which certain aspects of reality can be modelled in a realistic fashion, while others are deliberately skewed, their effects caricatured or dampened according to the game's requirements.

The most intriguing way in which videogames are apparently becoming more 'realistic' is in the arcane world of physical modelling. Laser behaviour may be a fantastical paradigm, but such games nevertheless enforce very strict systems of gravity and motion. Videogames increasingly codify such natural laws, such as those of Newtonian physics and beyond, in ever more accurate ways. This sounds abstruse and technical, but you have already experienced it if you've ever played or seen a game even as old as Pong (1972). Pong was modelled on simple physics: the way the ball bounced off the bat obeyed the basic law 'angle of incidence equals angle of reflection'. Approach a stationary bat at an angle of forty-five degrees, and you'll leave it at the same angle. Elementary stuff. Similarly, Asteroids enjoyed a smattering of physics modelling in the fact that your spacecraft had inertia: you carried on moving across the screen even when your engines stopped firing. And mastering this inertial control system (later refined and made much trickier in games like Thrust) was part of what made the game so enjoyably challenging. Now processor speeds are such that ever more tiny variables can be computed 'on the fly' – near instantaneously, as and when required – to give the player a sense of interacting with objects that behave just as they would in the real world.

At the vanguard of physics modelling is a company called Mathengine. Their airy, relaxed Oxford headquarters is crammed with casual young mathematicians and physicists gazing intently at the screens of muscular computers. One displays a crude wireframe representation, in blocky green lines, of a human calf and foot. 'Modelling a simple ankle joint,' the programmer confides. This sort of thing will soon have applications in, for instance, football games: the virtual players will respond to physical knocks and tackles through a system based on detailed mechanical models of the human musculo-skeletal system, rather than through predetermined animations. Motion-capture techniques, based on filming human actors and digitising the results, synthesise 'realistic' movement from the outside, and so in-game possibilities are strictly limited to those that have been filmed in the development studio. Physical modelling, on the other hand, synthesises movement from the inside, from the interaction of fundamental parts, and so allows a theoretically infinite range of character movement.

Other Mathengine demonstrations include a ball bouncing on to a slatted rope bridge, whose resonant swings and twists differ every time according to where exactly the ball was dropped; and a string-puppet articulated elephant, controlled just as in reality by a wooden cross from which the strings hang, and which can be tilted on two axes by manipulating a motion-sensing joypad attached to the computer. One begins to have an ever stronger sense of moving *objects*, rather than mere patterns.

Mathengine provides a software development kit for games

designers and other industries which allows the developer to use 'real', very accurate and processor-cheap physics in his or her applications. If a game company is writing a racing game, for instance, using a kit like Mathengine's the car can be defined as a certain mass resting, through a suspension system, on four wheels, which have a certain frictional relationship with the road. From this very simple mathematical definition, it turns out that 'realistic' car behaviour, such as oversteer and understeer, load-shifting and tilting, comes for free. Whereas games developers used to have to 'kludge' the physics, to laboriously create something that approximated to realistic behaviour, physical modelling makes it all happen as behaviour emerging from a simple set of definitions.

And this process directly affects the videogame player's experience. As Mathengine's product manager Paul Topping puts it, 'dynamic properties are a very intuitive thing'. We are used to handling objects with mass, bounce and velocity in the real world, and we can predict their everyday interactions pretty well. You don't have to be Paul Newman to know roughly how a pool ball is going to bounce off a cushion; you don't have to be Glenn Gould to know that striking a piano key with force is going to produce a louder sound than if you'd caressed it. And anyone who plays tennis is automatically doing pretty complex parabolic calculus without any conscious thought. Appreciation of dynamic properties is hard-wired into the species – it's essential for survival. This, then, is one of the most basic ways in which videogames speak to us as the real world does, directly to the visceral, animal brain – even as they tease the higher imagination by building a universe which could never exist.

Furthermore, just as timing a good shot in tennis is a pleasure in itself, there is a direct link between convincing videogame dynamics and gameplay pleasure. A game which is more physically realistic is thereby, Topping says, 'more aesthetically pleasing', because the properly modelled game enables us pleasurably to exercise our physical intuition. 'All great games have physics in them – that's what gives it the lovely feel,' Topping points out. And this is just as true for classic games such as Defender or Asteroids as it is for modern racers like Gran

Turismo 2000. In Defender, you aim your ship to face left or right and then thrust, and the simple inertia means that you can flip around and fire at aliens while still travelling backwards; the subsequent application of forward thrust takes time to kick in. Even a very simple puzzle game such as Bust-A-Move exercises the intuitive knowledge of Pong-style (or, in the real world, squash-style) angular reflections, as bubbles may be bounced off the side walls to achieve tactically desirable formations that are impossible by aiming directly.

Even so, the physical systems that games can model so accurately are never totally 'realistic'. Just as with the operation of lasers, videogames deliberately load the dice one way or another. If you put a Formula One racing driver in front of an accurately modelled racing game, Topping says, he would still crash the car, because of the gulf between controllability and visual feedback. And an ordinary player would find the game merely boring and frustrating. So, Topping explains, 'You're gonna fake the physics. Increase friction, make the car smaller – you *choose* what you model properly.'

The lesson is that even with whiz-bang maths programming, a videogame in important ways remains defiantly unreal. Videogames' somewhat paradoxical fate is the ever more accurate modelling of things that don't, and couldn't, exist: a car which grips the road like Superglue, which bounces uncrumpled off roadside barriers; a massive spacecraft with the manoeuvrability of a bumble bee; a human being who can survive, bones intact, a three-hundred-foot fall into water. We don't want absolutely real situations in videogames. We can get that at home.

Let's stick together

Naturally, the player doesn't mind this fakery, this playing fast and loose with the laws of nature in the name of fun. But a critical requirement is that the game's system remains consistent, that it is internally coherent. Crucially, it is lack of coherence rather than unrealism which ruins a gameplaying experience. This is largely but not exclusively a phenomenon of more modern videogames, whose increasing complexity in terms of space, action and tasks clearly places a greater strain on the designer's duty to create a rock-solid underlying structure.

Videogame incoherence has three types: it can apply to causality, function or space. Incoherence of causality, firstly, appears, for example, in a driving game such as V-Rally (1997), where driving at full speed into another car causes a slight slowing down, but hitting a boulder at the road's edge leads to a spectacular vehicular somersault. Another example crops up in Tomb Raider III, where a rocket-launcher blows up one's enemies into pleasingly gory, fleshy chunks, but does no damage to a simple wooden door, for which one simply has to find a rusty old key. (Indeed, having travelled far from the austere near-perfection of its original incarnation, Tomb Raider III boasts many instructive examples of design incoherence.) In direct contrast, Quake III incorporates the hilarious but highly coherent idea of 'rocket-jumping'. You've got a rocket-launcher. If you point it at the floor and then fire as you jump, you'll be catapulted much higher into the air by the recoil of your foolishly potent weapon. Eminently reasonable.

Incoherence of function is more serious. In many games one encounters 'single-use' objects, such as a magic book that only works in a particular location or a cigarette lighter that can only be used to illuminate a certain room. Resident Evil typifies this lazy approach to game design, with all manner of special scrolls, gems, books and other things which are used once as puzzle-solving tokens and then forgotten about. Tomb Raider's rocket-launcher fails on this count too, because its use is artificially restricted in the game. If a game designer chooses to give the player a special object or weapon, it ought to work consistently and reliably through all appropriate circumstances in the game, or the believably unreal illusion is shattered.

By contrast, perfect coherence of function is great fun. It is just one virtue of Zelda 64* that, despite the colourfully huge gallimaufry of in-game objects, they are hardly ever single-use items; it is an unprecedentedly rich and varied yet highly

---

* Shorthand for the remainder of this book for Legend of Zelda: Ocarina of Time.

consistent gameworld. The titular ocarina, a clay flute, has a different function according to what tune is played on it: if Link plays certain songs he has learned (the gamer must physically play the notes using the control buttons), he may cause day to turn to night, invoke a storm, warp to a different place in the gameworld or cheer up a miserable rock-eating king. Link's hoverboots can be used in several different places for several different results. The bow and arrow might be used to kill a far-away enemy, or (in one brilliant problem) to melt a frozen switch by firing an arrow through the flame of a blazing torch while standing on a revolving platform.

But of course a bow and arrow isn't going to open locked doors. You wouldn't expect it to. The hookshot, a retracting chain device with a hook on the end, may be used to kill enemies, but it is also a means to get up to hard-to-reach places, Batman-style. Even here there is a thoughtful, stern consistency based on properties of physical substances: Link's hookshot will bounce off stone, but if it hits wood it will sink in and let him swing up. And the player can be sure that a burning stick will always light a torch, wherever it may be encountered.

The third type of incoherence is that of spatial management. Tomb Raider III adds to its heroine's series of possible moves – which already include implausibly high jumps and rolls – a crawl, so that the player can move around in low passageways. But at a certain stage in the game Lara finds herself at the end of a low tunnel, giving out on to a corridor. Try as the player might, it is impossible to get Lara out into that corridor, owing to the game's basic construction around a series of uniformly sized blocks. If the tunnel entrance were a full block above the corridor floor, Lara could get out. But the getting-out-of-a-tunnel animation requires her to lower herself fully down the side of the block while hanging from her hands, and the tunnel exit does not achieve the required altitude. So the move becomes impossible. This sort of inconsistency also rears its gory head in Resident Evil, where the player is not allowed simply to drop unwanted objects on the floor, but must stow them away in one of several chests – and, risibly, an object put in one chest may be retrieved from another chest three floors higher up in the building.

By these standards, Tomb Raider III and Resident Evil are arguably inferior to Space Invaders or Pong, both of which exhibit total consistency in the laws of the imaginary world. As Chris Crawford says in *The Art of Computer Game Design*, special-case rules (which roughly map on to our causal, functional and spatial incoherences) are bad: 'In the perfect game design, each rule is applied universally.' This is easy to verify if you consider the situation in other types of game – chess, for instance: Garry Kasparov would be profoundly, glaringly unimpressed if his opponent sought to stave off defeat by pronouncing that, actually, at this particular juncture, the black queen was not allowed to move diagonally.

Tomb Raider III also illustrates perfectly another potential danger of trying to increase 'realism' in a game – in this case by adding extra ranges of movement to a human character. Because the hero of Manic Miner lives in such a resolutely bizarre world, where flying electrified lavatories are the least of his worries, we do not worry that our character is able only to walk and to jump. But in the far more naturalistic milieu of the Tomb Raider series, the bolted-on possibilities of movement that are added in each sequel only serve to remind the player how odd it is that Lara can run, swim, crawl and jump, but cannot punch or kick an assailant, for instance. She cannot even sit down, although given her lecherously silicon-enhanced curves, it is probably just as well, for she would never get up again.

This is not to say that expanded physical possibilities in human characters are bad – in themselves they are good – but their introduction poses other problems of design that must be attended to. In Zelda 64, for instance, Link's inability to punch or kick is never an issue, for by the time he is first in danger he already permanently owns a sword. A sword is better than a fist, so the player doesn't feel that anything is missing. By contrast, Lara Croft often goes about unarmed among enemies, having had her guns confiscated, and so her unwillingness to punch and kick is frustrating.

To complain about these aspects in a game, of course, is not incompatible with happily accepting that the heroine must on occasion do battle with a slavering Tyrannosaurus rex.

There is a crucial difference between axiomatic principles of the fantastical world on the one hand – for instance, the laser behaviour considered earlier, or Manic Miner's winged cisterns – and inconsistencies in the fantastical system – such as Lara's rocket-launcher or Resident Evil's item boxes – on the other.

Life in plastic

Of Sweeney's* three certainties of life, videogames have so far largely eschewed birth and copulation. But, as if in sardonic compensation, they are triply teeming with death. And their particular reinvention of death is but one of a whole lexicon of happily irrealist principles that videogames have amassed over their history. Death in a videogame is multimodal: it means one thing for your enemies, another thing for certain other types of enemies, yet another for you. Shoot a space invader and he is gone for ever. Kill a dungeon skeleton in Zelda 64 and it is dust – but if you leave and then re-enter the room, it has horribly regenerated, there to be fought all over again. But what does death mean for you, the player? If the aliens' rain of bombs becomes overwhelming and one hits your ship, blowing it to pixellated smithereens, it is certainly bad news. But wait – suddenly a gleaming new ship appears at the bottom of the screen, under your control, and you can continue the never-ending battle from the point where you left off.

We are used to thinking of 'life' as a single, sacred thing, the totality of our experiences. But videogames redefine a 'life' as an expendable, iterable part of a larger campaign. In part this resembles the brutal calculus of war, where a human life, normally the definition of total value in peacetime, is arithmetised as being worth, say, one hundredth of the value of taking the next ridge. But videogames offer a multitude of lives to the same individual. It is instant reincarnation, though reincarnation in a body indistinguishable from the original. It is instant expiation for the sin of failure. The standard number of lives granted at the beginning of a game is three, which

---

* Protagonist of T. S. Eliot's *Sweeney Agonistes*, that is.

corresponds to the paradigmatic number of tries allowed in many other games, from a baseball hitter's number of strikes to a javelin-thrower's attempts at the gold, to the number of doors from which a contestant must choose in the American gameshow *Let's Make a Deal**, or the number of 'acts' or significant subdivisions of the protagonist's story in classical drama.† In a universe where guns have infinite ammunition and spacecraft infinite fuel, it is life itself which becomes a resource whose loss is survivable.

Yet a videogame 'life' is not just a resource but also a possible reward. Games such as Defender or Space Invaders offer 'extra lives' when a certain score is achieved (usually a multiple of ten or twenty thousand). It resembles an ethically inverted form of Buddhism. In the eastern philosophy, if you commit wrongs, your growing karmic debt means you are constantly reincarnated into a new existence in order to suffer anew. But whereas Buddhism's final aim is to jump off the exhausting carousel of constant reincarnation and to be no more, life in a videogame is always a good thing, and killing is the morally praiseworthy action required to resurrect it. The fact that simple survival edges the player closer, as the score increases, to an extra life argues that – as Nietzsche would have growled through his moustache after half an hour at the Robotron controls – what does not destroy you makes you stronger.

The concept of multiple videogame 'lives', then, bespeaks an arena of strategic experimentation in which a fatal mistake need not be your last; branches of a system can be multiply explored until all the lives are used up. But when that happens, the downside is grim indeed. The result in this final situation is not a simple death, but a violent ejaculation from the safety of the entire game universe. The *petit mort* of *Homo ludens*: Game Over.

Subsequent to this distribution of multiple 'lives', videogames began to introduce another highly unrealistic paradigm, again

---

* Source of the amusing 'Monty Hall Paradox' in probability theory. For an excellent explanation, see Deborah J. Bennett, *Randomness*.

† The claim that classical drama was born from the gameplaying instinct is made persuasively in Johann Huizinga, *Homo Ludens*.

disguised in deceptively ordinary language: that of 'health'. Whereas in Space Invaders or Asteroids the player's ship is destroyed by contact with one bomb, bullet or rock, later games further subdivide a life with a coloured bar representing 'health', which is degraded (to use an ugly late-twentieth-century military euphemism) by damage to the player's character. When the bar is completely emptied, the life is gone. Applied to spacecraft or other vehicles, this concept is understandable, as it could be thought to measure the integrity of the craft's hull or other analogue, flight-critical criteria. Yet from a doggedly literal point of view, it approaches risibility when applied to human characters. Lara Croft can take several bullets in the torso, or get savaged by a tiger, while losing only an eighth of her 'health'. Modern videogames, however, are so full of perilous situations that such a sliding scale, rather than simply being alive or dead, is crucial to the game's playability.

Health is also the primary means of adjudication in beat-'em-up games, where each combatant has an 'energy' meter that is depleted when the opponent lands a punch or a kick. The player whose energy is reduced to zero first is the loser. Of course this is unrealistic in that an axe blow to the head – in Soul Calibur, for instance – only takes off a fraction of your 'health'. Yet it is a causally incoherent system as well: a punch to the face does the same damage as a kick to the shin, although in real life it would be debilitating in a completely different way. This is another obvious future application for developments in physical modelling, when the game will 'know' automatically that a jolt to the head will affect vision and balance, whereas a leg trauma will affect locomotion and kicking ability.

The first steps towards this kind of more complex system have already been made in games like the fascinating Bushido Blade (1997), a more 'serious' weapon-based game in which one well-aimed blow with a katana or sledgehammer will – naturally – kill the opponent, while severe blows to a limb will disable him. The spectacle of two wonderfully animated virtual fighters in beautiful oriental robes shuffling about a cherry-tree garden on their knees because leg injuries mean that they can no longer stand is hugely amusing.

The wittiest use of the 'health' paradigm yet seen is in Metal Gear Solid (1998), an exploration game which initiated its own sub-genre, the 'sneak-'em-up'. The player has access to rafts of guns and bombs, but if she simply runs about firing, the guards will call for reinforcements and quickly go in for a kill. The gameplay necessarily becomes stealthy: guards and security cameras must be avoided wherever possible. In the game, the player controls a soldier, Solid Snake, who can be made to smoke a cigarette. The game provides the mandatory tobacco health warning, and while Snake is puffing away, his health meter slowly goes down. If you smoke for long enough, health reaches a minimal sliver on the bar, but it is impossible in the game to commit suicide by cigarette.

This raises an important point. The programmers of Metal Gear Solid have unfortunately not provided the option of smoking several cigarettes at once, or eating a whole pack, which would almost certainly kill you. It wasn't written in as a possibility, so you can't do it. Remember, in a videogame you can only perform such actions as the programmers have allowed for. This recalls Heidegger's notion of 'enframing' – that technology, far from being liberating, actually circum-scribes the possibilities of action. But a good videogame will allow predetermined actions to be combined in creative ways that certainly weren't deliberately predicted at the design stage. In chess, after all, you don't invent the forms of individual moves, you choose creatively among them and string them together in a strategy. This is the basic difference, if operating at a far less complex level, that we touched on in the last chapter, between beat-'em-ups, which provide many hundreds of individual actions but little freedom of combination, and something like Robotron, with two basic actions – move and fire – and strategy aplenty. Indeed, as Eugene Jarvis, program-mer of Robotron and Defender, told J. C. Herz about someone he watched playing the latter game: 'He was doing things I never envisioned, never thought of, tactics I never dreamed of.'

Meanwhile, back to smoking. Metal Gear Solid stresses that it's bad for you, but if Snake hasn't found some infrared goggles, he needs to smoke a cigarette in order to render visible a web of security beams that will set off alarms if he breaks them; and if he smokes while using the sniper rifle, his aim is steadier. In this way, with its alluring mix of peril and desirability, smoking in Metal Gear Solid, as in life, is sublime.* In a more general sense, it is an example of how health can be traded for other benefits concerning the game objective. The idea of health sacrifice is a relatively new one; it appears in a much cruder fashion in the Tomb Raider games, where if Lara is in a recessed pit filled with spikes or barbed wire, she can avoid injury by walking carefully, but to get out of the pit she is forced to jump and therefore lacerate her legs.

Most games featuring a health bar also provide some means for the player to restore her health, rather than face an inexorable slide towards loss of life. Pick up a mystical 'medikit' and bullet wounds are healed, all injuries forgotten, stamina replenished. Medikits and other health-restoring devices are further examples of a class of items in the gameworld which usually obey none of the gameworld's usual physical rules: power-ups. They can be items on the floor to be picked up, or amorphous blobs of energy floating in the air to be driven or flown through.

Power-ups in general enhance the abilities of the player's character in the game: aside from restoring health or granting an extra life, they may also increase speed, envelop the player's ship in a temporary shield (which mysteriously stops bullets from entering, but allows the player to shoot outwards) or furnish the player with one of an arsenal of extra-destructive weapons with which to meet the next enemy onslaught. In their instantaneous and nakedly magical effect, power-ups partake of a totally different ontology from anything else on the screen. Their mode and effect is purely relational, redefining the logic of how the player's character and the enemies interact.

---

* See the intoxicating Richard Klein, *Cigarettes Are Sublime* (1993; London: 1995).

Out of control

What's the most glaringly unreal aspect of videogames? It's a cybernetic thing. Cybernetics is the study of control systems (from the Greek *kubernētēs*, meaning 'steersman'). And videogame control systems are for the most part radically removed, in structural terms, from what happens on the screen. I have so far been talking about how videogames manipulate the imaginative involvement of the player, in the ruses and paradigms of their unreal worlds. But the videogame is not simply a cerebral or visual experience; just as importantly it is a physical involvement – the tactile success or otherwise of the human–machine interface. Some games recommend the use of a peripheral: an extra piece of interface hardware that plugs into the console or PC. For driving games this would be a steering wheel, complete with floor pedals; for Time Crisis the player buys an actual lightgun with which to shoot at the television screen. Yet most games are still controlled with curiously alienating devices: a standard joystick or 'joypad', or a computer mouse and keyboard.

We saw one way in which this can hobble gameplay in the last chapter, when it was noted that beat-'em-ups rely on memorised combinations of button-presses to perform almost arbitrary series of martial arts moves. Sports games, too, suffer from a particularly limiting cybernetic dissonance. The swing of a golf club, for instance, is accomplished in videogames simply by pressing buttons at the right time while observing 'power meters'. All manner of ball tricks, spins and tackle evasions are called up in a football game by particular combinations of buttons. This is clearly not ideal for convincing involvement with the action. But there is no reason why such an arrangement should persist.

Early sports games like Daley Thompson's Decathlon actually boasted a far more compelling physical interface with the notorious 'joystick-waggling' method: the faster you could waggle your joystick from side to side, the faster your character would sprint or skate. This system has been resurrected for Konami's brilliant multi-player athletics game International

Track and Field 2 (1999), except that the player must now press two buttons alternately at very high speed. But Sony's present-day controller for the PlayStation, the Dual Shock pad with two thumb-controlled analogue joysticks, has so far been woefully underused in just the types of game it could revolutionise in a similar way.

An analogue joystick provides far greater sensitivity and range of control. The old-style digital joysticks only recognised 'on' or 'off' states of any particular direction; the analogue joystick recognises degrees of change. You can move, for example, slightly right or fully right, with degrees in between, which may correspond to various velocities between a slow walk and a run, or various rotational positions of a steering wheel. The cybernetic possibilities are rich and largely unexplored.

A tennis game, for instance, could use one stick for your character's movement over the court, and the other to control directly the movement of the racquet arm when playing a shot. Move the stick faster, and you play a more powerful stroke; move it in a curve, and you impart spin. Similarly, in a boxing game, each stick could be programmed to control directly the movement of an arm. This seems such an obvious idea that it is astonishing that software companies do not so far implement it generally. The first, and so far only, use of the idea occurs in the splendid gadget-festooned exploration game Ape Escape (1999), in which the player must row an inflatable dinghy downstream by rotating both sticks, each controlling a separate oar; sub-games offer direct control of skis or, indeed, arms in 'Monkey Boxing'. Analogue control is becoming a new standard. The standard controller for Sega's Dreamcast console only provides one analogue stick instead of Sony's two, which is a bad oversight, although its dual triggers are both analogue. Sony's PlayStation2 controller, meanwhile, boasts analogue response on all its buttons, opening up intriguing new gameplay possibilities.

Another fairly recent cybernetic innovation has certainly enhanced the 'feel' of many videogames: force feedback. Sony's Dual Shock controller is so named because the videogame can tell it to vibrate or 'rumble' in the player's hands. This vibrational feedback can be used in a driving game, to simulate the shuddering of braking or a skid into a gravel pit; it can add a physical dimension to damage done to the player's character by bullet or blunt instrument; in Metal Gear Solid, a game which makes splendidly creative use of this extra mode of information, it even simulates the thumping of the main character's heartbeat when he is looking through the scope of his sniper rifle – the rhythmical juddering of the control pad justifiably makes it difficult to aim accurately. We can expect that in future controllers will provide more subtle gradations of vibration, as well as physically resisting the player's movement and even, as hypothesised in Kurt Andersen's 1999 novel *Turn of the Century*, changing temperature according to the action onscreen.

Perhaps the most enjoyable recent cybernetic novelty is that offered by Konami's fabulously eccentric Dance Dance Revolution (now known in the West by the inferior title Dancing Stage), in which the player must use her whole body to control the game. It consists of actually dancing, on a pressure-sensitive floormat, in time to pumping techno music blaring from the speakers. The screen simply shows a bunch of symbols floating downwards, and they correspond to squares on the floormat that must be hit by the feet at exactly the right moment. This speedy techno version of Twister provokes the thought that the best videogame interfaces are indeed those that are most intuitive (an idea that will crop up later in another context). No one needs to learn how to stamp on the floor, just as no one needs to learn how to turn a steering wheel or shoot a play gun.

In general, cybernetic developments will always increase the possibilities of closer and more pleasurable interaction with a videogame. In just the same way that a motor-industry journalist might say one car 'feels' nicer to drive than another, there is a particular pleasure to be had simply from engaging in a responsive control system, whether in videogames or in real life. It is no accident, then, that Nintendo's Shigeru Miyamoto, widely regarded as the 'God of videogames' (in Jeremy Smith's phrase), not only designs software but actually designs the controllers for each new Nintendo system in order to maximise gameplay potential.

When I spoke to Richard Darling of British developers Codemasters about what makes a game 'fun', he echoed Paul Topping's admiration of early physics-based games such as Thrust: 'You're flying that little space rocket around and you pick up a ball and it's on the end of a pole with a weight, and the way it swings and the way your thrust and acceleration affects the swing and the motion and everything is extremely intuitive. It's complex, but it's intuitive.' But more than that, according to Darling, Thrust was also cybernetically clever:

> The control system is *deep* – in that anyone can pick it up and play it; you've got a thrust button and you rotate left and rotate right. Now if that was *move* left, move right and move forward, the gameplay would be extremely limited. But the fact that what you're actually doing is thrusting, which is accelerating you, and you can *rotate* to any angle, and *thrust* at any angle, means that the learning curve in becoming an expert at the control system is very long.
>
> That was true of Super Mario Bros as well. It seems like a simple 'press a button to jump, run left, run right' game, but if you analyse it, you actually *accelerated* left and right up to a maximum speed, and when you jumped, the amount of time you held the button down for determined how high you jumped. Therefore there was an awful lot of skill in running along over a hole, jumping up on to a platform and landing on it without falling off the other side. It was actually an extremely skilful thing to do.

What about total immersion? Virtual reality systems have been around for many years and no doubt will soon be affordable and efficient. Some combination of headset (such as Sony's Glasstron monitors), motion-sensitive data gloves and so on will enable the player to become totally immersed in a game, just as the science fiction movies have been telling us for decades. Will this, then, become the dominant means of videogame control? Perhaps; but if so, the spirit of Heidegger will rise again to warn that such cybernetic hegemony will necessarily *narrow* the field of possibilities. Immersive VR will be fine for exploration games, driving games, 3D space shoot-'em-ups and so on. But what happens to the pleasurable unreality of human-body physics? How will such a system enable the player to somersault like Lara Croft, to climb sheer walls, to swim a hundred feet down in icy Arctic rivers or to finish off a brutal martial arts combination of smacks and punches by floating six feet into the air and delivering a round-house kick to the head?

Counter-intuitively, it seems for the moment that the perfect videogame 'feel' requires the ever-increasing imaginative and physical involvement of the player to stop somewhere short of full bodily immersion. After all, a sense of pleasurable control implies some modicum of *separation*: you are apart from what you are controlling. You don't actually want to *be* there, per-forming the dynamically exaggerated and physically perilous moves yourself; it would be exhausting and painful. Remember, you don't want boring, invisible lasers; you don't want a For-mula One car that takes years of training to drive; and you don't want to die after taking just one bullet. You don't *want* it to be too real.

The purpose of a videogame, then, is never to simulate real life, but to offer the gift of play. In a videogame, we are citizens of an invisible city where there is no danger, only challenge. And our videogame metropolis, like any city, is teeming and multifaceted. We have already sketched out a rough map of its geography. Later in this book we shall look at its architecture, dig below its tarmac to the pipes and cables that keep it running, and stroll around in its forest of signs. But for the moment we want to know just what kind of industry buzzes behind those imposing towers. Is this a city of words, a modern Alexandria, or a city of images, a virtual Hollywood?

Look over on that street corner: a camera crew, smoking under black plastic cloaks, huddled in the neon-flecked rain. Let's go and ask them.

4

ELECTRIC SHEEP

A spectre is haunting Tinseltown. We have seen how successful videogames already compete in financial terms with the figures grossed by Hollywood blockbusters. And one increasingly popular term of praise for a certain sort of exploration videogame is to say that it is like an 'interactive film'. On the summer 1999 release of Silent Hill, a horror videogame in which you play the character of a man searching a deserted American town for his missing daughter, one journalist claimed that this game 'fully exploited' the developments towards 'fully interactive cinema'. The media buzz is that cinema and videogames are on convergent paths. If this is true, Hollywood ought to be worried that videogames are going to swallow it whole.

Some of the world's best videogame developers happily admit that they lean heavily on styles of action and decor drawn from popular cinema. Hideo Kojima, the brilliant designer of Metal Gear Solid who comes on like a twenty-first-century Beck, dressing up for interviews in garish PVC outfits and tinted shades, has joked that whereas most people are 70 per cent water, he is 70 per cent movies. Konami's publicity for Silent Hill, meanwhile, claimed 'cinematic quality' as a virtue, noting that its developers cited David Cronenberg, Stephen King and David Lynch as aesthetic influences.

So what in fact makes Silent Hill like a film? Well, it has an impressive introductory video sequence, pre-rendered with high-quality computer graphics workstations, which tells the story of how your character suffers a car crash and wakes up in the ghostly small town with his daughter missing. This sequence is indeed very filmic, with fast cutting and weird camera angles. However, it's not part of the game, even though one British entertainment magazine which featured a piece on Silent Hill clearly based its judgement of the game's 'filmic' quality entirely on this video sequence.

During the game itself, the part you actually get to play, the graphics are of a far inferior quality, and occasional scenes of scripted dialogue between characters are incompetently written and amazingly badly acted. Some films have a 'so bad it's good' quality, but this hack attempt at drama is just so bad it's appalling. If it's supposed to be like a film in this way, it's a film you wouldn't ever want to see.

However, what Silent Hill does successfully breed from its cinematic forebears is quite simple: a powerful sense of atmosphere. Tense wandering in dark environments is interrupted with shocks, sudden appearances of blood-curdling monsters. Silence is interrupted by grating noise, making you jump and increasing your nervousness. The same sort of atmospheric virtue is present in the Resident Evil series of zombie videogames, which themselves are the subject of interesting cross-media developments. It was long rumoured that George Romero was to make a live-action film based on Resident Evil, which would have been apt, not only because he directed a high-budget television commercial for the second game in the franchise, but because the Resident Evil games themselves cheerfully lift wholesale the camera angles and action sequences from Romero's own classic zombie flicks such as *Dawn of the Dead.*

Why is it particularly the horror genre, and to a lesser extent science fiction, that largely provides the aesthetic compost for supposedly 'filmlike' videogames? No one has yet claimed that a videogame is like a good comedy film (though it may be funny in other ways, as is Grim Fandango, a rococo puzzle-solving RPG with delightful cartoonish graphics), or that a videogame tells a heartbreaking romance. The answer is that the horror genre can easily do away with character and plot; it is the detail of the monsters, the rhythm of the tension and shocks that matter. Plot and character are things videogames find very difficult to deal with.

The fact is that Silent Hill and Resident Evil resemble each other far more than they resemble any film you care to name. But will this necessarily always be the case, or could the much-hyped 'convergence' between films and videogames become a reality?

The gift of sound and vision

Videogames are superficially like films in one major respect, which is that they communicate to the player through eyes *and* ears. Just as film crews include specialised audio technicians for the post-production dubbing of sound effects, the sound design of videogames too is a mini-art in itself, and development companies also employ composers to provide musical soundtracks. At first, this looks very like film industry practice, but it soon becomes clear that deployment of the audio arts cannot always follow similar lines in the two media.

The reason why sound design is important in videogames is quite simple: if a laser makes a pleasing, fizzy hum, and if an exploding enemy makes a particularly satisfying boom, then the game is just more fun to play. Defender (1980) had particularly avant-garde sound design for its time, with its near sub-bass rumblings and eldritch alien buzzings offset by the heroic, almost melodic sound of your ship's weapon fending off the vicious hordes. Purely abstract sonic invention such as Defender's was partly necessitated by the comparative crudeness, in those days, of the videogame machine's sound chip. But now that videogame systems can read huge amounts of digitally encoded sound straight off a CD, sound design has largely moved in a more conventional direction, using 'samples' (digital recordings) to reproduce actual, real-world sounds. A modern development company might devote many hours to accurate sampling of different cars' engine noises for a driving game, to make the whole audio-visual experience as immersive and (deceptively) 'authentic' as possible.

This concentration on 'real' sounds in general parallels what movies do. But just as a film with terrific abstract sound design, like David Lynch's *Lost Highway*, is highly refreshing to the ears, so I think this attitude of 'realism' is narrow-minded in a videogame context. The best audio engineering now seems to be constrained to highly generic videogames such as space shoot-'em-ups or science fiction racers, where the fantasy world can justifiably be accompanied by fantasy sound, all manner of lovingly crafted blips and whooshes. An instance of particularly good contemporary work is in the otherwise rather shallow shooter Omega Boost, where, if you bump into enemies, a grating metallic clang enhances the momentary discomfort, and spacecraft whoosh past you to fabulously alien stereo effect. The sonic mayhem (with these effects unfortunately competing with a musical score of Japanese heavy metal) effectively increases the level of sweating tension in the player.

Such a strong division between games which enjoy 'real', sampled sounds and games with an invented sonic architecture I think is unfortunate. Surely, if videogame developers were to experiment, say, with weird and unexpected sound effects to accompany supposedly 'realistic' visual action, this might open up new avenues of strangeness and even comedy – the amusing disjunction of small action with epic sound, say – to future digital experiences. Videogames are best at imagining whole new worlds of their own, so why cannot they invent more new sounds to bring them to sensual life?

Moreover, given that in real life all sorts of information about our environment is constantly flooding into our ears, videogames ought perhaps to think of cleverer ways to let us use this gift in their imaginary worlds. After all, a videogame player, unlike someone watching a film, needs to use information from the senses to decide what to do next. Any sound can become a clue, a spur to action. One fascinating new idea has been tried by Rare, who in Perfect Dark (2000) have engineered a quasi-surround sound system which lets the attuned player know which direction enemies are in purely by listening to their footsteps.

This is one example of sound design that is not merely decorative, but functional. Many games, particularly in the popular horror genre, are already quite creative in using sound to enhance the player's involvement. Resident Evil, for instance, shows a superb handling of sound effects which is directly influenced by its movie forebears. One room is eerily silent, whereas a large galleried hall is ominously and stressfully dominated by the solemn ticking of a clock. When the moans of zombies suddenly float out of nowhere, or the silence is broken by the piercing sound of a smashing window, you know you had better run. Silent Hill, too, does this sort of thing very well. Early on in the game, the player's character is given a radio which seems to be broken, but it emits a nerve-fraying fortissimo jangling noise whenever a monster is approaching. The evocation of fear is deliciously heightened by this aural sign, as you run around panicking when the alarm goes off, not knowing from which direction the beast is going to approach through the omnipresent fog.

Videogames' musical soundtracks, too, are an important part of the player's aesthetic experience. But oddly, in the far-off days of the Commodore 64 and Amiga, videogame music was far more distinct as a stylistic genre than it is now. The composers generally had to wrestle with programming languages to force the most sophisticated sound possible out of woefully underpowered audio chips, and these strictures resulted in a flood of remarkably inventive videogame music. If polyphony – the number of notes it is possible to play at the same time – was restricted to, say, four notes, the musician might write a piece characterised by deliciously floaty buzzing arpeggios. And because the microcomputer's sound chip didn't have much inbuilt information to speak of – unlike a modern synthesiser, it didn't boast banks of ready-made instrument noises – the composer also had to invent the quality of each of the sounds he used. The star of this era was the musician Rob Hubbard, whose excellent soundtracks for old games – with their airbrushed, joyfully artificial aesthetic that mixed robotic beats with hummable tunes – have now been collectively preserved on a commercially available compact disc.

Nowadays, videogame soundtracks fall into two main classes: the compilation of licensed pop tracks, or the specially composed score. Slapping an existing pop record over a videogame, or a film, is a rather hit-or-miss affair: as we have seen, it worked wonders for early PlayStation games like WipE-out, but it can equally be grindingly inappropriate, the French heavy-rock songs on V-Rally 2 being an emetic case in point.

The alternative of a specially written score is now blessed with total sonic freedom, because videogame systems (apart from the poor Nintendo 64) now read music directly off a CD, so soundtracks are recorded with full banks of pro-quality digital instruments and no restrictions on epic breadth. Sometimes the music may even be recorded by a full orchestra of live musicians, as is the case with Outcast.

The problem with such scores, even when – as is increasingly the case – they are highly competent and pleasing pieces of music in their own right, is that, unlike the videogame's visuals, they are not interactive. A film score is written to accompany a predetermined and unchanging visual story. So it is recorded once and cast in stone. But videogames can change from one moment to the next depending on what the player does. One way round this is just to cut in a rather ugly fashion from a light-hearted piece of music to a doom-laden one when something bad happens onscreen. Microsoft have developed a system called Direct Music which hopes to automate this technique more smoothly. But all this means in practice is that the composer writes tiny little 'cells' of music a few bars long that are then algorithmically combined into longer episodes by the processing engine. (Avant-garde classical musicians had exactly this idea of combining cells in the 1960s.)

The best videogame scores circumvent this knotty problem altogether by *not* attempting to be continuous, film-like soundtracks at all. Instead, music is used as another kind of atmosphere-heightening information. The rather beautiful title music of the Tomb Raider games features undulating orchestral strings with a lovely oboe tune. But within the game, the mood and instrumentation change dramatically, according to the fictional context. The celebrated Venice level of Tomb Raider II, for example, features a superb piece of pastiche baroque. In these games, music's appearance is much rarer than it is in your average film, and when the speakers burst into a fast cello motif or a clatter of electronic percussion, you know that something exciting is going to happen and you look round rapidly for an enemy to avoid, or watch in awe as another fabulous vaulted ceiling stretches up above you, and then the music fades away again, leaving you with the drips of condensation from the walls or the rumbling of some ominous nearby machinery. When music in a game is this good, less is often more.

So music in a videogame does not work in exactly the same ways as music in a film. In a game, sound can be functional, a means of providing information which the player then acts on. But what about the visuals? Do videogames present information to our eyes in the same way as films?

Ciné qua non?

Since the upstart videogame form shattered film's monopoly on the moving image, the two media have been engaged in a wary stand-off. As their powers of graphical realisation have increased, videogames have begun superficially to look a bit more like films, while films have become more interested in videogames as visual furnishing and conceptual subject matter. Videogames have lovingly appropriated set-piece forms from the cinematic milieux of horror, action and science fiction (the enormous monster, the car chase, the space dogfight), while films have stolen ever more brazenly from videogames' hyper-kinetic grammar (the exaggerated sound effects, the disregard for classical gravitational laws) in executing those same forms on the silver screen.

It is, of course, understandable that the mass media, in having to deal with the vast but to them incomprehensible culture of videogames, naturally reach for the vocabulary of film – apparently the nearest medium in visual terms – in order to describe such games as Silent Hill. But before we start positing a hybrid future of 'interactive movies', it would be as well to take a cold mental shower by looking at what actually exists in film–videogame crossover form.

Disney's *Tron* (1982) was the first film actively to engage in an aesthetic dialogue with videogames, arguably as a symptom of Tinseltown's increasing insecurity about its silicon rival – for at the time, just before their first market crash, videogames were grossing more in America than the Hollywood cinema and gambling put together. *Tron* is still probably the best film of its kind. The shallow, primary-colour fable about a gameplaying wunderkind beamed into cyberspace to do battle with an evil programmer was based around live-action interpretations of existing videogame formats (most notably the 'light cycle' race), and then soon became a licensed arcade videogame in its own right.

For videogame companies, film licences are often a sure winner. Studios generally acquire the videogame rights to a film, such as *Batman*, *Rambo*, *Aliens*, or *Raiders of the Lost Ark*, and then produce a painfully substandard platform game or shoot-'em-up that might borrow a certain visual style from one or two of the film's scenes but has nothing to do with the storyline. In 1983, famously, Atari, having acquired the rights to produce an *ET* videogame, was so confident of its success that it produced nearly six million copies. One fly in the ointment: the game was terrible. Gamers aren't stupid. Most of the cartridges were eventually buried in a landfill site in New Mexico, where one hopes they will eventually provide some amusement for archaeologists in the distant future.

Films based on videogames are even worse, as anyone will testify who has giggled throughout the truly spectacular artistic abyss that is *Street Fighter: the Movie*, starring sex-kitten Jean-Claude Van Damme and renowned pugilist Kylie Minogue. *Mortal Kombat* was not much better, and Bob Hoskins displayed rather less animation than his pixellated counterpart in *Super Mario Bros*. Nothing daunted, Paramount is making a film of *Tomb Raider*, although Angelina Jolie, the actress hired to play Lara Croft, might be expected to have a hard time replicating the digital heroine's acrobatic moves.

Of course, the *Tomb Raider* film-makers will use digital trickery to achieve such effects. Post-production computer manipulation of the film image is increasingly common; director George Lucas even prefers to modify his actors' performances digitally, so that a performer's frown in take six might be mapped on to his forehead in take three. Interestingly, some of the first technical demonstrations of Sony's PlayStation2 console in Tokyo concentrated on animating the muscles of a highly detailed human face in exactly the same way. In this purely cosmetic respect, it is true that videogames are converging with films.

The commercial praxis of the two industries is also looking more and more similar. The relative simplicity of computer and videogame systems in the 1970s and 1980s meant that a game was often written by just one person over a period of a few months. The graphics design, gameplay design and programming were all done by the same red-eyed multitasker, and some of them – Matthew Smith, Andrew Braybrook, Geoff Crammond, David Braben – became wealthy stars. Videogames had a relatively long period in which the *auteur* theory was actually true.

But now all that has changed. Just as a film is a collaborative effort between many different specialists – director, cinematographer, actors, composer, set designer, costumier, dolly grip, best boy and so forth – so videogame 'studios' today employ concept designers, animators, 3D artists, tool developers, programmers, composers, writers, character designers and a host of other experts in relatively hermetic fields. The first stage in development of a videogame at British designers Core, for example, consists of the writing of several hundred pages of a 'Game Design Document', which is rather like a (non-linear) script for a film: the game's characters are introduced through drawings and verbal sketches; the gameplay concept is elaborated; and example situations are described. A top game will now take around two years to develop, with a budget of anything up to tens of millions of dollars – which is Hollywood blockbuster money. And the rewards can be equally impressive.

Meanwhile, Japanese videogame giant Square is moving the other way, making an entirely digital feature film based on its bestselling Final Fantasy games. Videogames and the cinema nowadays certainly look like close media competitors.

Perhaps this perceived competition is one reason why when videogames themselves feature in films they are so often shorthand for moral or cognitive vacancy, or actual destructive tendencies. Russ Meyer shows a woman playing Pong at the beginning of *Beneath the Valley of the Ultravixens* precisely to indicate her anomie and lack of sexual interest in her partner. Meanwhile, the superb slice of 1980s teen paranoia *Wargames* features a young geek hero who hacks into the Pentagon's military computer system because he thinks he's going to get to play some cool videogames; in fact, he nearly starts a global nuclear war. Generally, if a movie shows a child playing videogames in his bedroom, the message is that this antisocial kid needs to get out more.

Other films extrapolate some hypothetical videogame future in order to make more or less successful points about man's increasingly intimate relationship with technology. The abomination that is *The Lawnmower Man* typifies Hollywood's prurient fascination with the oxymoronic and irremediably adolescent concept of 'virtual sex'. More thoughtful is David Cronenberg's orthographically eccentric *eXistenZ*, which pictures a bio-mechanical future whose characters jack into an animal game 'pod' via a slimy spinal socket, and toys in a rather facile but entertaining way with the problems of competing realities.

But preeminent in this filmic tradition is *The Matrix*, which, despite competition from *The Phantom Menace*, was most people's choice for science fiction film of 1999. With a cunning script incorporating a kaleidoscope of Homeric, Christian and Gibsonian references, it starred Keanu Reeves as a computer hacker who learns that the world is something like an enormous game of SimCity run by computers to keep us enslaved. In its exaggeratedly dynamic kung-fu scenes, in which actors float through the air and smash each other through walls, *The Matrix* contains the most successful translations to date of certain videogame paradigms to the celluloid medium. (This film also reminds us that the concept of 'virtual reality' is itself a very old idea, for Descartes conceived of a *malin génie*, or evil demon, which, exactly like the computers in *The Matrix*, caused him to have the thoughts and perceptions he ordinarily believed to be signs of a real, external world.)

The primary influence on *The Matrix*'s sort of hyperkinetic action is still a filmic one: the Hong Kong guns'n'kung-fu movie apotheosised by such cult directors and performers as John Woo and Chow Yun Fat. But the increasingly unrealistic dynamics of such films through the late 1980s and 1990s clearly owe a lot in turn to the rise of the videogame beat-'em-up such as Street Fighter, and in one such film this is explicitly acknowledged. The star of *City Hunter*, Jackie Chan, is at one point knocked into an arcade beat-'em-up machine, initiating a comic sequence in which Chan, dazed by the blow, imagines his assailant as different digitally generated characters from the videogame itself, finally winning the fight in the virtual world and so in the real one. Videogames repaid the compliment with Tekken 3 (1998), which contains, although the makers Namco explicitly deny this, playable characters that look as if they might be heavily influenced by Bruce Lee and Jackie Chan himself.

For their part, films have been very successful in influencing the look of certain types of videogame. The first great film tie-in (still only one of a handful today) was the videogame Star Wars (1983), a three-dimensional space shoot-'em-up which abstracted elements from certain battle scenes in the film and turned them into simple game objectives. The most impressive visual aspect of these action sequences in the film was the shower of red and green laser bolts, and it is these that were most easily translated into early videogame graphics, while John Williams's pompously brilliant score, mixed with high-pitched R2–D2 wibbles, pumped from the arcade speakers. The game did not replicate the movie, but stole those parts of the movie (the action sequences) that could be successfully reimagined as videogame forms. And the lure of the *Star Wars* franchise is such that every console and computer-game platform since then has been home to a game based on the film. They have covered nearly every conceivable genre: platform, 3D shooting, role-playing – even, lamentably, beat-'em-up, in Masters of Teras Kasi for the PlayStation.

One of the most seminal modern influences, not just on videogames but on all forms of science fiction, is the film *Blade Runner*. This is partly due to aesthetic considerations – the popular style of futuristic tech-noir – but for videogames it has also had, until the current generation of extremely powerful machines, a technological payoff. For the vision of neon-soaked streets at night in a skyscraper-studded, futuristic Tokyo was particularly amenable to videogames' limited powers of representation. The night-time setting meant the processor had less to draw, could fill large areas of the scene with black; neon lighting is gaudy and luminous in a way that computer graphics can easily imitate; and the absence of vegetation freed the machine from the very processor-hungry task of creating a convincing tree with hundreds of leaves and different shades of green. A game such as G-Police, one of the most blatant videogame homages to the visuals of the *Blade Runner* city yet, welcomed these in-built visual limitations of the tech-noir genre thankfully, since it had so much else on its silicon mind.

As well as influencing hundreds of other videogames, mostly futuristic shoot-'em-ups, *Blade Runner* has also been made into a rather successful adventure game in its own right. But we have seen already that influential currents between the two media do not run only one way. And this turns out to be true even of Scott's own remarkable film: one of the production designers on *Blade Runner* has said that his work was inspired by the cabinet art on – what else? – an arcade videogame.

But while creative aesthetic interpollination between films and videogames may have positive results, the attempt at wholesale translation from one medium to the other is usually doomed. If you make a film based on a videogame world, you instantly lose what is most essential to the videogame experience. One problem is that pleasurably unreal visual qualities will be lost. Good software simulation of grass, for instance, can, in its necessary stylisation, be more aesthetically interesting than a field of real grass on film. Jeremy Smith, managing director of Core Design, is very decided on this point:

> For me, driving a touring car in a race game, I don't want a photorealistic car in there, I want a computer-generated car. I think it would spoil it as soon as you put a proper car in there. I think in that, the interaction between the movie and the videogame is a step in the wrong direction. These things need to be generated by a computer. Okay, you can get them looking absolutely gorgeous, with fantastic shading and all these beautiful effects, but fundamentally I'm still looking at an arcade game.

And the difference works the other way: even Bob Hoskins in a padded suit is not as lovably squat as the real Mario.

Yet even if you make your film entirely digitally, along the lines of *Toy Story* or *A Bug's Life*, a second, major problem remains. In *Star Wars, Episode 1: The Phantom Menace*, the plot stops for ten minutes for the technically remarkable 'pod-racing' scene, in which the young Anakin Skywalker races a turbo-charged hovercraft around the rocky Tattooine desert. Critics of the film complained that this was just like a videogame, but the point is precisely that it wasn't *anything* like a videogame. Because the viewer is not in control. The pod-racing sequence was nothing more than an extended advert for the actual videogame that was based on it. You couldn't *play* the movie, so it was far inferior in terms of high-speed thrills.

Of course, films become works of art in their own right by involving the spectator emotionally. But there is precious little emotional material in an action-oriented videogame for the film-maker to latch on to. A film based on a game, therefore, is likely to be utterly impoverished in two ways: not only by failing to provide the fundamental attraction of the videogame experience, but by failing to exploit what the medium of film itself is best at doing.

Videogames, in fact, have the better of this strange relationship, in that they are able to suck into themselves more aspects of the filmic art without compromising their *raison d'être*. For one thing, more and more videogames now contain mini-'films' in their own right. Known as FMV sequences ('full-motion video'), these are almost always computer-generated scenes that advance the plot around which the game is based, such as in Final Fantasy VIII or Tomb Raider: The Last Revelation. The visuals might be digital, but they are voiced by real actors and graced with filmic scores. They function like the proverbial carrot and stick: the player must successfully complete a portion of the game before the next 'film' sequence is activated, providing an opportunity to relax and rest those tired wrists. FMV sequences can be graceful and beautiful in their own right (especially in the Final Fantasy games, where they alone can eat up $4 million of the budget), but they are something of a red herring. These sequences are simply there to be watched; they cannot be played with. They are merely tinsel around the real gameplay.

The question remains: what kind of cinematic action happens, not as self-contained intervallic episodes, but in the thick of videogame play itself?

Camera obscura

When videogames were flat, two-dimensional affairs, the player was furnished with a God-like objective viewpoint. The game-world of Pong or Space Invaders is laid out flat before the eye; everything takes place in the same horizontal plane. You can see everything at once, because you can see the entire universe. The problem once three-dimensional games became the norm was that in a solid world every viewpoint is subjective, and no viewpoint enables you to see everything. So videogames began to offer the player a choice of windows on their worlds that could be switched at will, depending on the task in hand. In a seemingly robust analogy with film, they are known as player-controlled 'cameras'.

If it can be argued that the film camera in some sense *creates* the onscreen world rather than passively recording it,* such a theory can be taken rather more literally with videogames. For, of course, there is nothing really there for the videogame 'camera' to shoot in the first place. Instead, there is a complex mathematical model held in computer memory which only ever erupts into visual 'solidity' for an instant, before fading away and being replaced with the next frame. The world is drawn perspectivally from one moment to the next, depending on the camera settings the player has chosen.

Videogame cameras ('cams' for short) have fairly recently settled into a group of standardised viewpoints. 'Follow cam' is usually offered in driving or flying games, and sets the viewpoint to a position behind and slightly above the vehicle under

---

* While André Bazin famously likened the film image to a 'window on the world', on the analogy with Renaissance theories of geometrical perspective; other film critics, such as Pascal Bonitzer, insisted that the film world could never extend outside the frame and so constituted a microuniverse in its own right.

the player's control. Sometimes this is differentiated from a 'chase cam', the latter taking a tighter and lower view to enhance the feeling of speed. The same genres also offer a 'cockpit cam', which puts the player in the hotseat, right at the virtual controls. G-Police (1997), a helicopter gunship sci-fi shoot-'em-up, makes available an 'aerial cam' which looks perpendicularly down on proceedings from a great height. Three-dimensional exploration games, meanwhile, generally offer elevated cams at each point of the compass that may be switched at will. They will also offer the player either a temporary first-person viewpoint – as in Mario 64, where you can look through Mario's eyes to line up a tricky narrow path – or a 'shoulder cam' as in Tomb Raider. The latter is a curious invention which provides a viewpoint which is very near to the character's own, yet is still an external one, peeping impishly through the eyes of a virtual stalker over Lara's shapely trapezium.

Why is it important for modern 3D videogames to provide this multiplicity of viewing angles? There are two answers: one functional and one aesthetic. Consider a real-life experience – say, watching a tennis match. If you watch it from the side and near the ground, you will see different aspects of the game from someone watching higher up at one end of the court. The spectator watching from the latter viewpoint, the classic television angle, has an averagely good view of all the lines and can appreciate cross-court angles. By contrast, the side-on spectator has a limited experience of these aspects, but he is much better placed to appreciate the varying arcs of the balls through the air, the niceties of topspin and slice, and the sheer length and speed of the shots.

Given that viewing angles have such an effect on the experience of spectatorship, how much more important must they be when you are actively involved in the game? Imagine if you were asked by an eccentric scientist to play a game of snooker wearing a VDU headset wired so that your point of view was situated on the ceiling, looking straight down on to the table. It would be a completely different experience, because you wouldn't be able to sight down the line of the balls while cueing. In fact, before the advent of efficient 3D realisation, several videogame versions of snooker and pool were produced that replicated exactly this thought experiment, with a top-down view.

Such games were pointless, but what is more interesting is that owing to this viewpoint differential they didn't merely fail to replicate accurately the experience of snooker or pool, they actually became entirely different sorts of game. Martin Amis expertly catches this point when he dismisses one early example, Video Hustler, as 'like playing marbles'. A similar sort of disjunction might be argued to operate in G-Police, where the multiplicity of viewpoints on offer creates different game styles within the same environment; the aerial cam, especially, which is more useful than the standard perspectival cockpit cam for lining up bombing raids on ground targets, harks back to classic two-dimensional top-down shoot-'em-ups such as Xevious.

Normally, of course, we don't encounter these sorts of problems in real life, because our eyes are (sensible, prescient Nature) hard-wired into our bodies. It is only the creative alienation of videogames, which translates physical action *here* (on this piece of plastic, in my living room) into visual effect *there* (in this otherworldly arena, at once viewed through my eyes and mediated through the prosthetic, virtual eyes of the videogame camera), which throws up such novel perceptual conundrums.

But ignoring for the moment the difference between watching the action of a film and implementing the action of a videogame, presumably this 'camera' analogy between the media still holds to some extent? No, it does not. Videogame camerawork was developed in order to enable the player to see the action from the most useful angle. In Mario 64, for instance, the player must often rotate the camera to a different compass point, or select a view from slightly further away, in order to guide the rotund plumber across a particularly narrow bridge or up a series of tough platforms.

Cinematic camerawork of the kind that is immediately noticeable or stylish, however, often depends for its effect on *hiding* something from the viewer, *not* letting you see everything. When the detective mounts the staircase of the Bates house in *Psycho*, Hitchcock deliberately chooses a very tight

Fig. 6. Resident Evil 2: claustrophobic camera angles don't always help your battle against the undead (© 1998 Capcom/Virgin Interactive Entertainment)

shot on his hand moving up the bannister, inducing tension through dramatic irony, as we know what awaits him at the top of the stairs, although he does not. But there can be no dramatic irony in videogames, because dramatic irony depends on a knowledge differential between spectator and protagonist – yet in a videogame the player is both spectator and protagonist at once.

True, some videogames attempt to replicate this kind of stylised shot-choice, most notably Resident Evil 2 (see fig. 6). But in a videogame, as opposed to a movie, this becomes a fraudulent and frustrating method of inducing tension: the player can get killed by zombies not because the environment is cleverly designed but because he was deliberately hindered from seeing them coming until it was too late. And, crucially, Resident Evil 2 doesn't let you choose the shots in the way Mario 64 does. As with film, shots are done *to* you. Silent Hill, meanwhile, sometimes lets the player control the camera when walking around the streets, but dive into a dim alley and the tilted overhead shot is the only perspective you'll get. And this shows how a purely filmic notion of camerawork cannot work in a videogame context. Film manipulates the viewer, but a game depends on being manipulable.

There is an even more fundamental formal distinction to be made between the structures of visual imagery in films and videogames. Modern film relies for its storytelling and conceptual effect on a highly sophisticated grammar of montage, a technique invented in cinema's youth, and perfected by Sergei Eisenstein. In simple terms, it describes the process of 'cutting together' discontinuous shots – something so common now in dynamic visual media that we hardly notice it at all.

Here is an example from any standard television commercial. A car turns a corner, coming towards the viewer, seen from a helicopter's altitude; in the next shot our eyes are at fender level and a car is moving away. Because we are culturally attuned to montage, we automatically see this as the same car performing one continuous movement. Yet it is easy to imagine that a person who had never seen film or television might assume that these were identical-looking but different vehicles. This is how montage creates a sense of rhythm and motion, but such an approach would be fatal in a videogame, where the player has to control the car, and thus requires a continuous, unbroken viewpoint – either a cockpit cam or follow cam. This is essential for easy, intuitive navigation; if the camera cuts to a different position so that your vehicle appears to be going the other way, the physical videogame controls will suddenly be reversed in their effects. You're going to crash nastily.

Sometimes videogame camera positions change automatically rather than at the player's behest; even so, when they do, they are not performing traditional montage but trying to give the player a better view of the action under his control. This is the case in the Tomb Raider games, for instance. Such changes of view, however, can and often do employ other quasi-filmic techniques such as tracking and panning. Metal Gear Solid is given a particularly 'cinematic' feel by touches such as these: whenever the hero backs up against a wall to

Fig. 7. Metal Gear Solid: a low cinematic angle as Snake (left) hides from a guard (© 1998 Konami)

hide from an enemy guard, the camera, which normally takes a functional aerial viewpoint, swoops in to about shin level to frame the player's character and the guard walking past (see fig. 7). But function always takes precedence over such stylish touches: when the hero moves away again, the camera reverts to its normal view, enabling the player to see more of the environment. True montage, meanwhile, is still not used. An action movie would, for instance, cut from a close-up of the hero's face to his point of view of approaching enemies, then back to a mid-shot of the hero with gun drawn, whereas such scenes in Metal Gear Solid's gameplay necessarily take place in long shot. Metal Gear Solid is a great videogame with quasi-filmic visual gimmickry, but it is nothing like an interactive movie.

Most of the work done by automatic videogame cameras, indeed, is largely modelled on a different medium altogether, and this brings us to the second, aesthetic rationale for such visual systems. The kind of montage seen in a car commercial does crop up in videogames, but only *after* the action has finished. This is the burgeoning phenomenon of the videogame 'replay'. Gran Turismo enables the player to watch a race he has just driven, with virtual cameras placed at spectacular angles on every bend. The reins are handed over to the digital director. The effect is thrilling, and clearly drawn not from film but from the style of television sports coverage. Similar replays accompany goals scored in the football game Euro 2000, and slavering slow-motion reiterates the final, lethal combinations of kicks and punches when a fighter in Tekken 3 is brutally floored. Television sports directors have understood for a long while that, when it comes to the electronic *mise en scène* of fast movement in three dimensions, several heads are better than one; the cutting together of different viewpoints gives a better and more visceral understanding of the action.

Videogames, meanwhile, approach the condition of film most closely when delivering that most sportive of filmic scenes, the car chase. The excellent free-roaming car-chase game Driver (1999) even goes so far as to allow the player, in 'Film Director' mode, to set up his own camera angles and cut together a unique car-chase sequence from the section of game that has just been played. Whereas videogame play is pure, evanescent kinesis, the replay is an event to be savoured after the fact, a sequence that is considered interesting enough to be watched as well as experienced first-hand.

Here, however, the term 'replay' is particularly misleading. Play is still primary; what comes next is not a 'replay', a playing again, but a *watching*. The carnival of camera angles in a videogame replay does not impinge at all on the basic functional requirements of in-game viewpoints. The two are properly separate 'modes' of the game. But this is exactly what I meant earlier when suggesting that videogames are potentially a more flexible form than film. Such borrowings from cinematic techniques can indeed enhance the visual experience of a game without compromising its unique intensity.

You've been framed

When videogame 'versions' of films do work, it is by creating a completely different experience that branches off from the same scenario as its parent movie. Goldeneye 007 (1997), for instance, is a first-person shooter that casts the player as James Bond. You are required to complete certain missions that are loosely based on the plot of the film: infiltrate an underground compound and blow things up; reprogram a satellite; rescue Natalya from a speeding train; and so on. Such sections of the plot generally happen at the end of a mission, and they happen *to* the player. The game does not let the player change the plot: for instance, to the dismay and fury of many addicts, you cannot decide that vulnerable, annoying Natalya has outlived her usefulness and shoot her in order to make a quick getaway. The game signals failure and forces you to play the mission again. Such plot nuggets, therefore, mean little more in the videogame context than excuses for the action of the next mission to move elsewhere.

But Goldeneye's strength is that it manages to cut and paste all its filmic influences – the faces of actors Sean Bean, Robbie Coltrane and so on are digitised and mapped on to the in-game characters – on to a mode of action that is pure videogame, with the accent heavily on stealthy shooting, and nothing in the way of sipping Martinis or seducing Russian women. Particularly successful is the way in which locations from the film, such as the main satellite control room, have been not just represented but fully recreated in three dimensions in the game. This fully investigable architecture is what the videogame can uniquely offer. When watching a movie, you cannot go and look round a corner unless the plot and the director take you that way. But in Goldeneye you can explore areas from every conceivable angle. Indeed, one aficionado of the game, on see-ing the film again, commented: 'I thought, "I *know* this place – I know it better than the characters do."' In the cinema, the world is projected *at* you; in a videogame, you are projected *into* the world.

This virtue of videogames is so seductive that on occasion

it can override all other formal deficiencies. Games like Myst and Riven were rightly derided by the videogame cognoscenti for having tediously simplistic gameplay properties, yet they sold in their millions precisely because they are rather beautifully pure exploration games. The player wanders around gorgeously designed virtual environments with fabulously detailed landscapes, water lapping against jetties and mysterious dark buildings. J. C. Herz is exactly right in labelling the appeal of these games as that of 'virtual tourism': 'Myst put you into a world you might actually want to visit, if you only had the money and time [. . .] It was an escape destination.'

The fundamental point in comparing this aspect of videogames with the movies is that, for instance, Goldeneye the videogame offers a different and incommensurable sort of pleasure compared with that of *Goldeneye* the film. For the moment it is hard to see how videogames and cinema could ever converge without losing the essential virtues of both. Cinema – especially good action cinema, which, as we have seen, has the closest links with videogames – is first and foremost a ride, like a fairground rollercoaster, part of whose pleasure is exactly that you are not steering, and you cannot decide to slow down. A videogame, on the other hand, is an activity. Watching someone else with a videogame, to non-players, is terribly boring. And even watching the most 'cinematic' of videogames is still like watching a really bad, low-resolution film. A videogame is there to be played.

There is one exception to the rule that videogames are boring to watch, and it is exemplified by the inventive beauty of the Crash Bandicoot games. Here it is apparent that, for all the talk of war between videogames and movies, the former have already won a stunning victory over one genre of film: the animated cartoon. The golden age of Looney Tunes was always a fertile ground from which videogames could reap certain mechanical ideas: the comedy of Mario and Luigi bashing their enemies with huge mallets in the 1980s is a direct homage to such exaggerated cartoon violence as that found in *Tom and Jerry*.

Now, with vastly increased graphical power, the multi-million-selling Crash Bandicoot 3 (see fig. 8) is as gorgeously

Fig. 8. Crash Bandicoot 3: a cartoon you can play with (© 1998 Sony Computer Entertainment)

coloured, smoothly animated and thoroughly entertaining as many Warner Bros examples. (While it is a very simple game to play, it is superior to cleverer examples like Ape Escape, Donkey Kong 64 or Spyro 2 in terms of sheer visual splendour.) Crash 3 is particularly successful in replicating and extending the tradition of humorous cartoon deaths – which, like videogame deaths, are only ever temporary. The eponymous orange marsupial, Crash, can get flattened into two dimensions by a rolling boulder and will wobble around piteously; he can get blown up by a mine and jump, singed and yowling, into the air; he can fall down a crevasse and have his ghost hauled heavenwards by an angel; or he can bump into a malign puffer fish and suddenly balloon to twice his size.

It is perhaps no coincidence that since videogames have been able to offer a detailed world of humorous action similar to that of the traditional cartoon, with the added killer ingredient of control, animated cartoons themselves have changed in order to survive. Cartoons such as *South Park* or *The Simpsons* no longer rely solely on pure kinetic comedy, but excel in the scabrous comedy of situation and character. Hence it is easy to see how the disgraceful videogame adaptation of South Park (1998) totally missed the point, offering as it did boring first-person shooter sequences with weapons such as the cow-launcher.

If film, as Jean-Luc Godard said, is 'truth, twenty-four times a second', then modern videogames are lies that hit the nervous system at two and a half times the frequency. Videogames, as we have seen, have borrowed from movie visuals. But films, too, have borrowed from videogame dynamics. Such proximities, however, are purely cosmetic, far outweighed by the structural dissimilarities. Videogames, far from being an inferior type of film, are something different altogether. The comparison between the forms – initially so inviting because they both look like they are doing similar things – is in the final analysis an informatively limited one.

Here is one description of the cinematic experience itself: Walter Benjamin's poetic appreciation of the perceptually liberating effect of early film:

> Our taverns and our metropolitan streets, our railroad stations and our factories appeared to have us locked up hopelessly. Then came the film and burst this prison-world asunder by the dynamite of the tenth of a second, so that now, in the midst of its far-flung ruins and debris, we calmly and adventurously go travelling.

Videogames are still a very young medium. Yet videogames already – it can hardly be denied – constitute a type of entertainment every bit as revolutionary, in its form, as cinema was for Benjamin. If it's adventurous travelling the chthonic prisoner is after, videogames can deliver in spades, for the player is free to wander at will around an imaginary world, meet interesting people and burst things asunder by the dynamite of the sixtieth of a second.

Benjamin's reference to 'far-flung ruins and debris' is, of course, far more deeply ambivalent about the desirability of such a detonation. And there is more to say about the negative interpretation of such destruction in videogames. For the moment I should point out that, though the videogame world may currently be enslaved to Hollywood aesthetics, there is no reason why this should not change in the future. Director David Cronenberg has said: 'In the graphic sense, many videogames can already be viewed as art, but overall I see a propensity to imitate Hollywood, which could be termed the "anti-art". Great videogame designers may have to struggle against this trend.'

If Hollywood is home to the anti-art that videogames must resist, where better to continue our investigations?

5

NEVER-ENDING
STORIES

A tale of two cities

Los Angeles is a game of SimCity played by a maniac. Six-lane
freeways gridlocked with sports-utility vehicles pump out
untold cubic tonnes of exhaust fumes, enveloping the city in
a permanent yellow smog. It's more or less compulsory to drive
any distance more than ten metres, but you're not allowed to
smoke a cigarette. In fact, thanks to designer Will Wright's
inbuilt bias towards public transport, it wouldn't actually be
possible to build Los Angeles in his videogame. This satirical
dystopia is too weird to be anything but real.

It's also the venue for the world's largest annual videogame
trade show, E3. The bustling steel-and-concrete cathedral of
the Los Angeles Convention Center is roaring with the combined sound effects and apocalyptic music of hundreds of new
games on display. This is where videogame companies show
off their latest glories of manipulable *son et lumière*, with hundreds of PlayStations, Dreamcasts and Nintendo 64 consoles
hooked up to television monitors running soon-to-be-released
products. Sony's triumphal stand features ten-metre-high
inflatable models of cutesy game characters Spyro the Dragon
and Um Jammer Lammy (a cartoon girl who plays heavy-metal
guitar, obviously). Nintendo's section of the hall projects the
playable images of Star Wars, Episode I: Pod Racer on to, yes,
a cinema-sized screen, while a room given over to Perfect Dark
features helpful blonde women gliding among the gamers,
dressed in black PVC and white jodhpurs and suggestively

stroking their leather whips (Perfect Dark, an espionage-themed first-person shooter, is strictly speaking not a game about horse-riding, but I don't see anybody complaining). Elsewhere, a Planet of the Apes videogame is promoted with the help of a bamboo cage imprisoning semi-naked women in animal-skin bikinis.

Refreshed or repelled by such marketing schlock and an endless supply of burgers, hot dogs, soft drinks and coffee over the four days of the show, journalists, designers, retailers and publishers scurry around the vast acreage of the various videogame halls to meet and do business, and to play as many of the games as possible in five- or ten-minute bursts. People happily queue in line for twenty minutes to try out the most promising new videogames, and the constant bustle and electronic noise starts claiming victims alarmingly early on in the course of the event. The popular outdoor café area is regularly full of half-comatose men and women sprawled in plastic chairs with a small mountain of promotional carrier bags strewn over the ground. Many of them suck hungrily on cigarettes with an expression of bliss peculiar to the Californian tobacco aficionado, everywhere hounded by the law. I notice this, of course, because that's where I stagger myself every few hours.

Everybody who's anybody in the industry turns up at E3. So I have gone to Los Angeles too, in an attempt to take the temperature of the videogame industry. And in one way, it's running pretty high. This year, producers are more concerned than usual about the question of 'violence'; parental lawsuits are in the air, and federal interference with their industry is thoroughly undesirable. Hence, the Dreamcast version of zombie-shooting game House of the Dead 2 is on demonstration without the game's cybernetic *sine qua non*, the lightgun. And as I wander the halls speaking to designers showing off their latest games, there is a marked tendency for them to make excuses. Yes, they say, this is a cutting-edge first-person shooter where you can put bullets through people's heads and blast their limbs off individually in gushes of beautifully animated blood, but that's not the point. You see, it's basically a really good *story*.

*   *   *

Storytelling is the second oldest profession. Epic poetry, drama, the novel and the cinema have all become expert in their different ways at the craft of telling a story. Why should videogames, then, be any different? Modern videogames have plots; they use voice actors for different 'characters'; there is usually a main protagonist who must accomplish specific tasks; the games boast self-contained, carefully scripted 'movies' in them.

So far, so once-upon-a-time. But as we've seen, videogames have an important quality which militates against easy conjunctions with other media such as film. That quality is interactivity. Of course, in one sense books themselves have always been highly interactive, depending on the reader's imagination to flesh out their worlds in colour and detail, but, unlike a film or a book, a videogame changes dynamically in response to the player's input. Surely this must mean something drastic for the traditional concept of a story, authored jealously by one godlike writer? Two extreme responses, for example, might be: videogames are so radically different from stories that there can be no comparison; or videogames have the magical, catalytic ingredient that will change our very conception of what a story is.

Now some theorists, such as the designers I met in LA, cleave to the latter view. They see in the unique quality of videogames a potential revolution, a liberation from the shackles of old, 'linear' storytelling. How? Well, according to a speculative essay by Chris Crawford, 'because the story is generated in real-time in direct response to the player's actions, the resultant story is customised to the needs and interests of the audience, and thereby more than makes up for any loss in polish with its greater emotional involvement'. (But the telephone directory is 'customised to the needs and interests of the audience' about as much as anything could be, yet it still doesn't make me cry or laugh. There has to be something more to the idea of storytelling than that.) Interactive narrative, or interactive storytelling, it is argued optimistically, is the entertainment medium of the future.

Well, the proselytisers are right in at least one weak sense, because it's certainly not the entertainment medium of the present. Not only has no convincing example of this new creature called 'interactive storytelling' yet been spotted in the wild, no one is even sure what it might look like. Like Albrecht Dürer and his confident rhinoceros, perhaps they've stuck the horn in the wrong place. Still, 'interactive storytelling' sounds like a fascinating idea. That disyllable 'active', in particular, makes us feel very modern. Intrapassive storylistening doesn't sound like half so much fun.

So how do videogames use stories? What kind of stories are they? And most importantly, is interactive storytelling the glorious future of videogames, or is it an imaginatively seductive entry in some fabulous illustrated bestiary?

Back to the future

The word 'story' itself covers a multitude of sins. Think of the cinema concept of the 'back-story'. A back-story happened in the 'past', and it determines the conditions and sets up the concerns of the present action. For instance, the back-story of *Blade Runner* is the invention, programming and rebellion of the replicants; the 'present' story is Deckard's attempts to find and kill them. Some films in fact are all about attempts by the characters in the present to find out what the back-story actually *is* – for instance, Hitchcock's *Vertigo*, or *The Usual Suspects* (what went on at the wharf? Who is Keyser Soze?).

For the purposes of talking about videogames, the 'back-story' is the diachronic story, and the story that happens in the fictional present is the synchronic story – an ongoing narrative constituted by the player's actions and decisions in real-time.*

Now synchronic and diachronic modes of story in other media are very often combined in the same narrative. For example, in the *Oedipus Rex* of Sophocles, the synchronic (present) story is about Oedipus as the King of Thebes trying to

---

* Of course, even what I am calling a 'synchronic' story unfolds over time, but since that period is far shorter – usually, in the fictional videogame universe, a few hours or days – I will let the term stand.

find out why his city is cursed. The diachronic (background) story, gradually revealed through Oedipus's dogged investigations, is that in the past Oedipus himself killed his father and slept with his mother. (This is the model, indeed, for all detective fiction: whodunnit is the diachronic story, while the process of investigation is the synchronic story.) In general, because a story in any medium must limit itself to a finite period of time, and cannot tell the entire history of the universe leading up to the events it describes, it must nearly always refer to some diachronic story – old Hamlet was murdered while asleep in the garden; a Jedi turned to the Dark Side and the Empire grew* – in the process of elaborating the synchronic one.

What does this mean for videogames? Well, it turns out that the delicate balance of story types is skewed in videogames: it is very heavily weighted towards the diachronic. Perhaps surprisingly, videogames have nearly always had a back-story, however simple. Robotron acquits itself diachronically with a post-nuclear fable about evil machines and saving the last human family; Doom's back-story is that the moon has been invaded by aliens; Donkey Kong is predicated on a princess's kidnapping.

Some diachronic stories, even in old games, are very complex, dipping freely into the myth kitty by basing themselves on Arthurian legend (Excalibur), Celtic sagas (Tir Na Nog and Dun Darach on the ZX Spectrum), Norse sagas (Valhalla), or Tolkien's Middle Earth (The Hobbit), not to mention science fiction and fantasy derivatives of these basic templates. But notice that these kinds of stories are, formally speaking, mostly more like folktales than novels. And folktales, according to Russian theorist Vladimir Propp, adhere to one of a handful of simple formulae. They are highly plot-driven and predicated on strong actions; what there is of a purely 'literary' character can be readily stripped away. That's ideal for computers. (It is hardly surprising, though obscurely disappointing, that no

---

* The theoretical problem with George Lucas's prequels is exactly that they plan to elaborate synchronically what was so suggestively mythical in the back-story of the original *Star Wars* films: how Anakin Skywalker became Darth Vader.

one has tried to make a videogame out of Nabokov's *Pale Fire*.)

But what kinds of synchronic stories do such games have? Very little to speak of. The 'story' of what the player actually *does* during the game would be merely a list of movements (up, down, run, shoot, open door, jump) – hardly something you'd want to sit down and actually read. At its most sophisticated it will be a highly skeletal version of a quest narrative. You look for something; you find it. The situation is even thinner with more action-oriented games whose diachronic stories are less rich with suggestion: the story of what a player does during a game of Robotron will just be a tedious list of movements and shootings, or more generously a higher-level, but still highly abstract – and uninvolving to anyone who is not the player – cyclical narrative about patterns of attack and rhythms of success and failure.

If these games can be said to have a 'story' at all, it is untranslatable – it is a purely kinetic one. The diachronic story of a videogame, however complex, is merely an excuse for the meat, the videogame action; while the synchronic story, as a story, is virtually nonexistent. This is not a criticism of videogames, not a sign of their impoverishment – it is simply pointing out that, in general, they are doing something totally different from traditional narrative forms.

But since a diachronic story is by definition unchangeable – remember, it happened in the past – it surely must be the synchronic story, the thing which the videogame player is able to change at will, which is essential to the possibility of 'interactive storytelling'. But we have just decided that many videogames so far don't have synchronic stories at all. So what's going on?

Well, Robotron and Valhalla are pretty old games. Things on first inspection look somewhat different with the modern multimedia extravaganzas. Gamers familiar with epics such as the Final Fantasy series will quickly voice this objection. For every so often in such games, an FMV (full-motion video) sequence – the computer-generated 'movie' nugget – pops up and moves the plot along. The narratives of the FMV sequences and the actual gameplay are contemporaneous: that is, the FMV is a synchronic storyline, and a very involved one it is too. The same thing occurs in Metal Gear Solid* – where the highly entertaining plot is as tightly scripted and twisty as most Hollywood action movies – in Zelda 64 and, to a lesser extent, in the Tomb Raider games. Here are games that do have synchronic stories. Do they constitute some form of interactive storytelling?

As we touched on in the last chapter, the thing about FMVs is that they are completely predetermined. The player must watch them, cannot take part in them interactively. These sequences are also known as 'cut-scenes' – appropriately, because they signal a discontinuous break between game-playing, which still has no story to speak of, and watching, which bears all the narrative load. In general the player runs around fighting, solving puzzles and exploring new areas, and once a certain amount of gameplay is completed, he is rewarded with a narrative sequence that is set in stone by the designer. This alternation of cut-scenes and playable action delivers a very traditional kind of storytelling yoked rather arbitrarily to essential videogame challenges of dexterity and spatial thought.

Why 'arbitrarily'? Well, it is as if you were reading a novel and forced by some jocund imp at the end of each chapter to win a game of table tennis before being allowed to get back to the story. Actually, with some games it's worse than that: it's the other way round. You really want a good, exciting game of ping-pong, but you have to read a chapter of some crashingly dull science-fantasy blockbuster every time you win a game. Where's the fun in that?

How many roads must a man walk down ...

Several videogames, however, are a little more sophisticated (in a purely narrative sense), in that they decide which FMV sequences to play at any particular time according to what the

---

* Although here they use the game engine's normal graphics, rather than the superior rendering of FMV. FMVs are just the most popular type of cut-scenes.

player has done so far. This is a small step towards narrative interactivity – but only a small one. In the space-combat game Colony Wars, for example, every few missions the player gets an FMV sequence detailing how the war is going: if gameplay has gone badly, a player's side is in disarray; if gameplay has gone well, a player's side is making victorious incursions into the enemy's solar system. But note that this overarching synchronic story is an extremely simple one: one side wins, the other fights back, somebody emerges as the war's victor. The plot in fact only branches in two directions at any given point, and there are only a handful of possible endings to the saga, depending on the player's overall skill.

One reason for this is that it would be prohibitively expensive and time-consuming for a studio to make the bank of hundreds or thousands of different cut-scenes needed to create satisfyingly complex stories by stringing together permutations of a handful of them. This problem of data intensiveness is likely never to be overcome. It is not a question of data storage, but data creation in the first place. It is simply impractical to write and pre-render that much FMV video.

The amount of work involved is not peculiar to the videogame form, either. Imagine an author writing an 'interactive story'. Let us say this story will be composed of only nine short chapters; at the end of each chapter (except the last), the reader will be offered a choice of eight different directions in which the story might go. That sounds pretty simple. Eight, nine – they're pretty small numbers. Unfortunately, if each possible plotline is to be truly independent of all the others, the number of chapters required by such a scheme is eight to the power of eight, or sixteen million, seven hundred and seventy thousand, two hundred and sixteen. Show me a writer who wants to work that hard and I'll choke on my Martini.

If you begin to adulterate this hyper-purist concept, though, and allow the different story-paths to cross each other or converge, so that they can 'share' chapters with each other, the numbers do get more manageable. But that in turn throws up its own unique storytelling problems. And they have already been encountered in prose writing. As noted earlier, the popularity of the ZX Spectrum and Commodore 64 computers in the early 1980s coincided with the rise of the *Fighting Fantasy* gamebooks by Ian Livingstone and Steve Jackson, as well as the American *Choose Your Own Adventure* series (by various authors).

Each numbered story nugget of a few hundred words ended with something between two and four choices; you made your choice and went to the next appropriate numbered section to see what happened. The *Fighting Fantasy* titles, such as *The Warlock of Firetop Mountain*, *Citadel of Chaos* and *Forest of Doom*, were generally darker and nastier, based on Dungeons & Dragons and with many more gory ways to die. Global sales eventually totalled more than fourteen million. (Ian Livingstone, now chairman of Eidos, in 1998 released the Tomb Raider-style videogame version of one of the early gamebooks, *Deathtrap Dungeon*. Steve Jackson, meanwhile, was involved in the design of God-game supremo Peter Molyneux's Black and White [2000].)

Now these books are entertaining children's pastimes, but as examples of 'interactive storytelling' they too are instructively limited. To keep the numbers manageable, very many sections of story in these gamebooks are shared by different plotlines. Yet, if an episode can be reached by means of several different previous ones, there is no way it can ever refer to its past – because it has no way of knowing what its past is, which is to say what particular route the reader took to get there. You end up with a species of story that is totally amnesiac, that has no sense of its own history. Try to think of a film or a novel in which at no point does a character reflect upon previous events within the synchronic story. Not easy, is it?

A second problem with shared story nuggets is increasing familiarity. The reader of a particular *Fighting Fantasy* book, after just a few 'plays', would soon learn to avoid number thirty-four if it was an option, because the Ganges demons lived there, and the game would end horribly. In such a situation, the player/reader's own memory is taking advantage of the book's amnesia to the detriment of the storytelling experience. A very similar sort of situation obtains in the sort of videogames that reward the wrong choice with instant death. You get killed in Tomb Raider, you reload the game and this time you don't run heedlessly down the path because you know about the spike-filled pit that killed you last time. Or you get shot to pieces in Metal Gear Solid and next time you remember to creep nervously past the security camera. If you know the consequences of your choice in advance, it is no longer a choice. A corner of the imaginary world has been cordoned off.

Erase and rewind

Knowledge gained through a previous play throws up a deep problem with the whole notion of 'interactive storytelling': what the fact of videogame replayability – in that you can always try again – means to narrative. One problem is that great stories depend for their effect on irreversibility* – and this is because life, too, is irreversible. The pity and terror that Aristotle says we feel as spectators to a tragedy are clearly dependent on our apprehension of circumstances that cannot be undone. If Oedipus, on learning of his unintended parricide and philomatria, were able to go back and undo his deeds in another 'play' of the story, there would be no tragedy, for he would live happily ever after. If Raskolnikov were able to undo his murders there would be nothing for Dostoyevsky to write about. The argument is, of course, equally true of farce. If Basil Fawlty had surreptitiously banked his horse-racing winnings so that Sibyl couldn't commandeer them, he wouldn't have been driven to such hilariously doomed attempts to keep the cash, and we wouldn't laugh at him. But in a videogame we can go back and change our actions if they turn out to have undesirable consequences.

Secondly, some choices just make better stories than others. If you are the hero in a videogame version of *Oedipus Rex*, and you think, 'Sod it, I don't care why my city is cursed, I'm off to the hills with Jocasta to live out my days in luxury', you're not going to get much of a story out of the game.

Some kinds of irreversibility, indeed, are actually anathema to good videogame design. A good exploration game, for example, should never let the player get irreversibly 'stuck' in a space from

---

* This argument is suggested by Alain and Frédéric Le Diberder in *L'Univers des Jeux Vidéo*.

which there is no escape (because, for example, he or she hasn't collected the right key yet), forcing her to switch off completely and reload. Although this is a feasible real-life situation for behatted and whipped adventurers, it is merely frustrating and boring in a videogame. The Tomb Raider games are admirable examples in this respect, as the level designers have always been careful to provide a way back to the more open environment: when the player gets stuck, she can be confident that there must be *some* way out that hasn't been spotted yet.

The fact that the videogame form is predicated strongly on such types of reversibility is one explanation, then, why the action tells no very compelling synchronic story. On the other hand, the FMV cut-scenes that move the plot along in the more ostensibly 'cinematic' types of game are full of irreversible factors that are out of the player's control – and it is precisely because of these irreversible factors that a videogame story can become involving. The death of a certain character in Final Fantasy VII is often cited as an example of videogames' power to induce emotional reactions – and if a player does so react, this is clearly because the death occurs in an FMV scene, and is irreversible: the player does not get a chance to resuscitate him. Similarly, the player's discovery in Zelda 64 that Link is not, as he thought, a real Kokiri elf is potentially poignant only insofar as the player can do nothing about it.

Such storytelling as so far exists in videogames, then, is not really very interactive. The player may interact with the environment in which the story takes place, but may not change the story at will. A good theoretical reason for this is pointed out by Olivier Masclef, the cheerfully erudite project director for Outcast (1999). 'You need to have talent to write a story,' he grins. 'I'm not saying [videogame] players don't have any talent – but it's not their job.' Over Diet Sprite and watery coffee in the Los Angeles Convention Center, he tells me about the way in which his own game approaches these problems.

Outcast is a fine example of the sort of quasi-'cinematic' narrative sweep that a videogame with a three-million-dollar budget can create. The player's character awakes in a strange alien world, and is identified by the inhabitants as a long-awaited prophet. He must win the trust of people in the game while embarking on a quest to find five religious artefacts. While exploring the game's gorgeously rendered organic-looking planets, the player may ride a two-legged camel, slap a robed elder, and now and then, of course, shoot enemies with very big guns. Masclef enthuses that such a game should ideally be like being 'thrown into a big, exotic movie'. The appeal of this sort of epic videogame is 'to be an action-movie hero'. The game's specially written two-hour musical score was recorded by the Moscow Radio Symphony Orchestra; twenty hours' worth of character dialogue was provided by sixteen different voice actors; as a reward for finishing the game, the player is given a full half-hour cut-scene to watch. There's a lot of story going on in this game, but how much of it is the player's business?

Our blond Belgian expert insists that a designer cannot simply leave the whole story up to the player. 'A totally open world is okay,' Masclef muses, 'but if you don't have high levels of dramatic changes, everything starts to seem the same. So above the non-linear play you have a totally linear storyline.' This, he thinks, is one way to address our theoretical concerns about non-linearity (that is, reversible, interactive stories). Non-linearity, Masclef agrees, leads to non-urgency: the player has no particular reason to do one thing rather than another. 'You've got to hook the player again. So when, say, ten per cent of the game is completed, we throw in a pre-planned event that changes things in a certain way. Generally [the story] is scripted and possibilities are locked in time.' This, then, is the traditional solution thus far in videogame history: the drama is provided by the pre-scripted story, the virtual exploration is interactive, and never the twain shall meet.

Cracked actors

But what makes Masclef's game more sophisticated than most is its approach to character. Now, of course, stories involve people (or at least intelligent, sentient lifeforms), and so any videogame with narrative pretensions must be populated with people other than the main character (the one under the player's control). These are known generally as NPCs, or non-playable characters. And just as it is largely the interactions between people that make a story interesting, so a good storytelling videogame ought to simulate believable exchanges between characters.

Character interactions can happen in cut-scenes as much as the designer likes, but a greater feeling of being immersed in the videogame world would naturally result if other characters reacted to the player's actions in a real-time, organic sense. Outcast is one game that is just beginning to scale this computational mountain. It is a problem of AI, of artificial intelligence: how do you make the computer-generated characters behave in a convincingly lifelike fashion?

Masclef's solution was found in the AI theories of Marvin Minsky. Outcast's 'Gaia' computational engine uses Minsky's concept of 'agents'. These are little mental homunculi with specialised jobs: one agent is for hunger, another agent is for curiosity, another is for fear, and so on. Weave enough of these agents together and you have a fairly crude model of a consciousness, but one which leads to surprisingly complex sets of behaviour. In Outcast the effects, though rudimentary, are enjoyable to see. As Masclef describes it: 'Say you make a big noise. If its agent of curiosity is bigger, the creature will investigate; if its agent of fear is bigger, he'll run away.' Meanwhile, if the player accidentally or deliberately kills a friendly alien, the rest of them have their agents of helpfulness instantly adjusted downwards: they will be far less inclined to help the player in his quest, or even to talk to him. Sure you can have a little fun with the rocket-launcher, but then Outcast quite surprisingly makes you feel guilty for having done so. Joyous death-dealing à la Quake this is not. In order to regain your friends' trust after such an aberration, Outcast sentences you to the equivalent of community service: giving money to beggars, for instance, or helping with agricultural work.

In the future, Masclef would like to see computer algorithms such as the agents expand and take on an ever larger role. 'We've developed very clever AI for the behaviours and the lifecycles of the characters, but sometimes the player doesn't see it,' Masclef says. 'Speech is one of the things that is not generated on the fly [in this game]. They speak this funky English – why not generate it on the fly? And then other characters' responses would be a continuum depending on your reputation and actions in the game.'

What a huge challenge for programmers. But the results would be worth it. It's all very well to try to script every possible interaction, but then – as we have seen – the game's story engineer has to write an awful lot to approach any semblance of interactivity. The artificial intelligence algorithms that are present embryonically in Outcast, however, while being very hard to set up initially, result thereafter in interesting and believable behaviour 'for free'. The videogame designer, like a deity, sets up laws of behaviour for his creatures, and then lets the processor do all the calculation to create the actual behaviour at any given point in the game. Algorithmic processes solve our problem of storytelling data intensiveness at a stroke.

In a certain crude sense, this has been the case for a long time. For instance, the enemy machines in Robotron are programmed with simple movement algorithms that tell them either to hunt down the player or go straight for the other humans on screen. But now that such movement rules are being combined with simulations of curiosity or fear, and if in the future they may even be accompanied by rules for communication, the illusion of other 'life' in the gameworld will be vastly enhanced.

A fascinating corollary of this arm's-length approach – set it up and let it roll – is that what happens in the videogame, though not random, then becomes highly unpredictable. This idea is seconded at Core Design's development studios, during the early stages of work on a beautiful PlayStation2 game which requires the player to herd eccentric cartoon wildlife. Never mind the humans; every creature in the forest, from insects to deer and cows, has its own specific web of AI algorithms. And this complexity leads to very rich and varied possibilities of behaviour. 'We may have written the game,' a programmer insists with amazed pride at his creation, 'but we don't know what's going to happen.'

These developments are analogous to Mathengine's work on the physical modelling of dynamic properties. And just as convincing feelings of bounciness, heft or inertia in virtual objects increase the aesthetic pleasure of the game, so will more convincing simulations of other wills, whether enemy or ally. The Holy Grail now for story-led videogames is nothing less than the physical modelling of personality.

Yes, this sounds like a tall order. But note that we do not need to believe in the cognitive science project of 'Strong AI' in order to become excited by these possibilities for videogames. 'Strong AI' is the position, much postulated in science fiction from *Blade Runner* and *Terminator* to *The Matrix*, that one day computers will be able to think for themselves. Now, just as with physical modelling, with NPCs you only ever need as much realism as is appropriate to the game. Remember, an accurate simulation of Formula One racing would be a bad game, and simplifications and elisions are part of the process of good game design.

Some simplifications, however, are more impoverishing than others. And as much as the behavioural possibilities of videogame NPCs (whether flesh, fish or fowl) are increasing, dramatic interactions are still going to be pretty one-sided unless the videogame player is allowed greater freedom and creativity in the exchange.

Outcast requires the player actually to 'speak' to other characters in the game; their responses vary from the helpful to the belligerent. Yet how are the player's lines chosen? You cannot simply say anything you like. Instead, you call up a menu screen which offers you a handful of possible conversational gambits, and you simply choose one with the joystick or keyboard. It is clear that, even if Olivier Masclef's ambition to have the computer generate the characters' responses automatically is fulfilled, the process will never feel like a conversation to the player as long as he is constricted by having to choose from a set of predetermined speechlets.

Superior though Outcast may be, the player can still only choose between conversational options that are offered to him by the computer. Whether these choices are predetermined by the designer or computed in real-time by the processor is irrelevant. The fact remains that the player still cannot do something that the game is not prepared to allow.

Talking it over

How could such freedom even be possible? To let a player 'say' anything he or she liked in a videogame conversation, the machine's processor would need, in short, to be able to parse natural language, to understand and respond to whatever was said to it in English (or American, Japanese, German, Finnish and so on), either via a keyboard interface or by analysing speech waves. This is such a massively difficult thing to get a computer to do that it actually constitutes one minimal requirement of Strong AI: the Turing Test.

And, needless to say, it hasn't been achieved yet. There are anecdotal reports of 'bots' – little mobile computer programs that roam the Internet★ – fooling people in chat rooms, but given the depressing level of conversational aptitude in such places, that is hardly surprising. But a computer that speaks your language, like HAL in *2001: A Space Odyssey*, is still – so far – a pipe dream.

In fact, videogames deliberately turned their back on the most promising avenue for success in this field in the late 1980s, for that is around the time when the classic text-based 'adventure' game was replaced by versions with pictures alone and no typing required. (This move was made for two largely commercial reasons: firstly, videogame manufacturers reckoned pretty moving pictures sold better than boring old words; secondly, videogames were increasingly played on consoles, such as the Nintendo Entertainment System, which didn't come with keyboards.) The adventure game, remember, is a puzzle game whose static problems are solved by rudimentary textual 'conversation'. The computer says something like, 'You are in a dark cavern. There is a door to the east, but it is locked. An orc appears, snarling hungrily.' The player would then type in UNLOCK DOOR. GO EAST, thus getting out of the way of the monster and calling up the computer's stored description of the next environment.

★ The term 'bot' is also used for the speechless but artificially 'intelligent' enemies in games such as Quake III.

The input language available to the adventure-game player began as a very rudimentary set of verbs: ADVENT's commands involved little more than directions, compass points, attacking, picking up and dropping things. Yet by the full bloom of the microprocessor revolution of the 1980s, the parsing engines of adventure games had reached a higher level of sophistication, able to respond accurately to prepositional and pronoun constructions, and inviting simple speech exchanges with NPCs. Players of the ZX Spectrum version of The Hobbit might remember frustratedly trying to use a wizard's muscle with the command TELL GANDALF 'BREAK DOOR'. At such times, of course, the bearded one was singularly unhelpful.

Richard Darling specifically remembers one program, Eliza, which was the fruit of early attempts to pass the Turing Test. It was originally written in the 1970s but cropped up on several home microcomputers in the 1980s: several versions of it are still available on the Internet. It played the part of a virtual psychotherapist. The user had a rudimentary conversation with it by typing answers to its questions, and Eliza would then respond to those answers and ask for further elaboration. 'Eliza was one of the really exciting events throughout the computer industry,' Darling recalls, 'because you could type to it and it wrote back to you. It's interesting, I think, that in the games world, AI hasn't to me actually exceeded that excitement level.'

With current videogame hardware thousands of times faster and more sophisticated, great strides could have been made towards incorporating more fluent language engines in games, and even steering them towards something approaching true conversation. But that evolutionary path was not taken. 'Unfortunately,' Richard Darling says, 'I think we've gone through a bit of a dark age as far as communication AI is concerned, but we'll hopefully come out of that soon.'

Instead, the kind of static puzzles that used to be typical of adventure games persist in what some call 'action adventures' (they belong in our genre of exploration games). How does this work? Well, a game such as Resident Evil, for example, is built on exactly the same kind of puzzles that were the meat and drink of text adventures in their heyday. A nasty plant monster bars the way: go find some weedkiller that you can splash on it. You must collect three books, or some crystals, or combine some herbs, or get more ammo for your gun. The only difference is that instead of typing in commands, you directly control the movement of your character, select items and use them by pressing specialised buttons on the joypad.

Resident Evil is in this way somewhat less sophisticated than Zork or Snowball, or any number of classic text adventures. Nostalgia aside, the comparison is instructive because of the ways in which each game executes aspects of a story. Adventure games on first sight seem to be very close to traditional stories. They were, after all, in the same medium: text. And their descriptions of locations and scenes (often very well written) stimulated the mental imagination in exactly the same way that the prose of a novel does.

Yet even they did not tell an 'interactive plot': locations were all prescripted, and though you had certain freedoms to explore, you were still exploring a determinate, linear world. And just as with more modern games, the uses and combinations of objects available were only those which had been deliberately foreseen by the designer. Resident Evil, on the other hand, imitates a different medium altogether: as we've seen, it tries to be like a film, making use of certain horror-movie camera angles and so on. And its most evocative language is the incoherent moaning of zombies.

The play's the thing

So what might the future hold? It is clear, for one thing, that mainstream videogames will never go back to the keyboard. (Games played on personal computers rather than on keyboard-free consoles such as the PlayStation account for only about 10 per cent of the total sold worldwide.) The text adventure, therefore, is dead as a dodo. But future games will probably start to incorporate accurate voice recognition and eventually, no doubt, sophisticated language parsing, so that you can actually 'talk' to other characters in the videogame world. Richard Darling agrees. 'And then with AI systems as we are now, that could be a huge leap in excitement levels, where you could actually communicate with AI people in a way that you believed to be pretty close to realistic.'

Sega's beautiful and fascinating oddity Seaman (2000), for the Dreamcast system, is an admirable first step to reclaiming this higher path for videogames. Described as a 'voice recognition pet', it requires the player to rear a hilariously bizarre fish with a man's head (straight out of Monty Python's *The Meaning of Life*) that swims around a digital aquarium. The player can speak into a microphone peripheral that plugs into the joypad, and Seaman answers back. For the moment, however, only half the job is done, for Seaman's responses are still all prescripted. Dynamic voice synthesis and language creation in response to a player's conversation is still, it seems, a long way off.

When it happens, it will certainly be a wonderfully rich form of interaction. But I don't think it will achieve the dream of interactive narrative. What it will revolutionise instead is Olivier Masclef's ambition of a 'dramatically interesting virtual world': it will bolster the illusion of actually being a character in an imaginary social context. Yet for the game to be able to surprise and move the player with its storyline, it must necessarily still keep certain plot developments out of the player's control. ('Could there be a truly interactive, democratic artform?' David Cronenberg wonders. 'My films certainly aren't democratic – their creation is more like a dictatorship.')

Like Tom Stoppard's Rosencrantz and Guildenstern, the future gameplayer might be an actor in a drama over which he has no control – for only then, as we have seen, is it a drama. The author, *pace* Roland Barthes, is not quite dead yet.

Pending some future computational revolution, then, in which a machine might be programmed to simulate a real human author, with a real author's consciousness, creativity and life experiences, truly interactive narrative is going to be out of reach. These are the (very difficult) minimum requirements, and they go beyond even the requirements of Strong AI. There are heuristic 'story-writing' programs already, but their output, although impressive in its syntactical sophistication, is worthless in literary terms. There is as yet no reason to think that solving the data intensiveness problem by applying algorithmic processes to the actual plot, rather than to character behaviour, will result in anything a human gameplayer would be interested in, emotionally or otherwise.

But this should not be surprising, or even disappointing. Because stories will always be things that people want to be told. If everyone wanted to make up their own story, why would they buy so many novels and cinema tickets? We like stories in general because they're *not* interactive.

Tie me up, tie me down

So should videogames totally abandon their current model of prescripted storyline interrupting interactive play? Not necessarily. While it certainly does not amount to 'interactive storytelling', it can still work remarkably well on its own account, under the same circumstances as any good story: when it is well written.

A good videogame story provides a powerful external motivation (external to the actual gameplay mechanics) for continuing to try to beat the system. A well-scripted game, such as Metal Gear Solid, keeps you playing because fundamentally, as E. M. Forster remarked of the primary appeal of the novel, you just want to know what happens next. It helps that Metal Gear Solid's cut-scenes of vocal dialogue are generally well-acted, and the multiple twists and turns of the thriller plot are highly enjoyable, dropping little hints as to the true nature of your mission and the organisation you work for, keeping you guessing as to how it will all turn out.

But Metal Gear Solid's true brilliance lies in its touches of humorous self-consciousness. It knows it's a game. One of your opponents, a pink-bodystockinged martial arts cyborg called Psycho Mantis, comments sarcastically on the other videogames you play (by reading the memory card in your console, which contains data saved from other games). And a helpful character will tell you at one point to pull your controller out of the PlayStation and put it in the other socket, so that Psycho will no longer be able to predict your movements and kill you quickly. Such clever devices ensure that the player is a happy slave: though he has no freedom to change the story, he has a lot of freedom in the gameplay itself, where many different creative solutions can be found to the game's problems. The unique pleasure of a videogame, after all, the one that no other medium can offer, is always going to be what happens *between* the episodes of the story.

The videogame industry knows just how successful this approach can be – and, increasingly, professional scriptwriters are being hired to work on high-budget productions for exactly these reasons. In the future, videogames will no doubt have much better stories, but it seems unlikely that we will be given much more freedom to change them than we already have in games like Perfect Dark, Zelda 64 or Metal Gear Solid. And above all, there will still need to be interesting tasks for the player to perform. Sega's Dreamcast game Shenmue, for example, looks absolutely gorgeous and has a suitably epic storyline, but the gameplay is somewhat limited.

What we want in general from a videogame story is not interactive narrative at all, but a sophisticated illusion that gives us pleasure without responsibility. Sure, it might be nice to feel like we really are infiltrating a terrorist compound in Alaska, or going on an exotic quest to find an archaeological artefact, and if prescripted story scenes can enhance this feeling of involvement, then they serve a useful purpose. If we can further choose to do certain things, and so see certain episodes of the story in a different order, then fine – but we *don't* want to have to make crucial narrative decisions that might, in effect, spoil the story for us. We want to have our cake and eat it.

A great deal of cake, not to mention roast chicken, salads and pizza piled high on hundreds of trestle tables, was consumed at Sony's 1999 E3 party, held in the lots of Sony Pictures in Culver City. This is where the throngs at the Los Angeles videogames fair went to wind down one evening – at least, those lucky enough to secure invitations. Before the stage was taken for a live performance by slacker-country rocker Beck, Ken Kutaragi, the engineering genius at Sony Japan who designed the PlayStation and its successor, gave an intriguing speech that concentrated on the advantages of 'new worlds' and 'characters'. He was cheered to the echo by the audience.

Kutaragi's concentration on 'character' rather than story-telling was informative. Developments in Los Angeles and elsewhere show a new pragmatism among videogame designers: concentrating on what they alone can provide, rather than chasing the fashionable dream of interactive narrative, or uncritically seeking convergence with the cinema. Instead, especially in their concentration on character, videogames are carefully strip-mining our conventional notions of narrative and storytelling for what can be usefully simulated in their own, utterly different, medium.

But how do videogames build the worlds that their characters inhabit?

6

SOLID GEOMETRY

Vector class

The world is made of glowing green and red lines. You are
seated in a cockpit, grasping a sculpted black lever in each
hand, thumbs hovering over the twin red fire buttons on top.
You are in a tank. Audio rumblings and sonar-like pings go
off around your ears as the other tanks on the battlefield seek
to destroy you. It's kill or be killed. It's a dream of perfect
destruction. You're playing Battlezone.

This arcade game, released by Atari in 1980, in which the
player must shoot other tanks and flying saucers while surviving
as long as possible, was a milestone in the history of videogame
imagery, and in the construction of videogame space itself. It
was the first really successful 'first-person' game, where the
screen showed the action from a perspectival point of view, as
if you were actually there. (There had been previous attempts
at perspective in games, notably in Night Driver, which used
moving white blocks on a black screen to evoke cats' eyes
and side bollards on a road, and in Star Raiders [1979], a
rudimentary 3D space shoot-'em-up, but Battlezone provided
an environment where the player had complete freedom of
movement over the ground in any direction.) And Battlezone
was also the defining moment of a style of graphical representation whose influence is still felt, even in the most modern
games of the new millennium.

The ghostly images of enemy tanks and flying saucers were
drawn in vector graphics. Whereas a television screen or a
modern computer monitor is a 'raster' display, consisting of
hundreds of horizontal arrays of dots which are drawn one at

a time, so that a diagonal line on screen always looks 'stepped', vector screens enabled a perfectly straight line to be drawn between any two points on the screen. Battlezone's universe was one of sharp-edged perfection.

But the most immediately noticeable thing about the game now is that its tanks and mountains are drawn only in luminous outline. You can see right through everything. This method became known as 'wireframe 3D'.* Where two planes of an object meet, a line is drawn, but the planes themselves have no surface, no solidity. Every object is drawn from simple geometrical objects such as triangles and rectangles. These are generally known as 'polygons'.

Wireframe 3D caught on after Battlezone, and several arcade classics borrowed this technology while making the leap from pervasive green to full colour, most notably Star Wars and, in excelsis, Tempest, whose abstract pyrotechnics drove one of the greatest shoot-'em-up games ever conceived.

The peculiar ascetic attraction of wireframe graphics (whose apotheosis coincided with the last days of vector displays, but persisted after they had gone, as raster monitors now had sufficient pixel resolution to draw pretty straight-looking diagonals) enabled the player to concentrate purely on the action in a defiantly alien, unreal and still featureless arena. For many people growing up on these machines, the pinpoint glowing geometries of these worlds became a new metaphor for the terrain of the imagination – the structures of logical thought incarnated in a beautiful dance of electrons.

Martin Amis wrote that Battlezone has 'the look of op or pop art and the feel of a genuine battlezone'. This intriguing comparison is instructive in its shortcomings. For unlike op art, which produces an illusion of movement in the abstract, static image, Battlezone has partly representational ambitions (that is a tank, that is a flying saucer), and produces an illusion of movement by stringing together simple static images at high

---

* The first 3D wireframe computer animation had actually been created nearly two decades previously, by Edward Zajac, an engineer working at Bell Labs, as part of an experiment to see whether an orbiting satellite could be stabilised so that one of its surfaces always faced Earth.

speed. Battlezone's defining aesthetic (owing in part to technical limitations at the time), on the other hand, and in contrast to pop art, is one of purely imaginary surfaces. Where pop art glories in colourful flat shading and razored curves, Battlezone evinces contempt for colour, for material, for substance itself. Such qualities, it murmurs seductively, are illusory anyway. The edge is everything: the frontier where one plane meets another, where turret joins body, where missile meets flank.

The look of Battlezone or Tempest was at the same time shockingly weird and comfortingly familiar, not from Warhol or Riley but from a much nearer and more disturbing medium. It was as if school mathematics lessons had come to life, benignly. No doubt Battlezone and its ilk had some influence on William Gibson's seminally incandescent descriptions of the Matrix (whence the 1999 film got its title). In *Neuromancer*, Gibson describes this computer-simulated world, where corporations are represented by 'green cubes' or a 'stepped scarlet pyramid', where the landscape consists of 'lines of light ranged in the nonspace of the mind, clusters and constellations of data. Like city lights, receding . . .' Battlezone was the first game to draw with those familiar schoolroom objects, polygons – and in that, it prefigured the firework geometries of cutting-edge games in the late 1990s and beyond.

Battlezone was at once fantastically complex, in the demands of reaction and strategy it placed on the player, and reassuringly simple. Here was a universe devoid of clutter, eternally shiny and new. Early dreams of virtual reality were always expressed visually in wireframe graphics for these very reasons (see *Tron*), and now that videogame graphics have moved on to fill in the wireframe skeletons with textured surfaces, and to smooth their hard-edged outlines, the wireframe aesthetic can be seen as one of the great futurist dreams of the late twentieth century.

Modern videogames themselves understand the loss and even grieve it, in witty ways: Metal Gear Solid, for instance, provides the player with a delicious 'VR Training Mode', in which strategies for the game proper are practised in a wireframe world, and moving among these glowing green rectilinear constructions feels, in a funny way, like a sort of homecoming.

The art of the new

From Space Invaders, to the creation of space itself. For many years the Holy Grail of videogame graphics engineers was a system of true three-dimensional action, a 'virtual' space that the player could inhabit.

The problem of representing three dimensions on a flat plane (in this case, the television screen) had already been worried about by painters for thousands of years. The earliest attempts at perspective that we know of are found in scenery painting for the Dionysian theatre at Athens in the fifth century BC (the Greeks called it *skenographia*), and foreshortening and shading developed with increasing sophistication up to and through the medieval period. But an exact theory of perspective in painting was not codified until *circa* 1420, when Filippo Brunelleschi systematised a mathematical method for what became known as 'scientific perspective'.

You know it already. Objects in the distance decrease in apparent size according to strictly defined ratios. Parallel lines converge at one or more 'vanishing points'.* Scientific perspective is universally familiar today, at least in the West. It is everywhere, and it just looks 'right'. When a child is taught to draw railway lines converging as they roll into the distance, she is learning scientific perspective. We are familiar with Escher's unsettling distortions of it. And scientific perspective is the kind on which most modern 3D videogames are constructed. In games such as Doom, where the screen supposedly shows the player's point of view in an imagined, putatively solid environment, the computer calculates – precisely according to the rules first devised by Brunelleschi and, later, elaborated by Alberti in his *On Painting* (1436) – the appropriate size and shape for all objects on the screen, depending on their distance from and angle to the hypothetical 'viewer'.

But along the way, videogames have rehearsed other histories

---

* This familiar term was not, in fact, coined (by Brook Taylor, in *Linear Perspective*) until nearly 300 years after the discovery of scientific perspective by painters.

of pictorial representation, and come up with imaginative and original visual strategies themselves. Moreover, as has been made abundantly clear in the mid- to late 1990s by the industry's numerous abortive attempts to convert old two-dimensional game paradigms into 3D space, videogame possibilities often depend totally on the form of representation chosen. It is hard to imagine a workable true-3D Asteroids or Defender. The critical problem is this: you can't see behind you. Of course, you can't in real life either, but then in real life you don't often find yourself piloting an arrow-shaped spaceship and blasting big rocks. The latest reiteration of Asteroids (1998), in fact, finally recognises this problem. The ships and rocks are reimagined as 'solid', multifaceted objects, but the playing area is a good old two-dimensional plane.

So what is the story of videogames' visual refinement? What shapes of world have sprouted from the silicon, and what might the future still hold?

Pushing the boundaries

The very earliest videogames, such as Spacewar and Pong, represented objects on a flat plane, the boundaries of which were those of the screen. The environment had no characteristics of its own: it was not terrain, but simply a function of the relations between objects (such as the perilous gravitational field surrounding the sun in Spacewar) or a means by which time could pass while one object travelled across the screen (the ball in Pong), so that everything did not happen simultaneously.

This was a mode of space purer than any that exists in the real universe. Its laws produced no frictional resistance, and it offered no decorative matter to distract from the task in hand. It was a pure dream of unhindered movement and harmonious action. More modern games have diluted this primal passion in a mania of hyper-representation. Certainly it is clear that as soon as more advanced graphical systems become available in the history of videogames, it is space that gets filled up, terraformed, converted into a game object itself. Perhaps in the end there was something disturbing about the alien vacuum.

In the early flat-plane games, the boundaries of the TV screen limited the play arena to a fixed, small size, and thus limited the type of action available to game designers. (Just as in real life, a game of football requires more space than a game of tennis.) The screen was a prison. But it didn't take long before ways were invented to gild the cage, and then burst its bars completely.

'Wraparound' screens were soon developed, as in Asteroids (1979), where the player's ship could, rather than bouncing off the screen edges, travel off one side of the screen and magically reappear on the other, providing increased fluidity of action. Now space was curved. Your disappearing ship would sail 'over' the top and zip around the (imaginary) back instantaneously before coming 'under' and rematerialising at the bottom. Topologically, the spatial arrangement of Asteroids, though it looked flat, was actually equivalent to the surface of a torus (a doughnut with a hole in the middle). While this curvature afforded the player greater freedoms of manoeuvrability, it also cunningly increased the sense of entrapment. For anyone who has watched their Asteroids ship career repeatedly across the screen time after time at full speed knows that there is no escape, however far you travel, from the implacable boulders.

The superficial limits of the screen were further eroded by the invention of scrolling. The term was borrowed, with semiconscious irony, from that pre-codex literary technology, the scroll, which may be unfurled horizontally or vertically, according to the dispensation of characters, in order to uncover more text than is currently viewable on the open section. We are now all familiar with the process of smoothly scrolling down a word-processing document or web page: videogames got there first.

Early scrolling games were mostly of the vertical shoot-'em-up genre. Rather than sit waiting for aliens to come knocking at one's defences, as in Space Invaders (1978), the player was in constant motion, rushing forever upwards on a long, linear strip of space, dodging and fighting enemies along the way. But most revolutionary was a type of space delineated by

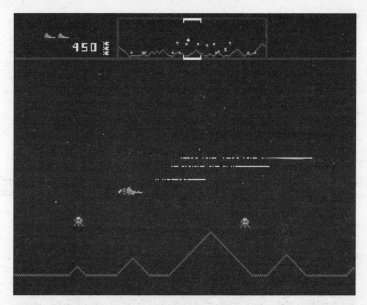

Fig. 9. Defender: swoop low over the mountains and defend the human race. The radar (top) shows the whole level space in miniature (© 1980 Williams)

the combination of horizontal scrolling with a variation on the wraparound concept.

This idea in fact featured one of the earliest scrolling games, Defender (1980 [see fig. 9]), for many reasons a classic of radical design, in which the player's ship is free to fly left or right, or simply to hover, spitting lasers at the evil hordes. When the ship is in motion, it remains in the centre of the screen; everything else scrolls by to give the illusion of movement. But fly far enough in one direction and the player approaches the original starting point, from the opposite direction. Horizontally, then, the play area is finite but unbounded.

Videogames had, with such forms as Defender's, somehow acquired a new dimension of action. It is certainly not the same space as in the old, static, one-screen games. Yet nor is it three-dimensional, for the player cannot fly 'into' or 'out of' the screen. The game demands, moreover, that the player watch two representations of the same space: one on the main playing area, and one on Defender's innovatively complex radar, a small subscreen which shows a wider section of the game universe at any one time so that attacks can be planned and threatened humans rescued. The arrangement of space on the primary screen is rather as if we found ourselves in the centre of a large circular strip, on to which is projected the battle action; when we scroll sideways, we are metaphorically turning our heads to investigate another area of the scene.

This spatial arrangement is indeed the perfect, unforeseeable fusion of two pre-cinema visual technologies: the Cyclorama of the 1840s, in which the viewer stands inside a circular drum painted with a continuous image; and the Kinematoscope, patented by Coleman Sellers in 1861, in which a series of photographs arranged around the inside of a revolving drum presents the illusion of movement to an observer focusing on a fixed area of the interior. Defender marries the endless, wraparound vista of the Cyclorama with the flickering animation of the Kinematoscope, although the vista itself is different in purpose. It is not the visual depiction of the cycloramic space that is important in the videogame – Defender's space is still mostly unindividuated – but the strategic opportunities it offers, the chance to come up behind the enemy.

Later games, such as R-Type (1988), took advantage of spare power to create an inventive impression of depth with 'parallax' scrolling. Imagine the viewer inside the circular strip described above, only now it is not one but several concentric circular strips, revolving at decreasing speeds as they increase in distance from the viewer. In a train, the observer notes that trackside posts flash by in an instant, while distant scenery rolls past in a more leisurely fashion. In order to imitate this effect of moving perspective, the game screen background now acquires several different flat planes, so that objects in the foreground plane sweep by more quickly than objects in the middle-distance plane, which in turn pass more quickly than objects (mountain ranges, clouds and the like) near the horizon. The term 'parallax' itself was, fittingly for a family of games that usually featured alien worlds, borrowed from astronomy.

It is important to emphasise again at this point that innovations such as wraparound and scrolling did not at once render earlier forms obsolete. The limitations of a fixed, bounded screen, for instance, are reimagined as positive gameplay virtues by the tense, claustrophobic design of Robotron (1982), in which the player's post-apocalyptic hero must do battle in a confined space with twenty, fifty or a hundred bloodthirsty automatons in order to save the last nuclear family on Earth. As the game's designer, Eugene Jarvis, explained to J. C. Herz: 'It was kind of about confinement. You are stuck on this screen. There's two hundred robots trying to mutilate you, and there's no place to hide ... You can't run down the hallway. You can't *go* anywhere else ... A lot of times, the games are about the limitations. Not only what you can do but what you *can't* do.'*

Points of view

In 1980, Battlezone's scientific perspective was still only one of many competing modes of representation available to the videogame designer. Games continued to perform on two-dimensional planes, scrolling in one or more directions, for years. In 1982, however, another new mode, which came to be known as 'isometric perspective', was popularised by Zaxxon (see fig. 10), a shoot-'em-up which scrolled, not simply vertically or horizontally, but diagonally up and to the right. 'Isometric' means 'constant measurements'. In architectural parlance, 'isometric projection' is the name given to a type of drawing in which all horizontal lines are drawn at an angle of thirty degrees to the horizontal plane of projection. In other words, parallel lines do not converge, and equal emphasis is

---

* Jarvis's point is further backed up by the fact that nine years after scrolling and perspectival representation were invented, along came Tetris, an ultra-simple affair which featured neither, but almost instantly became the world's most popular videogame. The modern success of Grand Theft Auto, too, has not been limited by its 'old-fashioned', top-down viewpoint.

Fig. 10. Zaxxon: isometric perspective and terraformed space (© Sega 1982)

given to all three planes. In videogame terms, this means that an illusion of solidity is created while preserving an external viewpoint. You could see three sides of an object rather than just one. And now, crucially, the game screen was not just a neutral arena; it had become an environment.

By means of simple jagged lines, Defender had created an illusion of planetary surface by sketching a mountain range; below the level of the mountains it was safe to drop off rescued humans. But the mountains worked only to delimit functional areas of the arena in this way; they were otherwise metaphorically 'behind' the player, and did not have to be negotiated. Later derivatives of the scrolling 2D shoot-'em-up, such as Scramble, did require the navigation of tortuous tunnels, but this design only in effect limited the play area, which remained as fluid and empty as ever. The player's ship in Zaxxon, however, while having as usual to deal with enemy aircraft, could also explode if it crashed into any of the numerous barrels, pylons and buildings poking up out of the ground. Movement was now nearly in three dimensions, with the introduction of controls to vary 'height' above the ground. Only the fact that motion was automatically one-way (a function of the scrolling) inhibited complete freedom of movement.

Isometric perspective was not a brand-new discovery. It is very similar, for instance, to the form of 'parallelism' (representation in which parallel lines do not converge) found in ancient Chinese art, whose high viewpoint and oddly elongated (to the modern eye) diagonals are reproduced by Zaxxon and its siblings. In this case it is irrelevant that isometricity doesn't resemble the way we see things in real life.* In videogames, isometric perspective enjoyed a phase as the most technologically sophisticated means of building a 3D world, for example on games such as Ant Attack, Highway Encounter and Knight Lore for the ZX Spectrum.

Foreshortening implies a subjective, individual viewpoint, so its absence in isometric graphics, along with the elevated position of survey, conspired to give the user a sense of playing God in these tiny universes. God could not yet move around – he was still glued to his chair – but he could see everything, he was in control, and he saw that it was good.

Isometric perspective still prospers in the huge genre of strategy gaming. In SimCity and Civilisation or Command and Conquer, the player controls numerous units (people, tanks, factories and so on) within a vast playing area. Construct this world in scientific perspective, without an omniscient overview, and you'd be totally lost among the details. In such games, you don't need to peer behind at the hidden surfaces of an arms factory, for instance, because it is a functional counter in the gameplay, defined solely by its use and potential.

Scientific perspective is not just one alternative mode of

---

* At any distance, that is. In fact, according to modern psychologists, when scrutinising objects that are very close in our visual field, convergence doesn't operate, and what we 'see' actually resembles parallelism more closely.

representation among others; it is not just an arbitrary artistic 'convention', but is wired into true theories of physics and biology. And its lure was irresistible to videogame designers who were searching for ever more elaborate ways to convince the player that she was not merely watching, but was really *in* that world.

Being there

People usually say that the first true 'immersive' 3D game was Wolfenstein 3D, released by iD in 1992. This did indeed kick-start a blossoming genre, the first-person shooter, where the screen displays the supposed viewpoint of the player's character wandering around an enemy-infested arena with a battery of projectile weaponry.*

Yet Battlezone, more than a decade previously, was in effect a first-person shooter, and the first-person viewpoint had even been crammed into a game released for the Sinclair ZX81 home computer, 3D Monster Maze, in which the player had to negotiate a black-and-white maze (drawn in a very low-resolution approximation of wireframe) while avoiding a marauding Tyrannosaurus rex; the entire game, a beautifully terrifying experience for any nine-year-old of the day (me, for instance), ran in a mere 16 kilobytes of code, which wouldn't be nearly enough to run even the joystick drivers for modern games.

Yet it was Wolfenstein which first situated the player in 'rooms', connected by doors, with walls receding realistically into the distance and other humans wandering around to be killed. (In this case they were Nazi officers, so no compunction need be felt about blasting them to their doom.) Wolfenstein's illusionism was rather crude: there was no texture to the floors or ceiling to aid the impression of forward movement – only the walls of the room moved; and the enemy soldiers were constructed by bit-mapped sprites, which means they were

---

* With wry names. In the follow-up, Doom, the most potent weapon was known by the acronym BFG: 'big fucking gun'.

basically flat drawings. When the enemies got nearer, they grew perspectivally by the simple means of enlarging every pixel in the drawing, so that they looked fuzzy and 'blocky'.

But another innovation Wolfenstein made has been copied by every first-person shooter since: at the bottom of the screen is a representation of hands clutching a gun, drawn foreshortened so that the gun appears to be pointing 'into' the screen. This was a clever effort to try to cross the barrier between onscreen action and the player's physical situation – those are my hands, so my head must be in this world too – and the animations of recoil and reloading have become ever more impressive.

But the purpose of this gun onscreen is purely cosmetic and psychological, rather than operational. It is not used for aiming, for while Wolfenstein and Doom have the gun pointing straight into the centre, other first-person shooters, such as Goldeneye, have it coming into the screen at an angle (usually from the right, which sadly compromises believability for lefties), so it is impossible to judge its precise direction and range. Of course, anyone actually using a gun points it dead ahead along the central axis of vision, rather than across the body; the videogame gun, however, is moved over to one side so as not to obscure the centre of the screen, where most of the action takes place, and a separate aiming cursor (usually small crosshairs) is provided for accuracy of shooting.

The makers of Wolfenstein went on to release the far more successful Doom, which added floor and ceiling textures as well as external locations, and then Quake, which further enhanced the illusion of a solid environment with solid, polygonal monsters. Suddenly, videogame space was inhabited, occupied by the enemy.

And it was all done with geometry. The triangles and oblongs of Battlezone are the same objects that make up a level of Half-Life (1998), only in the latter they are massively more numerous, and the surfaces are filled in. So why did polygons become the ubiquitous virtual bricks of videogames? Because, whatever the interesting or eccentric devices that had been thrown up along the way, videogames, as with the strain of Western art from the Renaissance up until the shock of

Fig. 11. House of the Dead 2: be afraid of geometry (© Sega 1999)

photography, were hell-bent on refining their powers of illusionistic deception.

Wireframe 3D was a nice start, but now it's old hat. Real tanks don't look like that. In two dimensions, you join the dots; in three dimensions, you join the lines. It was time to colour in the surfaces, and in the early 1990s game types such as aircraft combat simulators, driving games and more tank games began to do this, while polygonal animated human forms first appeared in videogames with the martial arts game Virtua Fighter. Remember: a polygon ('many sides') is any flat shape drawn with straight lines. A triangle, a square, an icosahedron – they are all polygons. Easy to draw. Easy, with a powerful chip, to draw an awful lot of them.

The bloody, rotting zombies in House of the Dead 2 (see fig. 11) are constructed from many differently shaded and shaped triangles, which foreshorten and morph when the figure moves exactly according to the rules of scientific perspective. The play of virtual light* off these baroque constructions gives

---

* Another coinage by William Gibson, in his novel of that name (1993).

them the appearance of solid objects in space in a way that flat graphic drawings (sprites) never accomplished. Shading of light and dark on a flat, static surface (for instance, in a painting) is sufficient to suggest depth and form, but videogames have the added challenge that they move, and 3D videogames allow objects to be seen from more than one angle. So the demonic form is defined as a mathematical solid, and then the computing engine can calculate all the shading and foreshortening automatically.

The fact that solid forms can be described by simple geometry (geometry literally means 'measuring the world') is an idea as old as Western civilisation. In the *Timaeus*, Plato's eponymous speaker reasons that the entire universe is made up of simple geometrical shapes that can be represented by the first four numbers: one is a point, two is a line, three is a triangle and four is the simplest non-spherical solid, a triangular pyramid. Numerological essays in cabbalism spring from the same idea, and from medieval times onwards religious thinkers hoped that applying geometrical analysis to the universe would enable them, in Stephen Hawking's retrospectively apt phrase, 'to know the mind of God'. In the thirteenth century, Roger Bacon praised the religious power of the developing tradition of 'geometric figuring' in painting; making the figures in religious scenes as lifelike as possible, he argued, could induce in the pious a sense of actually witnessing the events depicted.

Artists began to experiment with geometrical analyses of that most important form, the human body. Engravings by artists such as Dürer and Schön show how an understanding of corporeal proportion is aided by reducing the body to simple geometrical building blocks. But this method was not just a device or a trick. The Dutch artist Crispyn van der Passe, for instance, produced in 1643 a large encyclopedia of geometric figurings for such common subjects as stags and birds, and argued that the fact that all animals are reducible to simple Euclidean forms is attributable to divine Providence. The geometrical method revealed to the artists a deep, Timaean truth about the nature of the universe: as Ernst Gombrich describes it, 'The regular schema which we call an abstraction was therefore "found" by the artist in nature. It belongs to the laws of its being.'

On the one hand, then, polygonal videogames are using a very old tradition of illusionistic construction; on the other hand, they have revolutionised it. Because these polygons move. Every videogame, you see, constructs not only a space but a space-time. All 3D games are in this sense four-dimensional. And now the polygons become animated – literally, given a soul. A machine soul. Virtua Fighter 2 looks as though the figures in Schön's etching have suddenly come to life, participating in an epic ballet of crunching tibia. The pious geometrical idealism of the ancients has been lost along the way, replaced by the banally unphilosophical late twentieth-century idealism of the perfect body: fighting men with horrifically overdeveloped trapezoid muscles; fighting women with long legs, wasp waists and unfeasibly pert breasts. But though human beings do not actually look like this, they do *move* like this, and the tangible solidity of one leg sweeping in front of another, of a fist slamming into a chest, is a magic wrought by Plato's four numbers.

Just as Timaeus argues further that the four numbers (or atoms) that make up the cosmos correspond to the four elements in ancient Greek cosmogony (earth, wind, fire and water), so modern polygons can be made to draw every kind of substance on the videogame screen: rocky outcrops, sure, but also lakes, blazing torches, grass, even snow. And games no longer have the chunky, android look of those in the polygonal vanguard, like Virtua Fighter 2. Usefully, the more sides you can afford to devote to a polygon – which can also be thought of as drawing a polygon with more and more basic triangles – the more curved it looks (because the straight lines connecting each point are so short).

The more polygons a processor can draw on the screen at any one time, therefore, the more rounded and 'organic' will seem the environments and the characters within them, as in markedly more 'realistic'-looking games such as Zelda 64, Tomb Raider: The Last Revelation or Quake III: Arena. And polygons' very ubiquity will lead to their immolation. Sony's PlayStation2 draws about seventy million polygons per second, which is roughly equivalent to the total number of pixels on the screen.* Hardware is thus getting very close to being able to provide so many polygons that to all intents and purposes they will soon vanish, collapsing back into the original cosmic building blocks. They will become, in effect, the modest, invisible atoms of videogame reality.

The user illusion

But even with modern videogames' zillions of polygons – and their weird mathematical progeny: voxels, non-uniform rational B-splines and other computational flora† – they still need to make use of tricks and misdirections borrowed from painting in order to achieve the dream of fooling the player into believing in an imaginary world.

These are tricks that persuade us we are looking *into* the screen or canvas, rather than just looking *at* it. In the real world, we perceive depth because we have two eyes: each receives a slightly different perspective on the scene and our brain blends them into a stereoscopic image. But a flat representation such as that in paintings or videogames can still offer a lot of information about depth, partly through scientific perspective, and partly through other 'indirect' means, taking advantage of the fact that in binocular vision at distances of more than about fifty feet, we do not perceive depth directly anyway. The fact that we routinely rely on cues other than the direct perception of depth is easy to demonstrate if you close one eye and look at people a hundred yards away. You don't immediately think they are midgets.

Videogames use many of the same tricks that painters have

---

* The number of polygons drawn per second is a theoretical maximum, of course, ignoring shading and lighting effects, and we are assuming a screen resolution of a million pixels at a framerate of 60 fps.

† Voxels is short for 'volumetric pixels' – tiny graphical building blocks that are already three-dimensional; B-splines are curved surfaces described not by polygonal approximations, but by clumps of polynomial equations.

used over the centuries. One hoary old device much used in the Renaissance was a chequerboard-patterned floor of alternating light and dark squares receding 'into' the painting's background. This is exactly the same *trompe-l'oeil* that crops up to enhance the sense of movement in games like WipEout 2097.

As well as scientific perspective, there are artistic traditions of overlapping contours, aerial perspective, dispensation of light and shade and interpretation of relative size. Most of these are self-explanatory, apart from the term 'aerial perspective'. This was coined by Leonardo Da Vinci; it has nothing to do with geometry but describes the effect of distance upon colour. Because light of different wavelengths is scattered in different ratios by travelling through the atmosphere, distant objects appear blue (bright distant objects, on the other hand, appear red, because more light from the blue end of the spectrum is lost – hence the spectacular colours of sunsets). It is also, familiarly, the case that distant objects do not appear so sharply defined in outline.

Once videogames, then, had learned to render distant mountain ranges, castles, bridges and so on in a bluish fuzz, as is done so expertly in Goldeneye, the illusion of distance within the gameworld was immediately enhanced. Sony's PlayStation2 console now automatically computes such blurrings if desired, to provide a spectacular illusion of 'depth of field', allowing the videogame designer to introduce many pleasing effects of focus.

Fuzzy blue things are less processor-hungry than sharp multicoloured things, too. With finite processing resources, videogames also have the option of shrouding the playing area in fog so that the player's range of vision (and thus what the computer has to draw) is markedly limited. Objects or monsters can loom out of the mist with stylish effect, passing smoothly from blued-out fuzz to sharp delineation. Often, fog and general darkness make an effective means to heighten tension in horror-related gameplay, for instance in Silent Hill (see fig. 12), a good example of how technical limitations can be turned to positive aesthetic effect.

Some technical limitations, however, run deeper. The mode of scientific perspective, whether in videogames or traditional

Solid Geometry

Fig. 12. Silent Hill: fog and snow heighten the tension (© 1999 Konami)

art, inevitably involves some choices and compromises about how to display visual information. One of the well-attested problems of representation in scientific perspective is that of marginal distortion. Projective geometry speaks of a 'picture plane' in front of the viewer. Imagine it as a window looking on to a garden.* Light rays from objects are said to subtend angles at the eye: this simply denotes how many degrees of our visual field they take up. But objects also have 'plane projections', which is their apparent size on the picture plane – the size you would draw the snoozing cat on the garden wall if you traced her outline on the window.

Now usually, any object B which subtends a larger view angle than object A has a correspondingly larger plane projection. This is common artistic sense: it looks bigger, so you draw

---

* The term 'perspective' itself actually comes from the Latin for 'to look through' – to look through something like a transparent picture plane, or window.

it bigger. But there are certain cases where view angle and plane projection do not tally. The simplest instance is a drawing of a sphere that is to one side of our vision. It subtends a smaller view angle than a sphere directly in front of us, but it has a larger plane projection. According to true perspective, therefore, it should have an elliptical, not a circular, outline. This is how we see, but it would 'look wrong' to draw it thus. (Consider how odd a photograph looks taken with a 'fish-eye' lens, even though it represents our field of vision more accurately than standard equipment.) Renaissance painters already knew that these sorts of compromises had to be made. A book on the subject argued that 'il ne faut pas dessiner n'y peinder com[m]e l'oeil voit'.*

In general, painting avoids the confusions of marginal distortion by two methods: combining several slightly different viewpoints (especially in large canvases), or keeping the angle of vision relatively narrow. The reason why such discrepancies occur is that in real life we never actually keep our viewpoint 'fixed' in one place for any great period of time; our eyes dart and flit over the scene in a series of saccades, building up an overarching picture out of fragments. If we were to concentrate attention on our sidelined sphere by looking directly at it for a fraction of a second, we would confirm that its outline really is round and not elliptical.

Videogames presented in a first-person viewpoint thus far have failed to overcome these problems, and their hyperbolic claims to a sort of 'realism' must therefore be qualified. Perspectival limitations are far more salient and noticeable in first-person shooters, which unlike most paintings are predicated on fast, aggressive responses. To avoid marginal distortions, for instance, videogames, like paintings, keep the angle of vision artificially narrow. But this has the side-effect of removing from the player's arsenal one of his most valuable real-life abilities in a hunting or evasion situation: that is, to apprehend things, especially sudden movement, with peripheral vision. Furthermore, the clumsy apparatus with which the gameplayer

---

* 'One should not draw or paint exactly as the eye sees.' Bosse, *Traité des pratiques géometrales et perspectives* (1665).

has to wrestle in order merely to look in different directions – moving a mouse or joystick – can never compete in terms of speed or intuitiveness with our natural, almost unwilled eye movements. As the field of view in a Quake-style videogame is artificially restricted vertically as well as horizontally, it takes a conscious decision and a mechanical fiddle just to glance down at the floor directly in front of you, to make sure you are not going to tread in some fatal ooze, break a trip-wire or fall down a satirical pit.

While videogames are still played out on flat television screens or monitors, therefore, and while the interface remains so doggedly mechanical, a critical level of realism will never be achieved, and the experience of playing Quake and its siblings will always be more like remote-controlling a robot with tunnel vision rather than being there yourself. Of course, remote-controlling a robot (or a dune buggy, or an orange marsupial) can be fun and interesting in itself, but this is a large obstacle to greater immersion of the player in the virtual world. Only coin-op arcade games such as Sega's fabulous Ferrari 335 Challenge (1999) have the resources to address this problem by using three large screens, with the two outside ones angled towards the player, thus giving an excellent illusion of wide-angle vision.

The third way

One creative and novel way, however, in which videogames have expanded the three-dimensional horizons and given the player a feeling of having more 'room' to move around, is with the so-called 'third-person' 3D style. Most famously exemplified by the Tomb Raider games (see fig. 13), this is a perspectival construction in which the player can see the character under control, and the representational viewpoint itself is a completely disembodied one.

Disembodied? I mean that the view we are given corresponds to no actual pair of eyes in the gameworld. The point of view from which we see Lara Croft is constantly moving, swooping, creeping up behind her and giddily soaring above, even diving

Fig. 13. Tomb Raider 3: the third-person perspective — we watch Lara watching her surroundings (here, an imaginary London wharf) (© and ™ 1998 Core Design Limited; all rights reserved)

below the putative floor level. We are spying on Lara even when she is alone in the caves. The player can choose to zoom in to a point just behind her shoulder, nearly sharing her point of view, in order to guide her more accurately across a chasm, but she remains oblivious. Tomb Raider plays a lovely joke in one level, indeed, which features a figure who imitates in detail all of Lara's movements. You assume it's an enemy, and try to shoot while dodging, panic-stricken, around the room, until suddenly it clicks. Lara is standing in front of a giant mirror. And of course only she is reflected, because the pair of eyes through which you are watching her in the digital world is invisible.

The important aspect of Tomb Raider's representational style, in fact, is that the modus operandi has been borrowed not from painting but from the cinema: the player's point of view is explicitly defined, as we saw, as that of a 'camera', whose movements can often be controlled as if the player were a phantom movie director, floating about on an invisible crane.

The external view of the player's character, although putatively less 'realistic', is very often more desirable in gameplay terms than the fashionable first-person view. Just as old-school blasters like Asteroids or Defender are only playable games in two dimensions, because the player is given an overview of the action surrounding his ship, so Tomb Raider enables the player to navigate far more easily and intuitively around the playing areas, because she can see immediately how close Lara is to a side wall, or just how far away that nasty spiked ditch is.

Brave new worlds

This brief history of the construction of space in videogames has suggested two things. One is that videogames have to some degree repeated histories of representation in art, on jittery, caffeine-fuelled fast-forward. But it is immediately apparent that so far, they have only reached a surprisingly early stage in that development, for by the eighteenth century in painting the classical ideal of beauty based on some cosmic mathematical order was already being challenged, and the shortcomings of perspective were already being identified. Videogame scenery, being an artefact of computers, is clearly still in thrall to the god of mathematics. Of the myriad post-perspectival ways of seeing such as impressionism or cubism, there is as yet no sign in the apprentice draughtsmanship of videogames.

One can imagine, for instance, a far more ambitious game along the lines of Tomb Raider, in which adventures in different times and places would be rendered in the appropriate style. Tomb raiding among the freshly built pyramids would draw the world in the statuesquely side-on, information-stuffed mode of ancient Egyptian art; Lara's exploits in early twentieth-century Paris would present objects as fabulous collages of their shapes apprehended under different viewing angles; Machiavellian derring-do at the court of the Medicis would most likely occur in doomy chiaroscuro, with something disturbingly off-key about the relationship between foreground and background; and if Lara were shrunk to sub-atomic size, she could journey among the full eleven dimensions that we are currently assured constitute reality.

There is no question that such a game could be built; it is a question of whether there exists the vision to build it – and, of course, whether anyone would want to play it. Such a mixture of styles in our hypothetical game, of course, would – and this is the second thing we have learned – necessitate a mixture of different sorts of gameplay. The Egyptian level might be a sophisticated melding of role-playing with platform genres, whereas the cubist level would imply more of an abstract puzzle game. And this is one of the main ways in which videogame representation differs from that in painting. No artist would now deliberately draw in the inaccurate perspective of the thirteenth century, a mode of representation which has really been superseded and replaced by a correct mode of endeavour. But as we have seen, videogames may still use isometric perspective, or wireframe 3D, or flat scrolling, depending on the type of gameplay experience they wish to offer. In this way, videogames are fortunate in that their entire artistic history in terms of spatial representation is, as yet, still available in the present. Two-dimensional videogames live on, for example, in software for the Gameboy, the most successful videogame system ever made.

The choice of spatial mode, of course, which includes the choice even of whether or how far to be representational at all (Doom versus Tetris), is bound up intimately with the question of what kind of game the designers intend to make. One result of the increasing detail and colour available with newer technologies is that this decision is becoming increasingly weighted towards the representational: videogames are becoming ever more creatively iconic.

A development studio these days first builds a world, then populates it with characters. So who are these virtual people, and what do they want from us?

7

FALSE IDOLS

Dress code

Chiba City: a sprawling, industrial town in the humid, rainy Japanese spring, where downbeat pockets of hardware shops, Pachinko parlours and lean-to noodle shacks are carved up by multi-lane highways. Cars don't stop to admire the view; they are always going somewhere else. Usually to the south, to Makuhari, Japan's own vision of the future now. Makuhari is a coastal district reclaimed from the sea and built from scratch within a decade: lowering steel-and-glass skyscrapers, webs of swirling concrete walkways, and acres of space on ground level – liminal expanses of perfectly clean and geometrically patterned paving which in Los Angeles would be instantly carved up into parking lots, but which here have precisely no function except a symbolic one: to emphasise and celebrate the area's gigantism of scale.

Makuhari, in its odd flatness of texture, its aggressively rectilinear architecture and its constellation of rosy aircraft-warning lights winking from the buildings at night, looks just like a city out of a videogame. It is a shrine to techno-optimism. Walking around, you feel that for all its perfection it is still somehow provisional, that Makuhari is in fact waiting for the foot-dragging future to arrive before it can flower in its full sci-fi glory. It was this district of Chiba which led William Gibson, in his Sprawl novels, to posit the city as his physical setting for the tales of corporate cyber-rapacity coexisting uneasily with a radical hacker underground.

Fittingly, Makuhari is also the location for the biannual videogame industry festival, the Tokyo Game Show. For more than twenty years, Japan has been the leading centre of videogame development in the world, both technologically and artistically. So the Tokyo Game Show is the calendar's most important event. A lot of what's big in Japan now will trickle down into Western gaming paradigms in a year or two. And the Japanese have a very particular approach to the design of character in videogames. So I'm going to brave the crush and see for myself.

Inside Makuhari Messe, the vast national exhibition centre (whose undulating roof gives it the appearance of eight hi-tech railway stations shoved together), more than a hundred and sixty thousand Japanese men, women and children have come over the two public days of the exhibition in March 1999 to see and play the newest videogames, the ones that will be launched in the next six months. Each hardware or software company has its own stand in the enormous, roaring halls, all competing with their neighbours to attract the gamers' attention with gigantic neon signs, hundred-strong ranks of TV monitors with consoles lined up underneath them, constant blasts of game sound effects and music, and professional software 'spokespeople': glamorous Japanese women dressed in skin-tight PVC, silver miniskirts or Lycra bikinis who smile, hand out leaflets and pose for batteries of photographers. (The show presents an award to 'the most excellent companion lady'.)

Just as in Los Angeles, at the E3 show, the big companies advertise themselves with their videogame mascots – the stars of their top games. But whereas Sony, for instance, contents itself in America with huge inflatables of Spyro the Dragon and Crash Bandicoot, in Japan it offers a live stage show, with a rock band fronted by performers in the cuddly, furry costumes of Um Jammer Lammy and Parappa the Rapper. These two forms of entertainment marketing have quite different functions: Sony's American inflatables point backwards inevitably, merely illustratively, towards the games from which they are taken; the prancing figures in Japan, however, imply that game characters have a continuing inner life elsewhere.

In fact, game characters are everywhere. For the Tokyo Game Show also features a contest for visitors: come dressed as your favourite videogame idol. Young Japanese men and women wander round as black-clad soldiers (many bandanna'd Solid Snakes this year after the huge success of Metal Gear Solid), scary-masked orcs from dungeon RPGs, or blonde S&M princesses with fishnet stockings and leather harnesses. These game fans pay costume obeisance to their virtual heroes and heroines with a lack of self-consciousness that is remarkable to Western eyes. Game characters are also available everywhere in the form of Action Man-style figurines, or on collectors' cards. They feature in posters, on T-shirts; in Japan, a videogame character can be an idol as much as a pop star or an actor in the West. One of the major criteria, therefore, for a game's success in Japan is that it contains good characters.

Here, by the way, is another important difference between videogames and films. The star of a movie is chosen from a pre-existing pool of actors; you can dress them up in black Prada, shave their hair or teach them kung-fu (ideally all three), but at bottom you know what you're getting. The star of a videogame, though, at least of that type of videogame which incorporates characters at all, is invented: built completely from the ground up. A false idol indeed. Yet in another way a hyper-real one: for whereas a novelist, who also invents characters, will normally only need (or desire) to provide a few salient features of a person's appearance and let the reader's imagination do the rest, a videogame character must be determinedly individuated, given a complete, solid visual form.

Virtual megalocephaly

Of course this is also what happens in comic strips. In Japan, videogames have very strong aesthetic and commercial links with *manga* (comic books) and *anime* (animated cartoon films) – the massive Japanese toy and videogame corporation Bandai, for instance, is a major sponsor of animated programming. Whole books have been written about 'Japanimation' alone. But the most pertinent aspect of these comic forms for our purposes is their peculiar style of character drawing, which has a very strong influence on Japanese videogames. *Anime* in particular makes use of a bizarre, so-called 'deformed' style for its people: they have huge heads and eyes, and tiny torsos.

In the early days of videogames, technological considerations more or less forced designers into exactly the same style. The most influential early game to feature a fully humanoid, animated 'character' was Shigeru Miyamoto's Donkey Kong, with its era-defining moustachioed hero, later to be christened Mario. Because of the low resolution offered by videogame systems back then, character designers only had a limited amount of pixels – the little squares of light that make up the visual image – to play with. Miyamoto gave Jumpman (as he was then) a hat, simply because the technology couldn't enable animated hair; he wore dungarees just to differentiate his red arms from his blue body and legs. As Miyamoto says: 'Mario was born of rational design in the days of immature technology.'

More generally, both with Mario and with later characters, such considerations meant that, since the face and eyes are the richest physical loci of 'personality' – we concentrate on them in real life when talking to people; we commend portraits when they get the 'look' and expression right – it was natural to devote more resources and more space to them over the more purely functional parts of the physique.

Videogame characters thus grew up megalocephalic: with big heads and short bodies. This was also useful in terms of rich gameplay because most games of the era that featured 'characters' were two-dimensional platformers (or side-scrolling character-based shoot-'em-ups such as Metroid). So a squat body for the main character allowed more vertical 'room' to play with in the screen area – and as we observed in the last chapter, the type and amount of space available heavily influences gameplay possibilities.

What is interesting, however, is that this deformed style persists even in modern videogames, where it is perfectly possible with increased graphical muscle to produce proportionally more realistic avatars of human characters. When Japanese fans got their first look at Final Fantasy VIII there was palpable outrage, because it seemed the characters had been 'Westernised': no longer the cute, deformed people of FFVII but longer-limbed and more 'adult'-looking.

This is a widely held aesthetic preference among Japanese

gamers; in fact, it can be traced back to physical distortions of the human form in Japanese woodblock prints of the Edo period (1603–1868). Jeremy Smith, managing director of British developers Core Design, confides that feedback from the Japanese audience suggested that they wanted Lara Croft, virtual idol extraordinaire of the Tomb Raider series and the most high-profile icon of Western gaming, to be more 'manga-fied' – that is, for her body to conform more to 'deformed' standards. But Lara remained herself – still deformed, of course, but in a somewhat more subtle, and stereotypically Western, chesty-and-wasp-waisted fashion. By contrast, the most successful Western games by far in Japan at the time of writing are the Crash Bandicoot series. Crash is a cartoonish, wide-eyed, spiky-haired orange marsupial with an enormous head and toothy grin. He is already 'deformed', and fits in nicely.

But what is it about the deformed aesthetic that makes it so desirable? To most Western eyes, such characters look merely childlike and childish: 'cutesy'. But remember that unrealism in videogames need not be a handicap; it can be a positive, deliberate pleasure. The Japanese preference for 'deformed' physiques, in this case, is a logical extension of this idea to the human form itself. Unearthliness is part of the charm.

This idea in turn explains another peculiarly Japanese phenomenon: that of virtual 'girlfriends' and 'dating' videogames, in which the (almost always male) player tries to woo a deformed *anime*-style female character with massively enhanced breasts, eyes and legs. Several of these games, which in general do not cross over into the West at all, were on display in Makuhari, including one schoolday-romance RPG named Little Lovers: She So Game; the company's stand was decorated with large display boards on which were pinned life-size schoolgirl and sailor uniforms. Writer Robert Hamilton has supposed that young Japanese men, to go by the weighting of magazine sales (those sorts of glossy fanzines that Hamilton nicely terms 'devotional' literature) actually prefer deformed *anime* and videogame idols to human media stars for this reason: desire that can never in principle be reciprocated is thoroughly safe and free of any possible disappointment.

This phenomenon is known in Japan by the term of disapprobation *nijikon fetchi* – literally, 'two-dimensional fetish', though it more generally covers devotion to any form of *manga*, *anime* or three-dimensional videogame characters. An interesting symptom of this preference can be seen in the reception of the famous Japanese 'virtual idol' Kyoko Date, a thoroughly digital pop singer who was created in 1997 by software engineers collaborating with Japan's leading modelling agency, Horipro. It sounded like a great idea. But Date's first CD failed to meet sales expectations. Why? Because she was not deformed; she was overly realistic. Kyoko Date was built piecemeal from existing humans: a singing voice from one star, a talking voice from another actress, motion-captured dance routines and a combination of facial features mapped from photographs of famous models. Date thus actually looked too human.

The limitations of motion-capture animations (applying computerised sensors to the body of a human performer and then applying them to the videogame character) in a dynamic gameplay context are that they are too overdetermined and prescripted (just like preset 'combo' moves in beat-'em-ups, and just like prescribed 'narrative' interactions in story games). With Kyoko Date, we see further that motion capture is also aesthetically impoverishing, as it limits the achievable virtual movements and gestures to those that are physically possible in real life. But if all you are getting is 'realistic' movement, far better to watch an actual human dancer. Humans will always be much better at that sort of thing. And it is just not what videogames – or computer representation in general – are best at doing.

Gender genres

The phenomenon of *nijikon fetchi* raises questions about gender in videogames. Here, too, there are instructive comparisons to be made between Japan, the epicentre of videogame creativity, and Europe or America. It seems that Japanese developers create more games that women like to play. Demographics are to some extent determined by aesthetics.

False Idols

Statistical insights into videogaming in Japan are richly furnished by the 1997 *CESA* Games White Paper*. It reports that attendance at the 1997 Tokyo Game Show was 82 per cent male (while very heavily male-oriented, then, this still means nearly a fifth of attendees were female), while the median age of attendees was 25 to 29, and the most common occupation was that of 'office worker'. (Videogames, then, are not just for kids in Japan any more than they are in Britain or the US.) Meanwhile, the extent to which Japan is leading the West in terms of videogames' status as a mainstream entertainment medium is shown by a poll of 6,000 people, of whom more than a third (35 per cent) currently played videogames. Another fifth used to play them and probably will start again in the future, while an eighth had 'never played before, but would like to try depending on software'. Less than a third of the population (31.7 per cent) responded that they had 'never played before and had no wish to do so'.

Now, Japanese women who are interested in videogames have notably different preferences from the men. When asked to rank their favourite titles, more than three times as many women as men nominated the Pokémon ('Pocket Monster') series (12.7 per cent versus 3.9 per cent). These games, unleashed upon the British market in the 1999 Christmas season, are cartoonish virtual bestiaries, in which lovable monsters may be reared, played with and battled against each other. Generically, they are more like God games (in the sense that they are 'process toys') than action games. On the other hand, ten times as many men as women enjoyed the horse-racing simulation Derby Stallion games (8.6 per cent versus 0.8 per cent), which are straight-ahead recreations of (televised) horse racing, complete with virtual betting.

Women also preferred Crash Bandicoot, the Super Mario games, Tetris, Parappa the Rapper, IQ (a puzzle game) and Donkey Kong. Men, on the other hand, preferred RPGs such as Dragon Quest, driving game Gran Turismo and beat-'em-up Tekken (the last two being nominated by no

---

* Japan's industry body, the Computer Entertainment Software Association.

women at all). One must be wary about easy inferences from such results: you could argue that women prefer nurturing-style games rather than violent ones, but there is a highly vocal 'Game Grrlz' movement in America which proves that women can frag* with the best of them.

What we can infer so far is just that these Japanese women simply have different aesthetic tastes: their preferred videogames are in general more quirky or brain-taxing than the straight-ahead genre preferences (driving, fighting, dungeon games) of the men. But notice also that, apart from abstract puzzle games such as Tetris and IQ, all those nominated by women feature good characters: Crash, Mario, Parappa the singing dog, or personable imaginary beasts. These women's preferred games are also notable for having relatively simple initial skill-set requirements: Tetris, especially, can be picked up in a matter of seconds. But of course, simple controls and rules do not preclude rich and complex gameplay, regardless of the player's gender.

Now, Tekken 3 and Gran Turismo are wonderful games in their own right, and plenty of women like them. One cannot denigrate their visceral fascination just because it seems to appeal, in general, more to men. But Brenda Laurel of Purple Moon Software, an American development studio which produces videogames aimed at young females, does exactly this: 'Girls' objection to computer games isn't what you'd expect. It's not that they're too violent, it's that they're too boring. They're extremely bored by them.' Are they? Not according to Game Grrl Nikki Douglas, who retorts: 'What exactly is boring about creative strategy and 3D virtual environments? [. . .] I'll tell you what boring is – it was waiting for those little cakes to come out of the Easy-Bake oven.'†

---

* In multiplayer first-person shoot-'em-ups such as Quake III or Half-Life: Team Fortress, a player does not 'kill' an opponent but 'frags' him. The term derives from the Vietnam war practice of mutinous soldiers 'accidentally' killing their superior officers with fragmentation grenades.
† The traditional gender debate in videogames is fought out at great length in the collection of articles edited by Cassell & Jenkins, *From Barbie to Mortal Kombat: Gender and Computer Games*.

False Idols

There is probably some kernel of truth in the claim that, since until recently almost all videogame designers have been men, the products will have appealed more to men than to women; just as, conversely, what is known in the publishing trade as 'women's fiction', written by women, sells more to women than to men. Yet even here it is impossible to factor out the undoubtedly huge effect of marketing – 'women's fiction' is targeted at women; 'men's videogames' are targeted at men (with often depressingly adolescent, sexist advertising)* – from any posited 'innate' preferences. Now that many more women are involved in the videogame design process worldwide, we may see in the near future that this fact, allied with better marketing, will erase it completely.

According to some American statistics, in fact, the perceived 'gap' has already vanished. In 1998 in the US, female buyers accounted for the sale of fully 49 per cent of PC games, and the purchasers of 51 per cent of console titles were women. Nearly half of online gamers are female. This in particular suggests that the social aspect of online gaming appeals particularly to women users. Nolan Bushnell suggested to me that 'The "game" for women is in fact the chat rooms. As a percentage of connected people women dominate the conversation of the Internet.' That might miss the bigger picture of videogame usage among women, but it does tally with the online statistics.

Yet it still seems as though many women are dissatisfied with the available games. 'Despite the growing numbers of female gamers, the gaming industry as a whole is not meeting their needs and not taking their interests and preferences into account. Given the enormous buying power that women have and will continue to have, this is a shortsighted mistake,' according to one writer.†

---

* Nintendo's British advertisement for the greatest videogame ever made, Zelda 64, ran on television during Christmas 1998. Its slogan was: 'Are you going to get the girl, or play like one?' In a just world, the agency 'creatives' who came up with this moronism would be forced to play Tekken all day with my sister, and suffer a comprehensive thrashing every time.

† Doctor K, of the website for female videogamers, www.womengamers.com

So what kinds of game do women prefer? The Japanese women polled preferred games with good characters – the lovable personalities of Crash or Parappa. But since many men also liked these games, we can really infer nothing about the difference between men and women. The informational arrow is pointing the other way: it tells us about the commercial success of certain aesthetic decisions made by game designers themselves. A game with good characters could appeal to everyone; but a game with characters that are bad (boring, unlikeable, stereotyped) won't on this evidence appeal to women any more than it does to men.

So what of future developments? By far the most radical suggestion is that those women polled by CESA simply seem to have some higher – and at present unfulfillable – expectations. This is borne out by the survey section entitled 'The Image of Desired Home Video Game Software', in which respondents were asked what kind of games they would like to see. Girls of 7 to 12, for example, would like 'a chatting game', while 16- to 18-year-olds envisage 'a game in which a user creates various stories and can be a leading role'. As with so much else, the potential success of both types of posited game of course depends on massive advances in computer artificial intelligence. (These Japanese women, it seems, would also prefer to use skills they already possess – say, those of conversation – in a videogame context, rather than learn a complex and hermetic set of rules that applies to one game, or one genre only.)

But dissatisfaction with current videogame abilities isn't monopolised by women. Male gamers, too, always want the next game to be better than the last one, to be doing something that was technologically unimaginable six months ago. This often means that they appear to be happy with a faster, prettier driving game. But is that really what they want, or is it just what the developers feed them?

The only thing we can be sure of for the moment is, reassuringly, that quality will out – that 'gender' differences are dissolved in the face of a truly great game, such as Mario 64 or Final Fantasy VII (the latter was ranked overall favourite by equal proportions of men and women CESA respondents).

False Idols

Videogame developers in future will appeal to more men and to more women, only as long as their games mature aesthetically.

Character building

Let us return to one clear aesthetic preference of the female (and many of the male) CESA respondents: for videogames which have good characters. What exactly does this mean, and why are good characters desirable in a game? How does a false idol induce real worship? It is a commercial fact that successful game characters really do shift units. Especially those, like Mario, that pop up in a whole series of different games over the years. Already by 1990, an American survey determined that the virtual Italian plumber was recognised by more American children than Mickey Mouse. By 1995, Mario games had sold a total of 120 million copies worldwide. A star character in a videogame also enables spin-off merchandising: Pac-Man duvet covers and television series; Lara Croft utility-wear; Solid Snake figurines.

A really successful character is not just a money-maker for software developers, either: as we've seen, it enables hardware companies to sell consoles. Witness the fact that Nintendo's N64 machine was delayed for a whole year while the finishing touches were put to the game Super Mario 64. Good characters become extremely valuable 'properties' in the industry. Sega's Megadrive took off on the back of Sonic the Hedgehog, and the massive financial success of British publisher Eidos is largely thanks to Lara Croft.

The first videogame 'character' of all was Pac-Man (1980). Before this epoch-making game, the player controlled space-ships, gun turrets or other mechanical devices. Suddenly, though, the player of Pac-Man controlled a *being*: an animated, eating thing. The game's designer, Toru Iwatani, says that he got the idea for Pac-Man's form after eating a slice of pizza, and seeing the shape that was left. Then: 'I designed Pac-Man to be the simplest character possible, without any features such as eyes or limbs. Rather than defining the image of Pac-Man for the player, I wanted to leave that to each player's imagination.'

Now at first sight there is a world of difference between Pac-Man and a modern videogame character such as Lara Croft (see fig. 14). That is certainly true if you regard them as traditional static pictures. But as we must keep reminding ourselves, videogames are a kinetic artform: many of their pleasures can only be realised through time. And on a very basic level, Pac-Man and Lara do in fact share one important attraction. If you swing the joystick to move Pac-Man around his maze, he opens and shuts his mouth automatically while on the move. If you press a button to make Lara walk forward, she walks in a fluid, hip-swinging motion that is the result of hundreds of frames of painstaking digital animation.

These are both examples (one ancient, one modern) of how characters give us videogaming pleasure: through a joyously exaggerated sense of control, or amplification of input. All you do is hold down a button, and you get to see this wonderfully complex, rich behaviour as a result. This is one very basic attraction of all types of interactivity, and it also seems to be a near-universal pleasure among humans in the modern industrialised world. Why do people enjoy driving cars? Amplification of input: you just lower your foot and suddenly you are moving at exhilarating speed.

This kind of attractiveness is true of all good characters in modern videogaming: a few simple controls result in absorbing, complex movements. Witness the beautiful bounces and skids of Mario in Mario 64, or the graceful, arcing somersaults and handstands of Lara in Tomb Raider III. Good characters are good largely by virtue of having a wide range of physical abilities, and by having those physical abilities particularly well animated. Just as we can often be surprised in the flesh by the beauty of a person whom we have previously seen only in photographs – because part of a human being's attractiveness lies in the choreography of facial expression and gesture – so, especially, a videogame character is of much less visual interest when frozen in time.

Even Lara Croft's creator, Toby Gard, recognises this. In an interview with *Edge* magazine, he said: 'All the successful characters have the same thing in common: a good game. You cannot have a good character in a crap game because then

Fig. 14. Lara Croft: a beautiful abstraction (© and ™ Core Design
Limited; all rights reserved)

Fig. 15. Sonic the Hedgehog: cat and mouse (from Sonic Adventure, © Sega 1999)

everyone would perceive the character as crap too. It's exactly the same as a character in a film. It's not the costume they are wearing or what their face looks like, it's what they do and how they do it.'

Now hang on, this must be overstating the case a little. After all, beardy full-time action hero Chuck Norris could probably perform the kung-fu stunts in *The Matrix* better than Keanu Reeves, but whom would you prefer to watch? And so in videogames, there must still be some interdependence between dynamic attractions and purely pictorial ones.

For a start, characters such as Crash Bandicoot or Sonic (see fig. 15) obviously borrow very heavily from the cartoon styles of Warner Bros and others: Sonic was allegedly created (after a honcho at Sega ordered that someone design them a character to compete with Nintendo's Mario) by a deliberate crossing of Felix the Cat with Mickey Mouse, while Crash obeys the cartoon tradition of animals that look nothing like their real-life counterparts. Both Crash and Sonic have big heads, saucer eyes, cheeky grins and small bodies. In this sense they are deformed, Japanese-style; yet such a cute stylisation is also used in Western cartoons. Perhaps they are attractive because their large heads and limitless curiosity remind us of children.

More proportionally humanoid 'good characters' – such as Lara Croft, Jin Kazama from Tekken 3, or Solid Snake from Metal Gear Solid – work (on this purely static, visual dimension) in a slightly different way, in that they borrow from cinematic conventions of costume and coolness. It is almost certainly no coincidence that Metal Gear Solid's cigarette-loving, husky-voiced hero shares one of his names with Kurt Russell's character in *Escape from New York*, Snake Pliskin. Jin Kazama in Tekken 3 is an idealised amalgam of body-building action grunts such as Schwarzenegger and martial arts movie heroes.

A good videogame character is one that the player, because of a fulfilled combination of dynamic and iconic criteria, likes – just as we like cartoon characters such as Dangermouse or Cartman. But since the character is under our control, if we like him (or her) we must also feel somehow protective, and anxious lest we cause the character harm through our own manual inadequacy. And so a good character, as well as being aesthetically pleasing, constitutes one very strong motivation for playing the videogame well: you want Mario to overcome his surreal obstacles; you want Lara to escape from those pesky dogs; you want Sophitia to hack Rock to bits. Jeremy Smith of Core Design remembers how Tomb Raider nearly featured a man:

> The original script and graphics that were done, it just *was* Indiana Jones, and I said 'Christ, you can't do that – we'll be sued from here to Timbuktu!' And they said, 'Yeah, I suppose you're right. We'll work on it.' And then literally two weeks later we had another project meeting and there was this *babe* there. I said, 'It's a woman – what are you doing?', and they said 'No, it's gonna really work.' Well, at that point, it really didn't make any difference. It was only when they really started to develop Lara – she

was animated and her hair was moving – it was like, 'Wow, you could actually quite relate to this!'

One apotheosis of this sort of emotional manipulation is in the classic puzzle game Lemmings, in which you must guide hundreds of stupid, suicidal little furry creatures home, reacting quickly to stop them falling off high ledges or being sliced in two by Heath Robinsonesque sadistic machines. The lemmings are only about fifteen pixels high, but the way their hair is bouncily animated and their naive faith in a safe world mean you've *got* to save them.

This protectiveness functions the same way whether the character is abstract and cartoony or humanlike and filmic. And of course we must still insist that the latter type of videogame character is not supposed to be 'realistic' any more than a deformed *anime* character is. Part of the very attraction is a certain glossy blankness – what Smith enthuses over as 'that computer look'. As videogame graphics become ever more sophisticated, the designers of the next generation of Tomb Raider games on PlayStation2 will surely be careful never to let Lara become too individuated. If she were to look photo-realistic, too much like an actual individual woman, what seductiveness she possesses would thereby be destroyed. Smith agrees:

> We feel that we can make Lara significantly different to the way she is now, without making her sort of real-life, by only going up to say twelve to fourteen hundred poly-gons. You don't *need* to go any higher than that – because you'll probably lose some of that feel for her, for how she is now. With PlayStation2 technology we'll be able to smooth her off, without changing the aesthetics that work. We can give her great facial expressions, and we'll be spending a lot of time on clothing technology and working out the physics of clothes – a cloak, a shirtsleeve . . .

But she'll never be thoroughly realistic. For Lara Croft is an abstraction, an animated conglomeration of sexual and attitudinal signs (breasts, hotpants, shades, thigh holsters) whose very blankness encourages the (male or female) player's psychological projection, and is exactly why she has enjoyed such remarkable success as a cultural icon. A good videogame character like Lara Croft or Mario is, in these ways, inexhaustible.

Some say life's the thing . . .

. . . but I prefer playing videogames. Time to dive once again into the bleep-ridden throngs of Makuhari, because it's not just in terms of character design that the Japanese industry is instructive. We can also learn from the esoteric flora and fauna of its videogame biosphere that never make it to the West. Talking about them one night after the show in a local sushi bar, Japanese student Gavin Rees offers this observation: 'The Japanese do not make the distinction between "form" and "content" that we do in the West.'

How so? Teruichi Aono, a professional Shogi player (a boardgame also known as 'Japanese chess'), has written about the Japanese art of flower-arranging that 'the feeling is not so much that this flower or that is in itself beautiful, but that a world of elegant beauty is to be found, for example, in the skilful gathering and arranging of flowers and pampas grass'. In the tea ceremony, too, the rules for which it can take ten years to learn, the point is not so much the content (the actual drink) as the form (the highly traditionalised methods of preparing it): 'The actions performed in carrying out the ceremony are as intricate as they are because the point is to feel the beauty involved in each and every movement.'

So, the point is not the flowers themselves; the point is not the tea. Form is its *own* content. And the Japanese words that describe such an aesthetic – *ma* (timing) and *aida* (balance) – are also used of forms of play such as Sumo and judo wrestling.

Within the adult age group, both sexes of respondents to the CESA survey nominate game ideas that illustrate the highly idiosyncratic Japanese approach to concepts of simulation. Videogame 'simulations' in the West, as we saw in Chapter 2, are generally highly complex games of combat flight or Grand Prix driving. They simulate fast, dynamic processes. In Japan, however, 'simulation' is a much more inclusive, and at first sight wildly eccentric, genre. At the 1999 Tokyo Game Show, videogame companies were offering new products in the wildly popular genres of fishing simulations (you wind a plastic rod connected to the console and catch virtual fish), gardening simulations (you water virtual plants) and train-driving simulations (you can drive a train round an accurately modelled 3D representation of the Yamanote line on Tokyo's subway system).

And the remit of videogame 'simulations' in Japan is sure to expand. Adult Japanese women, for example, want 'a simulation game of being a housewife, giving experience of leading a happy married life including housework, having/raising children, sex'; 'a simulation of buying a house'; 'a game in which the user raises a human baby'; 'a job simulation game'; 'a game in which the user can date actors/singers'; 'a simulation game of overseas travel'; 'a game of cooking in which the user finds ingredients, cooks and becomes a master chef'; or 'a climbing game in which the user tries to reach the summit. On the way rivers, valleys, birds and little animals appear.'

Now, this looks a little weird, to be sure; but just as with the deformed *anime* tradition, we must be careful not to imagine an unbridgeable cultural chasm where none exists. Again, in fact, this phenomenon of burgeoning 'simulation' genres is a logical progression of facets in Western videogaming, albeit one powered by a characteristically Japanese conceptual tradition.

Most Japanese people live in cramped accommodation in sprawling cities. The idea of escaping to a rural idyll and lazily casting off by a babbling stream is largely an unattainable fantasy, except for the wealthy. Yet in a culture where the form of an activity is held in such high esteem for its own sake, being able to recreate that form in a videogame context is, it seems, a decisively valuable pleasure.

This is not so different from a Western driving game. Most of us will never be able to hurl a Dodge Viper at two hundred miles an hour through the Tokyo suburbs. But we can play Gran Turismo, and as the form of the videogame becomes an ever more accurate analogue to the form of the real activity (with our provisos about playability), that is a better and better consolation. The gallimaufry of Japanese simulation games are attractive because they can provide the dynamic form of an activity even though the content (the physical paraphernalia of that activity: actual fish, or a real garden) are missing.

Now, of course, irrespective of their varying approaches to character design or formal realism, Japanese videogames are still, fundamentally, games. And Japanese people like to play as much as anyone else. One of their biggest leisure pastimes, in fact, has much to tell us next.

8

THE PLAYER OF GAMES

Tiny silver balls

After the luminous hi-tech orgy of Makuhari's videogame exhibition, let's stop off at a Pachinko parlour in Akihabara, or 'Electric Town', the Tokyo district that constitutes a paradise on earth for devotees of *denki seihin*, or consumer electronics. In the West, we have slot machines built around spinning wheels inscribed with cherries and numbers. In Japan they have Pachinko, a simple yet intriguing game played with tiny silver balls. It appeared in Japan in the 1920s, and is in some ways a forerunner of videogames themselves.

This particular arcade in Akihabara, one of about eighteen thousand in Japan as a whole, is nearly full, over its four floors (nearly four hundred machines), of Pachinko aficionados: power-suited, black-clad and stylish businesswomen in their lunch hour, lean elderly men in tatty suits dropping cigarette ash into the machines' integral ashtrays. Lined up in endless rows like workers on a factory conveyor belt, the players are nevertheless all alone, gazing intently at the machines in front of them. The air is electric with a thunderous clacking: the result of thousands upon thousands of silver balls hitting each other in a mesmerising dance.

The name Pachinko is supposedly derived from *pachi-pachi*, a Japanese term describing the clicking of small objects or the crackling of fire. The game is set up vertically: behind a covering pane of glass, hundreds of small pins are set perpendicularly into a board. When the knob is turned, a stream of tiny silver-coloured steel balls shoots out of a funnel at the lower left-hand corner, spraying up to the top and thence downwards, where they bounce off the pins (thus making the clattering noise). Lower down the board are a few special slots; if a ball bounces off the pins in the right way and falls into one of these, it sets off a computerised fruit-machine-style set of three 'wheels'. If these wheels come to rest at a desired combination, the player wins something. What is the prize? Uh, *more* tiny silver balls. They gush out of the bottom of the machine into a big plastic basket. From there they can be scooped back into the machine for more plays, after the initial hundred have been used up.

Now if you amass a great many balls, and you have the self-discipline not to shove them straight back in the machine, you can go to the back of the shop and exchange them for real stuff, like a toaster or a microwave oven. In fact, most Pachinko parlours operate a shady back-room where balls can be converted into cash. But this is, strictly speaking, illegal, for in Japan Pachinko is not officially regarded as a 'gambling' game.

The final monetary exchange is cleverly disguised, mediated by the tiny silver balls. But this deferral of the transaction is potentially endless, as a player will often reuse all the balls he has won and end up with nothing physical to show for the session – in which case nothing has been 'won' at all save an unquantifiable gameplaying pleasure. The transaction – the verifiable, quantifiable *content*, from an accountant's point of view – is secondary to the experience of the *form*, the pleasure of playing the machine exquisitely well. Pachinko is a primarily aesthetic experience.

With Western slot machines, the bottom line is how much money the thing spews out at the end. With pinball, with which Pachinko obviously has a lot in common mechanically, the object of the game is to amass a different kind of currency – the social capital (in French sociologist Pierre Bourdieu's terminology) of the arcade or bar: a high score. (Remember, the first successful arcade game was sited next to a pinball machine in a bar.) But Pachinko is purer than either of these alternatives. Players do not eye each other's piles of balls. They are fixated on their own machines, seemingly hypnotised.

This hypnotic effect of Pachinko is in part caused by the startling beauty of the showers of silver balls bouncing around the board. If you remember studying Brownian motion under a microscope at school – the jiggling, dodgem-like movement of tiny particles bouncing off others – the Pachinko balls offer the same kind of random-seeming fascination. In fact, neither Brownian motion nor that of Pachinko balls is random; they are both governed by physical laws that are, at least in principle, deterministic. But they are unpredictable, given the impossibility of measuring accurately each system's initial conditions (they exhibit chaotic behaviour).

Some Pachinko experts roam the halls with a gaze so intuitively attuned to the game that they can pick out machines whose pins are slightly bent from the constant battering of balls. These, they know, will pay out more often. But to minimise this advantage, parlour operators go round at closing time with a hammer, knocking all the bent pins back into line. So the Pachinko system can never be rationally mastered.

A lot of videogames rely in part on exactly the same teasing unpredictability as Pachinko. It is thoroughly deterministic, but a feeling of randomness is generated by our imperfect knowledge. 'We may have written the game, but we don't know what's going to happen.' You're never sure what's coming next, which is partly why you want to try again.

Pachinko further prefigures another deep pleasure of videogames in its method of control. The player holds a single, very sensitive knob; as it is turned clockwise the tiny silver balls are shot out from the funnel at increasing speed. The challenge for the player is to manipulate the control in order to find the optimal ball speed – the rate at which the greatest number of balls falls into the target slots. Unlike a fruit machine, then, where you merely pull an arm or hit a button and then wait, Pachinko marries its teasing randomness with a continuous control over one important variable of the system. So do videogames. That one variable is the behaviour of the player's own character (animal, humanoid or mechanical), battling in an otherwise unpredictable virtual world. As the Pachinko control is analogue, furthermore, the tiniest variation in its position can produce large effects in the chaotic system. And this is comparable to the 'deep controls' that Richard Darling enthuses over in games like Super Mario Bros.

Thirdly, and again as with videogames, Pachinko assaults

the player's senses with the balls' clacking, constant electronic music and a dazing miscellany of coloured, blinking lights and computerised animations. You play Pachinko for twenty minutes and you come away empty-handed – yet you know you've had some weird kind of fun. And it was Pachinko machines that were Taito's original business before they created Space Invaders.

Power tools

So far we have seen that videogames have *some* things in common with films, with paintings or with stories, without ever being quite the same sort of phenomenon. But the example of Pachinko should remind us that videogames are also part of a different lineage. The arcade, which today is normally a fluorescently lit space crammed with the latest monster videogame cabinets and their ever more inventive control mechanisms – lightguns, life-size kayak oars, motorised snowboards, electronic drumkits, big plastic horses – has changed little from a sociological point of view in around a hundred years.

Back in the late nineteenth century, penny arcades also lured in a cross-section of punters from all walks of life, especially in America, where they boasted coin-operated phonograph machines, sweet dispensers, kinetoscopes and even X-ray machines (the latter were phased out as public amusements after it was shown that repeated use led to death, by what we now know as radiation poisoning). The next generation of technological fads was led by the mutoscope, a quasi-cinematic device which was, however, controlled by a mechanical crank, so that the viewer was able to choose the speed at which the film was played, to stop it or even to send it spinning backwards.

Videogames are clearly part of a project that began more than a century ago, and whose aim was to domesticise the machine. Automatic textile-processing technology, for example, had only seventy years previously been causing an unimaginable upheaval in the lives of millions, forcing people out of work and instigating the formation of resistance groups such as the

Luddites.* The lesson was quickly learned. By the 1890s, the fruits of applied science were deliberately offered to the public in a markedly different way: not as labour-replacing devices, but simply as entertainments. Progress, the arcades argued, could be *fun*.

High technology today is thoroughly domesticised. The process is complete. Many living rooms are furnished with a television, video recorder and hi-fi system – not to mention, in twenty million European homes, a PlayStation, whose very name continues the proselytising argument: it is the antithesis of a workstation, a place where one taps seriously away at a beige PC on spreadsheets or word-processing software. A PlayStation puts the kind of computational power that was the stuff of science fiction just a few decades ago to the sole purpose of entertaining the user. Not only can it be argued that videogames played a significant part in quelling the fear of technology, they have made technology our friend, our playmate.

In this, videogames are again part of a larger tradition: this time, that of the technological prostheticisation of play in general. Tennis, for example, has been transformed over the past few decades by material racquet technologies and string-dampening. Serious chess players routinely use computer analysis and million-game CD-ROM databases to prepare for matches, or to work on correspondence games. Golfers may avail themselves of carbon-fibre clubs and balls coated with space-age Kevlar, so that they fly more truly through the air. The whole trainer industry is predicated on a promise that an extra air pocket, say, will somehow make you run faster. And serious running is now itself in part a game of numbers made possible only by timing devices that count in the thousandths of a second.

Role-playing videogames began as a technological pros-theticisation of the Dungeons & Dragons boardgame, with the computer taking over the onerous duties of numerical calculation. Many videogames have arisen in this way, building on pre-existing game formats. Time Crisis, for instance, the

---

* For an excellent history, see Kirkpatrick Sale, *Rebels Against the Future*.

lightgun game, is at heart nothing more than a technologically enhanced version of fairground duck-shooting with airgun pellets. Except that whereas the latter retains some pretence of monetary exchange – you might shoot enough ducks and win a cuddly toy – Time Crisis finishes the job begun by Pachinko, and offers nothing but purely sensual and psychological rewards for your cash. Another lightgun game, Point Blank, explicitly acknowledges this heritage by including a number of fairground-style shooting ranges to play at.

Fairground games in general, which are tests of skill packaged in a fizzingly *son et lumière* environment, are obviously another set of precursors to modern videogames. So, too, are fairground rides, in a different way, for they offer a very convincing illusion of danger: on a rollercoaster, you feel you must be plummeting to your death, but you know it is safe. Shigeru Miyamoto has said he is constantly playing on his audience's 'desire to realise something exhilarating but impossible in real life'.

A good example of this is Gran Turismo, which we touched on at the end of the last chapter. Now, not only will we rarely have the chance to race a Dodge Viper around Tokyo at two hundred miles an hour, but it would be extremely dangerous to do so. Doing the same thing in a videogame, however (practising the same *form*) ensures that if we crash, we do not die or get burned to death, but only lose the race and live to try again. (The relative safety of high-speed collisions, moreover, turns most racing videogames further into digital versions of the fairground dodgems.) So the rollercoaster and the videogame both offer the pleasurable, adrenalin-surging experience of danger, with none of the risk.

Other technologies have enhanced (or at least changed) games and sports, and videogames have enhanced (or at least built upon) the basic concepts of boardgames and fairground attractions. But though you can play chess with bits of mud, or football with scrunched-up newspaper and a few sweaters, you cannot play a modern videogame except by means of a machine.

It can be argued that all artforms are dependent on a certain level of technology. Writing in English, for instance, cannot take place without an alphabet, which is itself literally a technology (the word comes from the Greek meaning 'knowledge of a skill'). But in the modern sense of technology as a physical device or gadget, videogames clearly belong in the lineage that was started only relatively recently, with photography, in which the execution of the artwork (or form of entertainment) is impossible without certain complex apparatus.

Videogames' special virtue of interactivity, though, vastly increases this technological dependence until it attains a quality of symbiosis. You are perforce a happy accomplice. For though you can appreciate a photograph or watch a film quite happily without being able to operate a camera or cinema projector, you cannot play a videogame without using the technology yourself.

Now as far as we can tell, human beings have been playing games for a very long time. We have so far looked back a mere century and considered videogames' place in a technological history. But one would expect that some or other aspect of play is represented in game forms throughout civilised time.

Veni, vidi, lusi

The earliest games that we know of from ancient records are of two basic kinds: contests of, say, spear-throwing through rolling hoops, and boardgames of chance. The first is clearly socially useful, as a hunter society does well to the extent that accurate spear-throwing ensures a plentiful supply of food for the community. In modern industrial civilisation, such aptitudes are no longer essential for survival, but humans for some reason still derive pleasure from refining them. They are exactly those skills exercised by modern target videogames such as Time Crisis 2.

Games of chance, meanwhile, seem to have originated from a belief that divine will could be glimpsed through seemingly random machinations; the *I Ching*, for example, is a book of wisdom in which hexagrams are consulted according to a random sequence of twig manipulations. But most 'games of chance' are not totally aleatory: a player in an ancient game such as backgammon or dominoes must still use skill to decide which piece to play next, or where to put the counter. Over time, these simple forms of game seem to have evolved gradually so as to make more long-term cognitive demands of the player. Skill is transmuted into strategy.

'In the history of civilisation,' writes game historian Brian Sutton-Smith, 'games of strategy seem to have emerged when societies increased in complexity to such an extent that there was a need for diplomacy and strategic warfare.' He describes one of the earliest examples: mancala, or wari, which was an ancient Egyptian strategy game. Each player controls a number of counters on the board, and the game involves using numerical and strategic judgement to capture the opponent's pieces. Mancala is clearly a direct forerunner of the twentieth-century boardgame Risk, and in turn, technologically prostheticised and expanded, of real-time strategy videogames such as Command and Conquer: Tiberian Sun.

Here is an account of the 'judicial duel' in medieval English law:

> Though sometimes fought to the bitter end the judicial duel shows a tendency to assume the features of play. A certain formality is essential to it. The fact that it can be executed by hired fighters is itself an indication of its ritual character, for a ritual act will allow of performance by a substitute [. . .] Also, the regulations concerning the choice of weapons and the peculiar handicaps designed to give equal chances to unequal antagonists – as when a man fighting a woman has to stand in a pit up to his waist – are the regulations and handicaps appropriate to armed play. In the later Middle Ages, it would seem, the judicial duel generally ended without much harm done.*

This process, whereby combat is sublimated into a play-form, leads all the way to modern beat-'em-up videogames such as

---

* This description is taken from the cultural history of play by Johann Huizinga, *Homo Ludens*.

Tekken Tag Tournament or Soul Calibur, where the abstraction is complete. Here, too, the fighting is performed on the player's behalf by a digital 'substitute'; here, too, unequally skilled human players may have a sporting match by tweaking the videogame's built-in 'handicap' device. Not only has bloody violence been transformed into a choreography of light, but the animus between contestants that gave rise to the judicial trial is now but a folk memory underlying cheerful competitiveness. So the physical and jurisprudential content has leaked out over the years, but the form endures.

The very fact that such forms still induce pleasure when played as videogames today seems to demonstrate that, though they initially grew out of practical concerns, ancient games could never have been wholly functional exercises in the first place. In other words, whatever other purpose they served, games must always in part simply have been fun.

Even such apparently purist, abstract videogames as Tetris have some similarities with older forms of play. Tetris itself is from one angle a dynamic jigsaw, in its demands of shape-matching; its designer, Alexei Pajitnov, on the other hand, has said that his original formal inspiration was pentominoes, a family of puzzles involving twelve differently shaped blocks, each made up of five squares, from which the player must construct larger shapes – except the videogame challenge is again a dynamic one, introducing time pressure on the player.

And children have always made up their own 'exploration games', playing, for instance, in a deserted house and imbuing it with magical qualities. Now the technological prosthesis afforded by a videogame such as Tomb Raider or Zelda 64 allows such activity to be far more complex and cognitively challenging, so that the gamer really can, in Walter Benjamin's phrase, 'calmly and adventurously go travelling'. Again, Shigeru Miyamoto has said that he draws his inspiration from childhood memories of exploring the Kansai countryside around his home, finding caves and hidden paths through the woods.

History also tells us that seeing people at play has often angered those in power. In Saint-Omer in 1168, gameplayers were pilloried; in Bâle in 1386, a backgammon player who had ignored an injunction to avoid the game had his eyes put out;

the same punishment was common in fifteenth-century Amsterdam; and in Germany players might have limbs judicially amputated or be executed by drowning.* Martin Amis astutely pointed out in 1982 that the burgeoning criticism of videogames even then was simply a repeat of 'the heated debates about snooker and pool earlier in the century'.

Games are not serious, runs this argument, they are somehow intellectually degrading. Play, anthropologist Johann Huizinga happily concedes, is at base 'irrational'. Though certain games might require a very high-level exercise of reason (chess), there seems to be no rational excuse for playing in the first place. One is simply spellbound. But games, rather than being a wasteful offshoot, are central to the formation of culture. Huizinga believes that play underpins all forms of ritual, and even religion itself. Ancient Greek mythology, for example, has a tradition of 'theromorphia' – imagining people as beasts, like Zeus as a swan – and Huizinga argues that this can best be understood in terms of the play attitude. (This is, by the way, another play tradition that finds its way into modern videogames, for instance in the beat-'em-up game Bloody Roar 2, where the humanoid fighters turn into monsters in order to inflict ever more ridiculous damage upon each other.)

Huizinga's overarching contention in *Homo Ludens* is that play is indeed essential to civilised society. His final, polemical chapter holds that the modern world (he was writing in 1938) is anomic and impoverished precisely because games have been torn from their organic place at the heart of community and neatly cordoned off into such spheres as that of professional sports. If this is true, we should not be surprised that at the beginning of the third millennium, the eternal human need for play has sprouted once more in radical, electronic form, and will very soon constitute the world's largest entertainment industry.

This might even be a cause for optimism. Videogames allow for, are often specifically built for, a form of social play activity. Indeed, a great many gamers, including me, find videogaming

---

* For more on the bloody history of gameplayers' persecution, see *L'Univers des Jeux Vidéo*.

at its most pleasurable in such a context. At its smallest level, social videogaming involves two, three or four friends racing cars against each other or beating each other up through colourful digital surrogates on the screen. The videogame console is mediating and providing the visual forms for such contests, but the pleasure is largely a social one. Richard Darling of Codemasters agrees. 'One of the most enjoyable times that people have when they're playing games tends to be good multiplayer games – like Super Bomberman and Micro Machines,' he says. 'There's so much more fun in beating your friends and competing with your friends than doing the same thing with computer-controlled opponents.'

This is similar to the pleasure of playing doubles in tennis, or playing a rubber of bridge; perhaps it is closer, however, to that of boardgames, which have always been advertised as social tools, fun for friends and family. Indeed videogames might be seen in this way as the logical next step from boardgames. The history of the boardgame sees a gradual moving-away from the physical apparatus of the board, and an increased focus of attention on the players themselves, from the totally board-dependent games like chess and draughts, to games such as Monopoly or Risk where a lot of the action (alliance-forming and back-stabbing) takes place off the board, to Trivial Pursuit, where the board does little more than keep track of the score. Videogames extrapolate from this trend *ad infinitum*, because there is no physical stuff being moved around at all, just patterns of photons.

But the social aspect of boardgames and certain sports is multiplied innumerable times in the burgeoning phenomenon of online videogaming. Now there is a possibility of social play that is far greater than at any time before in human history. Users can connect games such as Quake III, Half-Life or Starcraft to an Internet server and play in real-time against hundreds or thousands of other people all over the globe. Sega's Dreamcast, of course, now incorporates a modem to facilitate precisely this activity.

Richard Darling sees immense possibilities for this phenomenon in the future, especially when it is widely available to more people than can afford thousand-dollar PCs.

With Dreamcast and PlayStation2, you'll be able to put the disc in, turn it on and just choose multiplayer, automatic connection to the network. Everything will be easy to choose and set up, and you can just play against other people. And although they're other people who you won't know initially, it won't take long before online communities emerge where there are other ways of communicating – online chat maybe, or voice discussions back and forth.

Or maybe, if it gets mass-market enough, the fact that you're connected online doesn't mean you have to be playing with people in South Africa, the United States, Zimbabwe or whatever – we could potentially log on to a Touring Cars multiplayer site and choose to play against people in Fulham. It might be that there are enough people so you could organise with your friends at work that you're all going to log on at eight o'clock in the evening and play selectively, just against each other. So it doesn't have to be like Internet communication is portrayed in the media, as people who are rather sad and lonely communicating with people they don't even know on other continents.

Videogames, clearly, are embedded in a deep and long tradition of play, and they borrow formally from many other games. Yet each borrowing is accompanied by a radical transmutation. From dominoes to pentominoes to Tetris; from spear-throwing to Time Crisis; from whist parties to thirty thousand people logged on to the Internet playing a science-fiction RPG: the videogame format takes something old and makes of it something startlingly new. But what kind of fun do videogames offer that is uniquely their own?

Get into the groove

There must be a reason why so many of the people I know who enjoy videogames describe racing a good lap in Colin McRae Rally or clearing waves in Defender as a 'Zen' experience. This is understood to be shorthand for a kind of high-speed meditation, an intense absorption in which the dynamic form of successful play becomes beautiful and satisfying. How exactly does such an experience come about?

One highly influential attempt at a logical interpretation of 'fun' has been made by psychologist Mihaly Csikszentmihalyi, with his concept of 'flow'. Csikszentmihalyi was interested in the fact that musicians, rock-climbers, chess players and other people engaged in very complex tasks reported an experience of ecstasy or bliss, losing track of time and losing the sense of self. He decided that, although on the face of it each activity was markedly different, all his subjects must be having the same sort of experience, which he termed 'flow'. In this state, 'action follows upon action according to an internal logic that seems to need no conscious intervention by the actor'. And 'there is little distinction between self and environment, between stimulus and response, or between past, present and future'.*

Now this sounds like fun. It sounds a lot like the 'Zen' experience of playing a good videogame. Interestingly, Csiksz- entmihalyi notes that flow experiences are attained when there is a perceived match between the demands of the activity and the subject's skills. Now why else would many videogames such as Metal Gear Solid let you change the difficulty level? Clearly it is boring to play a game that is too easy, and frustrating to play a game that is too hard. The same is true of, say, tennis or chess: playing someone who is far less competent than you is not much fun, as it's too easy to win (you don't need to play to the height of your abilities); playing someone far better than you is not much fun either, because you just get stomped on (you are made painfully aware of the inadequacy of your abilities). So pleasure seems subjectively to be optimal when the demands of the game and your skill levels are closely matched.

In a non-dangerous activity, I think the game's demands ought always to be pitched slightly higher than the player's skills. The only way to improve one's chess, for example, is regularly to play slightly stronger opponents. Because an

---

* Quoted in Satô Ikuya's fascinating history of *bosozoku*, or motorcycle gangs in Japan, who also apparently experience 'flow' during their races: *Kamikaze Biker: Parody and Anomy in Affluent Japan.*

important component of pursuing a flow activity over time is the simple pleasure of getting better. A pianist will attempt pieces that are just beyond the current level of her technique, and by practising them she will improve her technique to match their demands.

Pleasure increases up to a point according to difficulty. So it seems very likely that one crucial component of videogaming pleasure is in fact a certain level of anxiety. This sounds counterintuitive but is supported by simple experiments that report increased heartrate and adrenalin levels among videogame users. And my own experience is that even when demands and skill are generally matched, there are periods during the game when I am aware of a temporary, small mismatch between them – the game is asking slightly more of my skill than I feel confident of being able to deliver, and a large part of the game's pleasure lies in overcoming these regular challenges.

Now what about the 'feelings of complete control' which are said to accompany a flow experience? I think there is, again, something wrong with this way of putting it. We have said that videogames provide a particular pleasure of control, especially when they offer rich controls whose interaction allows for a great deal of variation, and when the controls result in amplification of input. How does this compare with the case of playing a piece of music at the piano? Here, too, the interaction of controls (keys and pedals) is a 'deep' one, offering a potentially infinite array of sonorities; here, too, amplification of input is at work, in that small movements of the fingers result in beautiful music.

But musicians know that there is another phenomenon at work, which is also appropriate to a discussion of videogame playing: muscle memory. When a pianist attempts a new piece, most of her attention is focused consciously on playing the right notes according to what is printed on the manuscript page, and working out precise fingerings for particularly difficult passages. But there is a point at which these visual instructions are no longer needed, when the player has so thoroughly learned the music that she does not consciously think about where to put her hands next. People also call this 'getting the music under your fingers'. It is only now, when the mechanics of playing have been assimilated, that the player can concentrate on performing the music.

The point is that the pianist begins really to play the music, and thereby enters into a 'flow' state, at precisely the stage when she is no longer consciously controlling the individual movements of fingers. It is as if the fingers themselves know what to do. That is what we mean by 'muscle memory'. The same thing happens when you drive a car or touch-type. But this is not a mysterious process for which we need to invoke flow or anything else: cognitive scientists have shown that practising complex sequences of finger movements actually rewires neuronal connections in the brain until they become automatic. A reduction in self-consciousness is naturally pursuant upon the observation that my critical 'self' is no longer controlling my mechanical finger movements, so that I feel to that extent absorbed into the music itself. And exactly the same process operates in videogames.

So here are two important observations about videogame pleasure. Firstly, when you are really 'in the groove' of a well-designed, fast-moving action game such as Robotron, Gran Turismo 2000 or Time Crisis 2, one of the reasons you feel so fluidly involved is that your muscle memory has taken over the mechanical business of operating buttons, joysticks, trigger or foot-pedals. This clearly has important implications for videogame designers. A videogame with a clunky or over-complex control system, such as G-Police – or, even worse, RC Stunt Copter* – is not as much fun to most players precisely to the extent that it is so much harder to get past the initial mechanical demands.

Secondly, the optimal match of demands and skills that we looked at earlier is the other factor that contributes materially to the pleasurable loss of self-consciousness, because if the brain is having to process a lot of information very quickly to keep up with the videogame's challenges, it is clearly going to

---

* A good candidate for the title of most pointlessly difficult videogame of the decade, this 'simulation' of a radio-controlled helicopter boasts such anti-intuitive and oversensitive controls that even seasoned videogame critics switched off in sheer frustration.

demote other considerations, such as keeping track of clock time or noticing that a foot has gone numb, right to the back burner until the challenges have been overcome.*

Videogames share deeply embedded aspects with many other sorts of games through history, yet they also share two components of pleasure with other common activities, such as piano-playing, that are not usually considered 'games' at all. (The videogame combines aspects of play and performance which nudge it in one sense nearer the family of sport. There are now regular world videogaming championships at which contestants from all over the world compete for prizes of hundreds of thousands of dollars.) But now we have uncovered some sources of videogame pleasure, it remains to be seen just how that pleasure is manipulated. How, in other words, does the machine play the man?

You win again

Videogames give you their full attention. They don't ignore you or say they're busy; they concentrate with rock-solid focus on what you 'say' to them through the mechanical interface. (Like psychotherapists, only at a smaller cost and with more quantifiable fun – Eliza, as we have seen, did actually take the role of a therapist in a text-based 'conversation' with the player.) The game is extremely interested in you.

Videogames also exemplify perfectly a general aspect of play: the temporary perfection, unattainable in the physical world, of absolute order. Nolan Bushnell says much the same thing: 'There is a completely controllable and understandable

---

* Now we have established this highly physical aspect to videogaming pleasure, by the way, it provides another nail in the coffin of the 'interactive storytelling' dream. Nolan Bushnell, the father of videogaming, made this incisive point to me: 'The big problem with interactive storytelling is a basic conflict. When telling a story one wants the listener to abandon his body and space and be swept along in a new place, time or world. When you ask a person to make a decision, you push that person back into his own body.'

universe that is predictable. Much more controllable than real life.' A videogame obeys a certain set of predictable rules of action, even if half the fun is finding out their unpredictable effects in particular situations. Martin Amis quotes the science fiction writer Isaac Asimov, invoking both the above motivations: 'Kids like the computer because it plays back [. . .] it's a pal, a friend, but it doesn't get mad, it doesn't say "I won't play", and it doesn't break the rules.'

Considerations such as these may bring the player to the table, but what keeps him playing? Well, psychologists have applied the term 'reinforcement' to denote the fact that, in general, any behaviour that is rewarded will be repeated in anticipation of more reward. 'The rat gets crunchy food, while the videogame player gets higher scores and free games,' explain the authors of *Mind at Play*, an early book on videogame psychology. But such rewards must be balanced. Videogames deliberately provide only partial reinforcement, because their rewards (attaining the next level; getting a new gadget, car or weapon to play with) are only intermittent; the gamer keeps hoping another one is just around the corner. In fact, this is another way of discussing the demand/skill match we talked about earlier. If a game provides continuous reinforcement, then it is too easy and boring. If, on the other hand, it is too hard, there will be no initial reinforcement and thus no reason to keep playing.

How do videogame designers achieve such a delicate balance? Such considerations are very important to Richard Darling. He argues that what makes an action game (driving, sports or shooting) fun is precisely this: 'The player's efforts being rewarded by achievements.' It's not so simple, however; Darling continues:

And those achievements need to appear to be worthwhile to the players, they need to be visible and valuable. Of course, people's perceptions of what's needed to make a game fun have been stretching and stretching as games have got better and better. A long time ago you had Space Invaders, where basically you move from one level to the next level and you're very excited because you've achieved the next level. In fact the next level was exactly the same as the last one but a little bit harder, but you're still very pleased: your score's gone up, you've moved to level two, and the same thing happened when you moved to level three, four and five. That had a simple reward system whereby you achieved a certain goal in the game and reached a discrete target and you got rewarded by a score and a level change.

In principle it's the same now, it's just that people's expectations are much greater than just wanting the score to be ticking up. If you move from one level to the next you want a new experience, new gameplay features, new things to be cropping up. So really our goal is to make sure that there's enough there to start off with so that people find our game exciting and interesting, but then the more they play the more they achieve, and they can't *constantly* be getting new rewards for all those achievements.

This is what the psychologists call 'partial reinforcement'. Yet presumably the videogame still has to keep something back to reward successful play?

It's always a big argument in game design, yeah, because the problem is, you see, when you release a game like that you get some people phoning up or writing in saying, 'Why didn't I have the Lister Storm [a model of racecar in Codemasters' TOCA 2] from the beginning? I've paid my money for the game and I can't drive a Lister Storm!' You know, you need to do X, Y and Z before you're going to get the Lister Storm, or the Jaguar XJ220. And they feel frustrated, so there is some pressure to open the game up and say, 'Look, you choose which car you like, race on whichever track you like', and make the whole game available from when you turn it on. But if you did that a lot of people wouldn't actually have any desire to drive the Lister Storm because there's no great progression in getting there.

In other words, there would be no great incentive to play the game and to get better at it.

But the videogame must not be too difficult: there must be some initial reinforcement for the player to want to keep going. Darling agrees: 'You need to be given rewards in a short enough timespan in order to encourage you to carry on and improve yourself.' Sailing between these two perils is no easy business.

It's a very difficult balance to strike. The way we've started to go in recent games is to have selectable levels of difficulty – but you still need to hold back rewards, I think, so that certain rewards are only available if you've chosen the expert level of difficulty. But at least somebody who's choosing the standard level can actually feel they've completed the game.

There are more cunning methods of doing it which we have tried in some games, which is to actually make the game adapt to how good you are. So, for example, in a racing game if you're driving along and you crash, and the pack goes ahead of you, you won't necessarily notice if they all slow down a bit so you get a chance to catch them up, and you feel like you're still in the game – whereas a good player wouldn't have crashed in the first place, and so the cars wouldn't have slowed down, so you can have a competitive time either way. But it's very difficult to keep it fair. For example, a good strategy to beat a game like that might be to deliberately hold back and stay at the back of the pack so all the computer cars slow down, and then on the last straight just put your foot down and cruise past them and win. You've got to be very careful with the logic of what's happening to make sure that a better driver will always do better.

One problem which videogame designers are very aware of is the wide spectrum of gameplaying skill among their potential customers. But, with careful programming of difficulty settings and reward distribution, they can make a product which is optimally challenging and satisfying to all. Darling regrets, for instance, that TOCA 2 probably appealed only to the upper

50 per cent of gameplayers in skill terms, and that a 'novice' who had just bought a PlayStation and tried to play the game would have quickly become frustrated and disillusioned. Obviously, it makes good commercial sense for his team to be working on this problem with the next instalment in the series: 'Anybody's achievement should be rewarded even if it's a hopeless achievement compared to an expert.' To be sure, this is a happy form of democracy.

This peculiar motivational system of pleasurable rewards is something that sets videogames apart from any other kind of game we know. If you get better at Trivial Pursuit, Risk, tennis, dominoes, chess or football, your increased sense of power and self-respect is the only reward on offer. The game remains the same. (The transaction of capital in the coin-op arcade game seems to be a positive if still strictly extrinsic phenomenon. The psychologist authors of *Mind at Play*, Geoffrey and Elizabeth Loftus, wrote that paying money for a videogame actually increases the pleasure one derives from it. This is due to 'cognitive dissonance': faced with incompatible beliefs, the brain acts so as to reduce the conflict. Videogames take your money and give you nothing tangible in return ... they must really be fun!)

But whereas chess or football remains the same kind of game no matter how good you are, modern videogames, as Richard Darling points out, change as you get better. Attaining a new level in Tomb Raider III means having a whole new virtual world to explore, moving from India to the rain-soaked rooftops of London. Collect enough coins in Ape Escape and you can play an entirely new mini-game on skis. Many videogames even keep something back after you have finished them, in order to encourage you to play the game again, only this time under new rules. Metal Gear Solid, for example, rewards the player with a 'stealth' suit, so that you can have enormous fun playing through the environments as an invisible, death-dealing hero. Beat-'em-ups such as Tekken 3 or Soul Calibur, meanwhile, cleverly spread rewards between their two-player modes (two humans fighting each other's digital surrogates – the genre's *raison d'être*) – and their solo modes (player versus machine), in that success in the latter unlocks new characters that can be pitted against each other in the social context.

Videogames in this sense are meta-games: the manipulation and achievement of such visual, dynamic and cybernetic rewards is another, higher-level game in itself. A well-designed videogame, such as Zelda 64, can approach the condition of a work of art simply by virtue of the way such rich, protean transformations in the game's very structure are linked together for the gameplayer's pleasure. The ways in which you can see more stuff and do more stuff are a joy, a reward in themselves. Perhaps they mirror the process of the rich and speedy acquisition of skills and experiences that we all went through as small children.

This idea suggests another course of action as we plunge deeper into the videogame metropolis. Along the way, we have measured the city's space, heard its stories and read its history. We have seen how we interact with videogames. So what exactly are the nuts and bolts of this process? When we talk to videogames and they talk to us, what language is this conversation in?

By its signs shall you know a city.

9

SIGNS OF LIFE

A jaundiced figure floats across the screen. He is constantly searching for things to eat. We are looking at a neo-Marxist parable of late capitalism. He is the pure consumer. With his obsessively gaping maw, he clearly wants only one thing: to feel whole, at peace with himself. He perhaps surmises that if he eats enough – in other words, buys enough industrially produced goods – he will attain this state of perfect selfhood, perfect roundness. But it can never happen. He is doomed forever to metaphysical emptiness. It is a tragic fable in primary colours.

You may well have played this game: it's called Pac-Man. Videogames, like anything else, can be read in many different ways. A videogame may not be a 'text', but it is true that videogames talk to the player in a special sort of language, one which the experienced user knows by heart. And this isn't a verbal language, it's a graphical one. Videogames talk to us with signs.

It is one of the fascinations of videogames as a form, indeed, that they constitute a kaleidoscopic, *prestissimo* exercise in semiotics, which is the ever-changing interaction of signs. More than advertising or the Internet, videogames, in their immense speed and complexity, have to that extent become the most sophisticated systems of communication of meaning that the culture has yet seen. Now if that sounds like an overstatement, videogame action does not have overarching 'meaning' in the way a novel or a film does; it is untranslatable, like music. Our scrutiny should instead be focused on the fast-moving low-level 'meanings' that enable us to understand the videogame system.

We have seen how videogames distort reality for their own

purposes, creating in the process a world of deliberate unrealism. But how does it hang together? And how does it speak to the player?

I am what I eat

Consider the playing screen of Pac-Man (see fig. 16). What do we see? A maze-like structure of tubular walls, the paths lined with dots of two distinct sizes; four jelly-like blobs with what look like wide eyes; a disc with a slice taken out of it. Above the maze are a line of text and two sets of numbers; below it are more discs and what looks like a brace of cherries. Now, considering this image solely as a picture, why do some paths in the maze have dots while others are empty? Why is there one disc inside the maze and others, slightly smaller, outside it? And what has all this to do with fruit? It is confusing, arcane. The game screen is inscrutable when approached as simple representation; it demands to be read as a symbolic system.

Take that little disc. That is Pac-Man himself, the character under the player's control. He doesn't look like a man, he looks like something you'd stick on the rim of your glass of gin and tonic. (Toru Iwatani in fact, as we learned, was inspired by partially eaten pizza.) Nevertheless, the crude yellow shape is agreed to stand for Pac-Man. It is therefore a symbol. A symbol is a sign whose meaning is determined by social convention, like a number, a theatre ticket or the word 'starling'. Charles Sanders Peirce, besides leading a notoriously libertine life, also found time to invent most of modern semiotics. He defined a symbol thus: 'Symbols, or general signs [. . .] have become associated with their meanings by usage. Such are most words, and phrases, and speeches, and books, and libraries.'

But we know that an important part of any videogame character is its dynamic form, and, sure enough, Pac-Man's animation lets him partake of another kind of sign. As he moves around, the missing 'slice of pizza' expands and contracts, resembling a schematic mouth in profile. It actually *looks* like a mouth that is opening and closing. In this way, Pac-Man is

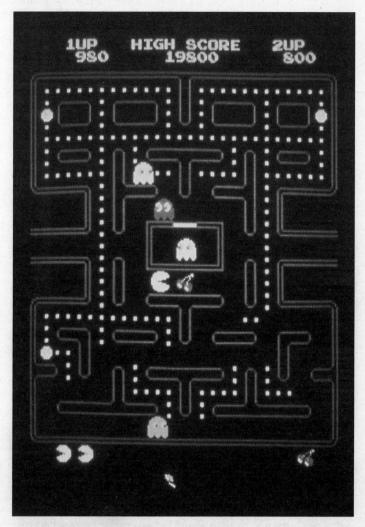

Fig. 16. Pac-Man: a parable of late capitalism, and a complex web of signs (© 1980 Namco Ltd; all rights reserved)

also to some extent an icon. Peirce defines an icon thus: '*Likenesses*, or icons [. . .] serve to convey ideas of the things they represent simply by imitating them.'

The third type of sign that we need to know about is the index. Imagine if Pac-Man's maze were a schematic map of an actual maze. In that case, it would be an index – basically, a pointer sign. In Peirce's terms: '*Indications*, or indices [. . .] show something about things, on account of their being physically connected with them. Such is a guidepost, which points down the road to be taken, or a relative pronoun, which is placed just after the name of the thing intended to be denoted.'

Pac-Man is both a symbol and, to a lesser extent, an icon. That's not unusual: in fact, many if not most signs are actually combinations in varying ratios of two or all three of these basic types. A map, for instance, is an index, in that it shares in and points to deep structural features of the landscape it describes, but it is also an icon, in that it simply looks like the terrain as seen from the air. The illuminated first letter of a medieval manuscript is both a symbol, in that it functions as a component of language, and an icon, in that it is an illustration. An Egyptian hieroglyph is an icon, in that it is a pictogram, but it is also a symbol, in that it has an agreed meaning.

So, Pac-Man is a symbol. 'His form,' the character's creator has noted, 'simply represents the personification of eating.' And indeed, Pac-Man is a game about eating. The dots littering his world are so perfectly symbolic as not to represent any object. They are there to be munched; that's all.

While we're on the subject of eating, note that the very theme of the game is at once infantile and politically loaded. It has been argued that Pac-Man was the first arcade game to be a substantial success with female gamers precisely because of this philosophy of consumption: eating is figured not as something to be wary of, but something to be celebrated, something (literally) empowering. However, it seems equally reasonable from this distance to read Pac-Man – a game from a country, Japan, that at the time was just beginning to claim a role as a global financial power – as a satire on a different kind of consumption: late twentieth-century capitalism. Hence our parable at the start of the chapter. For Pac-Man, consumption cannot end; no conceivable quantity of dots is enough. He will continue to search them out and eat them until he dies.

What about those jellies with eyes? They are symbols, but they are also more iconic than Pac-Man himself, in that their eyes are relatively well-defined. Pac-Man has no eyes at all, but the jellies, who are according to the game actually 'ghosts', have eyeballs with mobile pupils. Now, the ghosts are actually some of the most semiotically advanced items in the game – partaking of all three modes of sign – because their eyes also function indexically. Where the eyes are looking is where the ghost is going to go next. The eyes 'point'; they work as an index. This is a particularly important sign for the player to be able to read, as for most of the game she must avoid contact with the roaming ghosts on pain of death. (Pac-Man's death animation, by the way, slots admirably into our political theory of the game: his mouth opens wider and wider, passing the horizontal and continuing, until there is nothing left of him at all. In his mania of consumption, he has eaten himself.)

What about Pac-Man's little cousins below the playing area? By videogame convention, these represent the number of lives he has in reserve. While the Pac-Man in play is almost entirely symbolic, therefore, the smaller ones function both symbolically and indexically. As a group, they constitute an index of 'how many', in the same way as counting beans. This is an indexical function, remember, because the number of yellow discs is congruent with, or 'points to', the number of tries a player has left. There is a similar mix in the large dots (one might even call them blobs) near the corners of the maze. Like their smaller brothers, they are symbolic (of pure, abstract food), but their increased size also functions indexically. They are bigger in circumference, and hence they are bigger in utility – better for you. Pac-Man earns ten points every time he eats a regular dot, but fifty upon eating a blob.

The blobs have a further function: as power-ups. When Pac-Man eats a blob, he may for a short while turn and chase the ghosts that have thus far been pursuing him. We can now say that in semiotic terms, power-ups actually function as second-order signs – signs about signs. The blob itself is an agreed symbol for 'power-up' according to Pac-Man's game design, but the power-up itself has no independent existence. Funnily enough, this is one context in which a phrase from postmodern theory is particularly appropriate: a power-up is a 'floating signifier'. The power-up's meaning consists entirely in a change of the potential relations between the rest of the signs in the game over a pre-defined period of time.

This sounds forbiddingly abstract, but it is a very familiar paradigm in film, especially in science fiction cinema. For example, during the finale of the film *Aliens*, Ripley gets into a mechanical exoskeleton in the ship's loading bay in order to fight the beast more effectively. She has acquired a power-up. Now the relations of force between the heroine and her foe are redefined. But the difference is that in Pac-Man, the power-up is not an external tool or weapon but merely an idea, a temporary enhancement of the character's own essence.

A power-up can also be a simple gift of more time: an extra life. Now, Pac-Man gives you an extra life if you reach a score of 10,000. So at certain times, anything edible on the screen could become a power-up if it pushed your score over that magical figure. Look at the cherries below the playing area, for instance. They seem iconic (like fruit), but in fact they are indices: they indicate that shortly some cherries will appear temporarily in the middle of the screen. If Pac-Man eats those, they earn him 100 points, or ten times the value of a single dot. Now imagine that your score is 9,900, there are only three dots left in the maze, and there is a cherry sign below it. Rather than completing the level by eating the dots – worth a measly 30 points – you would be better advised to wait for the cherries to appear in the centre, because they will then operate symbolically as a power-up, giving you an extra life. In that situation the cherries signalling below the maze would be a *third-order* sign. They would be (deep breath) an index denoting the future appearance of a symbol about other symbols.

Now, all right, hang on. Pac-Man is a videogame, no? It's not rocket science. It has chirpy music, bright colours. You trundle round the maze eating dots and getting your own back on the ghosts. It is fun. It would be lunacy to suggest that someone playing Pac-Man is consciously doing all this semiotic calculus.

But this analysis does help in two ways. First, it demonstrates that videogames are complex systems rather than just simple toys. Secondly, and more importantly, it *does* in fact explain at one level what it means to play a videogame. Because it helps to reconstruct something the player is doing automatically – there can be no doubt that to play the game well she must understand how all the signs on the game screen interact, in just the ways we have described. Human beings are very good at reading complex systems of signs without having to describe to themselves what they are doing.

Now Pac-Man is twenty years old. We have seen how videogames have progressed since those days. We might expect, then, as videogames have increasingly enjoyed the power to build ever more convincing cities of the unreal, that their systems of semiotics, being the bricks and mortar of those edifices, have themselves become ever more complex and interesting. At first sight, though, it seems as if that isn't necessarily true.

Deep in conversation

From the playful web of signs in Pac-Man, modern videogames seem to have, in their increasing powers of graphical photorealism, become ever more pervasively iconic. Compare Pac-Man with the player's characters in Soul Calibur (see fig. 17); whereas Pac-Man is abstract, largely symbolic, Voldo (left) is a triumph of iconic or pictorial representation.

Now what does this do for the player's sense of involvement with the game? The unique feature of videogames, after all, in terms of the structure of their consumption as a medium of mass entertainment, is that we are not merely spectators but participants. And we participate by identifying with 'our' character on screen. A gameplayer whose ship has just exploded does not say ruefully, 'The ship just exploded'; he says, 'I died.' So might it be true that we cannot 'relate' to characters who are pictorially too well defined? J. C. Herz thinks so: 'Characters in Mortal Kombat have fingers and stubble. You watch them. Pac-Man has one black dot for an eye, and you *become* him.'

195

Fig. 17. Soul Calibur: fabulously iconic fighting ()

We might interpret this claim by suggesting that a game concentrating on the interplay of symbols is a richer experience than one involving mostly icons. A game of Snap, for instance, consists entirely of comparing icons (the pictures on the playing cards), whereas a game of chess is symbol manipulation *in excelsis*. The requirement of the player to treat game objects not merely as pictures but as symbols represents a greater cognitive challenge.

This is not to say, of course, that iconic arts such as photography and cinema do not stimulate the imagination at all. Of course they do (or can). But there is a difference in the faculty exercised. Looking at a photograph, one may invent a story around the scene, give the subjects inner lives and histories. The same thing operates in cinema, where we are required to reconstruct stories that have been fragmented through cuts and flashbacks, or to deduce the thought processes of a character by reading an actor's face. This process is hermeneutic: it is about interpretation.

But the imagination that videogames require of the player is a different process: it is pragmatic. It can be subdivided into two parts: 'imagining into' and 'imagining how'. 'Imagining how' because at every moment this operation precedes the dynamic challenge of being able to predict how one's actions will affect the system, and therefore what course of action is optimal; 'imagining into' because one needs to understand the rules of the semiotic system presented, and act as if those rules, and not the rules of the real world, applied to oneself. The requirement is to project the active (rather than just the spectating) consciousness into the semiotic realm. The videogame player is absorbed by the system: for the duration of the game, he lives among signs (another way of describing the dissolution of self-consciousness in the videogame experience).

The person playing Pac-Man, then, may be said in a sense to be having a conversation with the system on its own terms. Just as human conversation involves a two-way transfer of and reaction to symbols (words), so a symbolically rich videogame, or other symbolic games like chess, share the same structural basis, exercising the pragmatic imagination. And indeed, we can say that a videogame is better as its symbolic conversation becomes more interesting.

The aesthetic importance of symbols to videogames is played on in the commercial sphere too, in marketing imagery. The four 'action' buttons on the right of the PlayStation control pad are identified purely by abstract symbols: circle, square, triangle and X. These symbols have become so closely identified with the PlayStation and PlayStation2 hardware that Sony can release advertisements which identify themselves as such only by having the four symbols somewhere on the page. One particularly inventive image, 'Lovely Buttons' (press advertisement, 1999), simply shows a young man and woman in tight T-shirts, staring with blank sexual confidence into camera. Upon closer inspection, what appear to be their protuberant nipples are actually tiny, solid PlayStation symbols poking through the fabric. The advertisement carries no other information, textual or otherwise, to identify the brand as Sony. The symbols are all.

Time, gentlemen, please

Remember that a videogame is not a static 'text'; it is a dynamic form. And since videogames operate through time, another constituent of good symbolic conversation is obviously going to be its rhythm, or how the symbols combine over time.

The importance of rhythm is exemplified most nakedly in a style of videogame that was hugely popular at the 1999 Tokyo Game Show, which relies completely on it, combining a handful of symbols with complex temporal interaction. As we saw earlier, Konami's Dance Dance Revolution shows combinations of four arrows floating down the screen; when they reach the bottom line, the player must step on the corresponding arrows of a sensory floormat beneath the feet, in time to the banging techno music from the loudspeakers. Hundreds of young Japanese men and women were queueing up to show off their skills at this game, practising their moves groovily in line. The best of them combined the moves required by the game with their own creative gestures and twirls.

Beatmania, meanwhile, consists of five large buttons (styled like half an octave of a piano keyboard) and a mock DJ turntable; similarly, various combinations of these must be manipulated in time with their corresponding symbols floating down the screen. Other 'rhythm games', as they are known, include Parappa the Rapper, in which the player must help a paper-thin rapping dog undergo musical training from an onion; Guitar Freaks, playing on the Japanese penchant for heavy metal by requiring the user to strum a simplified rock axe; and Drummania, in which the player sits on a stool and hits electronic drum pads in time with symbols.

All these games show funny, colourful digital animations on their screens: pulsating cartoon embryos for a rave track; *anime* heroes performing six-string heroics – but these icons are completely irrelevant to the gameplay. But even these simple games boast a unique structure of semiotic interaction. Notice, for instance, that the symbols on the screen in Dance Dance Revolution are also functioning indexically, because they are pointing to the symbols which need to be stepped on by the player, and the symbols themselves (arrows pointing in four directions) are quite special in that they are utterly content-free – they do not stand for anything else in the context of the game.

Dance Dance Revolution and Beatmania are very literal applications of videogame rhythm. But rhythm is also important in games which are not explicitly predicated on musical interaction. Giving the keynote speech at the 1999 Game Developers' Conference in San Jose, Shigeru Miyamoto emphasised this point exactly: 'I feel that those directors who have been able to incorporate rhythm [. . .] in their games have been successful.' We can break this idea down into three components.

First, nearly all action games rely on the player's basic ability to use tactical timing, by which I mean pressing a certain button to produce an action at exactly the right time. Many old platform games such as Miyamoto's own Super Mario Bros, for instance, demand great accuracy in jumping and in controlling your character's skids so he doesn't fall off platforms. A racing game such as Sega Rally demands tactical timing in manipulating the joypad or wheel so that the player's car rounds a corner in a controlled skid. A beat-'em-up such as Soul Calibur rewards tactical timing if we begin our attacking move just at the moment when our opponent is in a vulnerable stance.

Tactical timing also incorporates demands of high-speed reaction: in this way, we rapidly take account of the sudden appearance of grenades flying towards us in Time Crisis 2, and we 'duck' by lifting our foot off a pedal before they hit. The expansive exploration game Shenmue, meanwhile, utilises a 'Quick-Time Event' system for certain periods of gameplay, which in contrast to the game's breathtaking visual sophistication is a revealingly crude instance of symbol manipulation through time. This occurs, for instance, when the hero is pursuing another character down a crowded Hong Kong market street. At regular intervals a symbol corresponding to one of the console buttons will flash on the screen; if the player fails to hit the corresponding control very quickly, his character will trip over a cart of tomatoes and thus lose his quarry.

As the period of time in question expands from tenths of a second to whole seconds, tactical timing bleeds slowly into a second component of videogame rhythm: strategic timing. A classic example of this is in the shoot-'em-up Defender. The player's basic weapon is a laser. To shoot down alien craft and swoop to rescue falling humans is a question of tactical timing. But you also have a limited supply of 'smart bombs', which instantly destroy everything in the screen area. Now as you only have three of these precious devices to start with, you must use them to your best advantage, in the situations where they will be most effective. That is strategic timing. The fact that destroying things earns you more points, and at certain scores you win another smart bomb or an extra life, makes a correct calculation even more potentially rewarding. As Martin Amis puts it: 'The score is actually part of the game, and the shape of many a ticklish gamble is determined by whether your score is, say, 20,980 or 29,980.'

Strategic timing is also required by the beautifully balanced beat-'em-up game Bushido Blade 2. Unlike most of its genre, this game incorporates one-hit kills: understandably, a well-aimed sledgehammer blow to your opponent's head will result in a pretty shower of blood and his instantaneous collapse. Two-player bouts of this game, then, are great fun because there is so much tension involved, and strategy determines which of three stances you hold your weapon in, and where in the three-dimensional arena you choose to fight. Strategic timing is also needed in more serious-minded driving games such as F1 World Grand Prix 2, where you must decide when to pull in your tired car for a pit-stop. And strategic timing is obviously crucial in the genre of God games or process toys, where fast reactions are subordinated to the intelligent deployment of resources over time.

The third way in which time and rhythm operate in videogames is at a high structural level, where I'll call it 'tempo'.* This describes, for instance, the ebb and flow of anxiety and satisfaction through the gameplaying experience. As games have become more complex and longer experiences, tempo plays an ever more important role in their pleasure.

---

* I am not using this word in its technical musical sense, where a closer analogy might be 'rubato'.

A game of Robotron or Defender, for example, induces a reasonably constant high level of stress for the ten or twenty minutes that it lasts. However, Tomb Raider III or Zelda 64, which can be played without restarting for hours on end, need to afford the player some breathing space at intervals, where there is no immediate danger, just as much as they need to invoke moments of extreme anxiety. This concept also involves Richard Darling's comments in the last chapter about the distribution of rewards throughout a videogame. They can't be constant (continuous reinforcement gets boring); they can't be spaced out too far (not enough reinforcement). And neither rewards nor periods of relative relaxation must be spaced regularly, or they become predictable, and the element of pleasurable surprise is lost.

A videogame designer must therefore consider the large-scale distribution of such aspects of his game and organise them to the best effect – then it will have good tempo. A brilliant example of this aspect of design is Resident Evil. Perhaps the greatest reason for the game's success is its virtuosic tempo: periods of wandering through deserted environments with a gnawing sense of unease are interrupted by startling high-adrenalin events, such as a vicious dog monster crashing through a window (see fig. 18). Tempo in this game relies on creative alternations of suspense (not giving you what you expect, holding back) and shock (giving you what you don't expect). As with its visual style, Resident Evil's tempo is also drawn from a movie template. The tempo of *Alien*, for example, works in exactly the same way: periods of nervous movement through the *Nostromo*'s service ducts punctuated by sudden, horrific appearances of the slimy xenomorph.

One final comment we can make on the timing of videogames' symbolic interactions is that just as games have graphical resolution – the number of little dots or pixels on the screen from which the image is built up – they also have temporal resolution, which describes the fluidity or otherwise of the image's movement through time. Now if a videogame suffers from 'jerky' animation, in that there are too few frames to the second, the player's absorption into the temporally based semiotic conversation will be injured; it is analogous to having

Fig. 18. Resident Evil: a shocking moment (© 1997 Capcom)

a conversation with a friend who pauses briefly after every word he utters. Even worse, in a high-speed driving or flying game, a low temporal resolution is just not giving the player enough information to make apt decisions. If you only see the road in snapshots every twenty metres, you cannot drive very accurately.

However powerful a computer processor, its resources will always be finite, so there will always be a trade-off between temporal resolution and graphical resolution. You can have very richly defined pictures which move jerkily, or slightly less detailed ones which move smoothly. *Quake III: Arena*, for example, is a beautiful example of how very high temporal resolution really sucks the player in. So frame-rate should never be sacrificed to visual detail.

Say something else

Modern videogames adore the icon. They draw ever more beautifully detailed worlds and characters. But they are not necessarily any less semiotically complex than Pac-Man, once you get behind the pictures. Nearly all signs are mixtures of the semiotic modes. In an iconic game such as Tomb Raider, it becomes clear that game objects such as doors and keys, while being good three-dimensional 'pictures' of their referents, actually operate mostly as symbols. For they are not granted 'realistic' physical attributes. As noted earlier in the book, a wooden door may not be blown up by a rocket-launcher, and a key may not be filed down to fit a different lock. A Tomb Raider door, therefore, operates as a symbol for 'exit' or 'threshold', a means of policing movement between pre-defined spaces, and a key operates symbolically a little like a minor power-up, a second-order sign denoting 'ability to use door'.

There are also clearly artificial symbolic conventions in the gameplay of the Tomb Raider world: for instance, if a stone block is a slightly different shade of brown or grey from its neighbours, that tonal contrast is operating as a symbol for 'pushable' – the player knows that Lara is able to push the block out of the way in order to climb up on to it, or to uncover a hidden passage. The 'medikits' that Lara finds scattered around, meanwhile, are iconic in that they look like little leather bags with a red cross painted on them – but their function is purely symbolic. We are not meant to imagine that Lara really sews up her bullet-wounds with the contents; they are conventional power-ups, restoring Lara's health in the time-honoured, blatantly artificial manner. For all its heightened graphic naturalism, then, the mechanics of the game still operate, just as in Pac-Man, as a symbolic system. The 'realistic' skin hides a semiotic cyborg.

The virtue of Tomb Raider is that, although the variety of symbolic interaction that it offers to the player – manipulating keys, doors and switches – is quite rudimentary and uninteresting, the way the player is required to interact with such symbols in the three dimensions of space is what makes the game a pleasurable challenge. Lara is a very nicely designed videogame character, as we have seen, because of the rich range of physical animations – rolling, somersaulting, running, climbing – she is capable of, and these acrobatic moves must be strung together with exquisite tactical timing to move her around the environments in which she operates.

But a game such as Zelda 64, historically a contemporary of Tomb Raider III, is even more entertaining, because it combines requirements of spatial navigation and tactical timing with a far greater semiotic richness, which consists in the much wider variety of sign combinations and the cognitive challenges they pose to the player. In the Forest Temple of Zelda 64, for example, a good deal of complex fun is had with the nature of an icon itself.

The environment is a crumbling old country house, full of dark nooks and shadows. Gilt-edged paintings of ghosts hang on the walls. The paintings are icons within the gameworld. But the ghosts inside suddenly come to life with a demonic chuckle. The player realises that he must shoot them with an arrow before the painting turns blank and the ghost flees to the painting behind him. So the pure icon has suddenly become a symbol to be fought.

A different part of the same Temple, meanwhile, sees the player facing another ghost portrait. Suddenly six stone blocks fall from the ceiling; each side of each block is painted with a different section of the ghost portrait hanging on the wall. The player's task is to move the blocks around within a strict time limit so that their arrangement recreates the painting, at which point the ghost is drawn into the open to be fought. So the painting, which as before starts out as a pure icon, then becomes an index, pointing at the desired arrangement of the blocks on the floor. And finally it becomes a symbol again, as the ghost turns into a real enemy. The fact that all this sophisticated semiotic play happens in a matter of seconds provides an enriching experience beyond simple puzzles of space and movement.

The masterful semiotic playground that is Zelda 64 also expands the language available to the player by means of its titular ocarina, a clay pipe which emits melodies according to which button on the controller is pressed, keyboard-style. Once you have learned certain melodies, you may cause day to turn to night, or invoke rain, or talk to your friend in the forest. The game helps the player by showing the tune on a stave, in traditional symbolic musical language, and also indexically showing, or pointing to, the particular button-symbols that will cause each note to sound. And the melodies work symbolically as a whole, in that they are just summarily agreed to be certain causal mechanisms in the gameworld.

This idea of a magical musical 'language' is immensely intriguing. The Pied Piper of Hamelin, of course, had the same gift, as did Orpheus, charming the dolphins with his lyre – it is a recurring theme in folktale and myth. Zelda 64, in fact, only scrapes the surface of its possibilities, as the effective melodies are already written into the game. But there is no reason why future videogames may not, with very clever programming, develop this idea, and have the environment react organically to musical themes that the player makes up.

The ocarina is an example, at base, of a power-up. Many power-ups, like this one, take the form of physical objects in the gameworld – gadgets – but functionally they remain the same sort of animal as the large blobs in Pac-Man: they are second-order signs effecting changes in the possible symbolic relationships of the game. The ocarina works in this way by expanding the player's symbolic language. Another Zelda 64 gadget, for instance, the hookshot (a sort of retractable grappling hook), enables the player to reach previously inaccessible areas by swinging up.

Now in general one wants to say 'the more gadgets the better'. The more ways in which a player is required to learn how to use a new gadget and thus expand her semiotic conversation with the game, the longer the game will be refreshing and surprising, delivering a sense of childlike discovery. The brilliant yet underrated Ape Escape (see fig. 19) is furnished with many such exceptionally imaginative gadgets: a monkey radar, which when waved in the direction of a rogue simian flashes and hoots, enabling the player to examine his prey close-up; a hula-hoop, which when spun round the waist enables the player's character to run extremely fast; a rotor,

Fig. 19. Ape Escape: monkeying around in the ice age (© 1999 Sony Computer Entertainment)

which when spun enables you to float up to previously inaccessible areas. But Ape Escape's crowning achievement is the radio-controlled car, which – bizarrely at first – offers *exactly* the same experience as working a real radio-controlled car. When you are first given this gadget, you just play with it, as you would with a real one. The form is identical. Herein lies one secret of the videogame's enormous potential: it is the universal toy. (Indeed, 1999's RC Stunt Copter is a videogame simulation of playing with a real radio-controlled helicopter, while No Cliché's Toy Commander lets you play with something like fifty different types – toy planes, tanks, racecars and so on – spread over an imaginary house.)

But wait a minute: Ape Escape's radio-controlled car, after all, doesn't really exist. It is racing round a virtual world, and an *anime*-styled orange-haired punk-boy is holding the car's controller box on screen. That's alienation without the pain. In fact, the tangible connection between the controls in your physical hands and the action of the little toy on screen is a clever semiotic trick that fools you into ever-increasing absorption into the cartoon world. A similar trick is worked by the videogame paradigm of the sniper rifle, introduced by MDK (1997), perfected by Goldeneye (1997) and then cropping up everywhere – for example in Metal Gear Solid (1999) and Perfect Dark (2000). This gadget zooms in on an area and lets you view it in close-up, usually for the purpose of delivering an exquisite head-shot to a bad guy. A virtual environment which reveals more detail when viewed telescopically is naturally more convincing than one which only works on one informational scale.

The exception to the rule that more gadgets are better is the bad case of the single-use object, which we came across earlier. The single-use object – for instance, a jewel which must be fitted into a crevice but is then forgotten about – is basically a rudimentary power-up, but as we saw it's also a special case of the dreaded 'functional incoherence'. By contrast, Metal Gear Solid superbly combines a large number of gadgets with a delicious freedom as to how they are used and reused in various situations. You may use a simple cardboard box to hide in, or to get yourself transported unwittingly by the enemy in a truck. When you meet your sharp-shooting nemesis, Sniper Wolf, for the second time, you can choose to battle her with the sniper rifle, or throw gallantry to the wind and fire off some Nikita guided missiles instead. If your aim is shaky, you can pop a tranquilliser, or smoke a cigarette. If you need to make some alarm beams visible, you can smoke a cigarette or use your infrared goggles – and so on.

A great game, we can say for the moment, will probably have one or both of the two semiotic virtues identified. The first is to set challenges that involve complex, rich interactions of signs. And the second is continually to expand the player's own vocabulary, to present the gift of freedom in negotiating those semiotic thickets.

Fig. 20. G-Police: the information superhighway (© 1997 Sony Computer Entertainment)

Information overlord

Now as signs are basically vehicles of meaning,* a videogame will, for its own part in the conversation, need to erect highly efficient, semiotic systems as it tries to present ever greater quantities of raw information to the player. That information can be broken up into different signs in different areas of the display.

Consider the screen of G-Police (see fig. 20). It shows a perspective construction of solid-looking buildings, roads, cars and other aircraft. In visual terms, this highly iconic construction is far closer to the film *Blade Runner* than it is to the videogame Pac-Man. But arrayed around the edges of the screen are ghostly, transparent figures that constitute a knotty

---

* Or actually, on readings such as the Saussurean one, *constitute* meaning by virtue of their arrangement.

system of signs which the player must read and react to in order to play the game competently. These figures are the game's 'HUD', or head-up display, which recreates an actual military technology whereby instrument readings are projected on to the cockpit window directly ahead of the pilot so that he doesn't have to look away for information.

Look at the screen. Top right is a number surrounded by a segmented, shaded ring. The number, a symbol, denotes the 'health' of your gunship: when it reaches zero, the craft is destroyed. Similarly the words at bottom right are symbols for the available weapons. But most of the gameplayer's information is also provided indexically: the shaded parts around the health number vanish in strict ratio to the decreasing number, with an overlaid symbolic order of rainbow colour, whereby green denotes maximum health, gradually turning to red for minimum. The shaded brackets at either side of screen centre, meanwhile, are indices: at left for craft speed (coloured above the middle for forward speed, below the middle for reverse); and at right for engine thrust. Again colour is overlaid symbolically, with a bright yellow for high forward velocities or accelerations, red for low ones, descending into blue and purple for reverse.

The signs at bottom left, meanwhile, furnish symbols (numbers) for altitude, but again provide the same information indexically, as an arrow pointing to subdivisions of a meter that rises and falls. Top centre is the player's radar, which works as a triumvirate of all three semiotic modes: symbolically, because each (green or red) dot is agreed to stand for a civilian or enemy craft; indexically, because the red triangle 'points to' the next mission objective; and iconically, because the whole arrangement is a simplified 'picture' of local space.

If it remains largely true that the interplay of symbols constitutes the richness of the gameplay itself,* there is a complementary truth that indices enjoy a greater importance in the business

---

* Although some videogames – in particular racing games like Ridge Racer Type 4 – can happily demote symbolism to a rather incidental property, if they provide enough interest solely with icons (beautiful scenery), indices (roadsigns and rev counters) and rhythm.

of providing feedback to the player on the basis of which he can determine his next action. It is more intuitively and speedily understandable to 'read' an indexical shape such as the remaining health segments than to read the numerical symbol, especially since the index provides, as the number does not, an instantly comprehensible representation of current health or speed as a ratio of the possible maximum. The reason is exactly the same as why your car's dashboard features an indexical speedometer: an arrow pointing to a certain point on a circular dial. A bald numerical display, such as that used by the odometer, is simply not instantaneous enough in its communication of critical data.

G-Police provides a polyphonic display of signs, and so, as already noted, it is a shame that its control system is too complex for fluid execution of the player's wishes. The badly designed language which the player is given erects a barrier between him and the world of the game.

Even in games that are less stuffed with quantitative information than G-Police and its simulation-style comrades, indices are still of great help in telling the player how to organise symbolic interactions. The best example is in exploration games which provide a map of the current environment. In Zelda 64, the player must find a map: it is an object in the gameworld that functions as a power-up. Once acquired, it can be viewed to help you find your way to new areas: it is graphically designed so as to look like a real parchment map (it's an icon); it 'points to' the salient structural features of the environment (it's an index); and it is marked with symbols that are agreed to stand for various crucial features: a treasure chest, the monster's lair. But here the player must switch between the map 'screen' and the gameworld. By contrast, the dinosaur-hunting first-person shooter Turok 2 intelligently enables the level map to be overlaid on to the iconically constructed environment, as if it were a transparency; thus, the player is reading all possible modes of sign at once.

Videogames have become so clever at displaying information in imaginative yet instantly intuitive ways that they have started to exhibit a kind of aesthetic techno-nostalgia. They are so far ahead of the race, compared to the dull and workmanlike interfaces of 'serious' software or most Internet pages, that they can footle around and have a bit of visual fun. This is most obvious in the panoply of support screens – option screens to set the player's preferences, to choose game modes or to save and load game data or pre-play mission briefings – all the prerequisites to play (which Shigeru Miyamoto calls a game's 'labour') that surround the action at the heart of even the simplest modern game.

G-Police 2: Weapons of Justice (1999), for example, is full of glowing green grids that sketch out a virtual graph-paper background to screens full of weapon and mission information; text spells itself out letter by letter accompanied by rapid high-pitched beeping. Control panels are given a metallic, quasi-solid sheen by the old effect of bas-relief, which renders the illusion of raised and hollowed surfaces with simple lines of highlight and shadow. The effect of all this is deliberately retro-gressive, harking back to an early 1980s era when such visual asceticism was in fact the technological cutting edge, for instance in the moody green-and-grey bas-relief of the brilliant shoot-'em-up Uridium for the Commodore 64. The modern Omega Boost, too, plays with screens full of crude, dancing alphanumeric characters, green wireframe data screens and deliberately fuzzy, old-school voice synthesis in its mission clips.

It is clear that videogames must differentiate themselves from the interfaces of 'serious' software: no one wants to come home, turn on a game and feel like they're still working at the office PC.* But the particular aesthetic phenomenon of techno-nostalgia is also working a very clever, stealthy trick. Just as Hamlet's deliberately archaic play-within-a-play enhances the audience's suspension of disbelief, in that the surrounding onstage action looks by comparison far more 'real', so the blatantly archaic technological design in some parts of the

---

* This is also the reason why, videogame journalists and hardcore system fetishists aside, PC-based videogames are far less popular than console-based ones – quite apart from the fact that the latter hardware is five times cheaper.

videogame make the cutting-edge visuals in the thick of the action seem even more novel and exciting.

Drawing you in

Modern videogames, as we have seen, glory in their graphical richness: spacecraft with scarred hulls, fighters with stubble, trees with individually swaying branches. But this does not necessarily reduce the player's involvement in the game. What spoils 'identification' is simply a lack of symbolic richness to suck you in. If a game with a beautiful graphical iconic construction also enjoys symbolic richness – as in Zelda 64 – it is a good game. Conversely, a game built entirely from abstract visual symbols can be a bad game if those symbols do not interact in interesting ways. Tic-Tac-Toe, played by arranging the abstract symbols X and O, is a boring game for exactly this reason, as well as the more general competitive reason that it is always a draw. Beatmania, however, combines a mere four symbols in compelling rhythmic ways and so is a good game.

But a good videogame character – a well-designed and attractive icon such as Sonic or Lara – can vastly increase our enjoyment of the game. So how can these two apparently contradictory claims be reconciled – on the one hand, that iconicism is irrelevant to gameplay; and on the other hand, that beautiful icons increase our enjoyment?

Well, the hermeneutic (in videogames, mostly iconic) and pragmatic (mostly symbolic) imaginations are not mutually exclusive. For instance, when reading a detective novel (hermeneutic), you are very likely to try to figure out how (pragmatic) the hero should proceed in his case. And the same is true of modern videogames. They just require more sophistication on our part to 'read' them properly: hermeneutic imagination for the gorgeous pictorialism, as well as pragmatic imagination for the symbolic interaction. The semiotic demands of videogames are becoming greater all round.

One irregular videogamer, an *habituée* of Pac-Man and Tetris, told me on playing Tomb Raider for the first time: 'I found I was *looking* at Lara rather than worrying what was going on in the game.' This is revealing: iconic modern games certainly hit you first with their pictures. But that's no bad thing, because if you like the icons, you are more likely to want to get to grips with the symbols. Good videogame characters please us visually and thus function as our motivation for continuing the struggle. They catch our interest simply because we like them, and would prefer to see them succeed.

In this way they are playing on our hermeneutic imagination – but of course we also need to exercise our pragmatic imagination when controlling them in order to help them overcome their problems. And here again we notice the desirable limits of videogame 'reality'. Remember that there is a limit on how purely, accurately iconic we want videogame characters to be: Lara Croft must always remain no woman in particular, for that is her charm. And we don't really want in a videogame to kill and mutilate very 'real'-looking people; for the game to remain innocent, visceral fun, they must remain partial symbols, retain that 'computer look'.

Modern videogames are in this way more seductive than ever, as thanks to their visual enhancement they challenge us doubly. The same gameplayer who couldn't help just watching Lara for a while also mused that she found it more disturbing when Lara died than when Pac-Man died, because she saw the character drown in a 'realistic' fashion. Modern games have the potential, as yet largely unfulfilled, to deliver a richer overall experience to the player.

The history of videogames' iconic powers, their increasing ability to draw a pretty world, has opened up new potential for semiotic richness. But good graphics cannot work alone: what matters in modern gameplay terms is the interaction of all three types of sign. A gorgeous game with nothing interesting to do is just a bad piece of software.

As videogames deliver richer visual experiences, it seems, ever more people will be willing to pick them up and play. A good modern exploration game such as Tomb Raider: The Last Revelation (Lara's penultimate outing on the original PlayStation) depends very heavily in this way on its iconic attractiveness. Jeremy Smith of Core enthuses over the possibilities offered by the next technological standard:

There are far more things you can do with Lara's hair, and with her clothing ... The leaves that you're going past or the vines are all moving and animating, and there may be water dripping off them on to a pool which is making a ripple effect. PlayStation2 can do this camera-blurring where you can home in on the central character and the view-distance at the back is blurred. Can you imagine the possibilities that that's going to open up? It's going to give you a depth of field that's so huge it's just like opening up a whole new door into gaming. Games are gonna have great depth – depth and atmosphere. Superb!

It certainly looks as though the more able a game is to draw an atmospheric, beautiful world – as in the frankly stunning Shenmue – the more willing the player will be to shuffle off his or her chthonic shackles and swim happily into that world, where he or she can then get to grips with its symbolic play.

What have we decided? That underneath the flashy graphics, cinematic cut-scenes, real-time physics, mythological back-stories and everything else, a videogame at bottom is still a highly artificial, purposely designed semiotic engine. And its purpose is not to simulate real life, but to offer the gift of playing a game. When we are at play, whether in front of a videogame screen, in a chess café, at the bowling alley or in the park, we are citizens of an invisible city, built of signs.

We should not find that so surprising, because man, after all, is the symbolic animal. And this is exactly what videogames celebrate, challenge and feed. It's no dumb accident that they appeared: once the technology was lying around, they simply *had* to happen. As Nolan Bushnell, the father of commercial videogaming, puts it drily, videogames arose out of a natural wish to 'make computers do fun things'. In this sense, they are an historically inevitable evolution of the play drive. To play a videogame is only human.

To win, of course, is divine.

10

THE PROMETHEUS ENGINE

God's gift

In the beginning, heaven and earth were married. Gaia (earth) and Uranus (the heavens) then gave birth to the Titans, the twelve gods of earliest times. They had dominion over all the cosmos. The youngest Titan, Kronos, married his sister Rhea, but he knew that he was fated to be supplanted by one of his children. In order to protect himself, he hit upon the strategy of eating them all, one by one, as they were born. However, when the last child, Zeus, fought his way from the womb, Rhea, sick of her wasted efforts, tricked her husband and gave him a stone to eat instead, hiding Zeus away in Crete. When Zeus grew up, he forced Kronos to disgorge the stone along with all his other eaten children. The Titanomachy ensued: a ten-year war between Zeus and his siblings on one side and the rest of the Titans on the other that shook the universe to its foundations.

There was one Titan battling on Zeus's side: Prometheus. His name means 'he who thinks ahead'. His insistence on using guile rather than brute force was laughed off by his fellow Titans, and so Prometheus abandoned them to their fate and made his ingenuity available to Zeus's faction. Thanks to Prometheus's strategic talent, Zeus won. He and his brothers and sisters took their thrones on Mount Olympus. The rest of the Titans, defeated, were consigned to the hell of Tartarus, while Prometheus's half-brother Atlas was forced to hold up the sky for all eternity.

Prometheus, alone of his kind now free, created men out of clay. Zeus, ever ready to pull the ladder up after himself, was afraid

215

that men in turn might seek to challenge his kingly position, and called for them to be utterly wiped out. *The Titan, however, loved his creations so dearly that he stole a spark from the forge of Hephaestus and carried it down to men, hidden in a stalk of fennel. Pyrotechnia, the art of fire, the source of all knowledge, was now man's.* Prometheus continued to improve the brutish lives of his creations by teaching them writing, astronomy, agriculture, sailing, medicine, mining and the interpretation of dreams. He also fooled Zeus into accepting the worst portion of meat from sacrificed animals: gristly bone was the gods' due, while men kept the edible flesh.

For these and other indiscretions, however, Prometheus was punished. The malignant Zeus had him chained to a rock, where a monstrous eagle gobbled at his exposed liver every day for thirty thousand years. In the Athenian drama usually attributed to Aeschylus, 'Prometheus Bound', the immortally pain-racked hero sums up his story: *'I gave a gift to mortals, and in that giving yoked myself to fate – to this! I filled a hollow reed with fire, stolen from heaven. I gave it to mortals. It sparked them, taught them cunning, filled their need. For that, now, I pay this price, chained, staked, wide open to the sky.'*

After an age of suffering, Prometheus was finally freed when Hercules shot the eagle-monster with his bow. From the surviving fragments of Aeschylus's sequel, it appears that Prometheus and Zeus were then to enjoy something of a reconciliation. More than two thousand years later, however, Shelley rewrote the ending in 'Prometheus Unbound', where Prometheus, the champion now of human imagination and sexuality, defeats the tyrannical god and casts him forever into the abyss. For the moment, man's inheritance is safe.

For what had Prometheus done in the first place? He had given men a power-up.

Burn this

The gift of fire. Like most children, I used to find battery-powered torches fascinating toys. I'd smuggle a torch into bed and turn it on after lights out, beaming whirling patterns on to the ceiling for what seemed like hours. The quality of light just before the batteries ran out was my favourite: a barely visible golden spectre, loopingly scrawling its message in a hiero-glyphic tongue. It was a mystery. The fiery glow of a tungsten filament powered by a couple of chunks of lead and acid some-how translated into this sensuous *show*.

The ancient Chinese, we are told, first invented fireworks – made fire a plaything. For centuries, fire-eaters travelled with circuses, making dragonish art from the destructive gift. To this day they give a thrillingly organic flavour even to such celebrations of technology-dependent entertainment as Manu-mission, the Babylonian techno palace on Ibiza. Lately, elec-tricity has become the preferred fire – eminently biddable and plastic – of the moderns. Electric light freed us from the tyranny of the dark, hastening the march of technology. The cinema came along and 'broke our prisons asunder': reality was recorded and recreated anywhere, through light.

Then there was television: a tumultuous inferno of electrons, arcanely marshalled and beaming more reality into each lucky home. Through the gift of fire in its latest incarnation, everyone was to have their horizons expanded, their minds cultivated, their hopes nurtured. That didn't last. The fire became not an illuminating flame but a cauterising one, dulling the nerves. You can shout at the television, but it will just keep on pumping out its moronising radiation. You can switch channels. You can switch off.

And now videogames – the television screen reclaimed for our control. What potential – if television replaced the log fire or the wireless as a focus of domestic attention, the videogame re-engineers the television's relentless blaze as a colourful zone of play, a new world to explore, a rich and strange place to pit your wits against the dazzling inventions of others. The pixels dance to your tune. You're not watching, you're *doing*. And when videogames are at their best, what you're doing is some-thing vastly more creatively challenging than watching a docu-soap or a quiz show. Your reasoning, reflexes and imagination are tested to exhilarating limits. That hunk of moulded plastic, that PlayStation or Dreamcast, is a magic box that allows you to play with fire. A Prometheus engine.

Bad company

Fire is not necessarily an unqualified good. It can burn. Back in 1982, the US Surgeon General, Dr C. Everett Koop, declared that videogames were evil entities that produced 'aberrations in childhood behaviour'. Then, videogames were abstract pixellated contests of timing and skill, but now they offer superbly detailed animations of blood and gore while you shoot an opponent's head off in Kingpin or mow down pedestrians in your car in Carmageddon. The latter game was grudgingly granted an 18 certificate in 1997 by the British Board of Film Classification, as the developers refused to change the colour of the victims' blood from red (too human) to green (acceptably zombie).

People are worried by such exultantly bad-taste imagery. Such scientific investigation as has been done into the possible negative effects of videogames is so far inconclusive. Patricia Greenfield's 1984 study, *Media and the Mind of the Child*, concluded that there was no such evidence, but then videogames were not nearly so graphically detailed as they are now. In more recent times, arguments that videogame playing temporarily increases aggression in children* are countered by other studies claiming evidence for the 'catharsis' hypothesis – that videogames provide a safe and beneficial outlet for aggressive feelings in a non-destructive context,† or that they contribute positively to a child's cognitive development.‡ The jury's still out.

---

* These arguments are given a witty and readable overview by Mark Griffiths in 'Video games and children's behaviour' in *Elusive Links*.

† This is the view, for instance, of G. I. Kestenbaum & L. Weinstein in 'Personality, psychopathology, and developmental issues in male adolescent video game use', in *Journal of the American Academy of Child Psychiatry 24*, pp. 325–37 (cited by Griffiths, op. cit.).

‡ Marsha Kinder writes in *Playing with Power in Movies, Television and Video Games* (p. 115) that she has observed her son playing videogames and argues that they enrich his development: 'I have noticed that the better Victor becomes at videogames, the more interested and skilful he is at drawing cartoons.'

Despite the absence of scientific consensus, there is a rising level of moral concern that parallels the outcry over 'video nasties' in the 1980s. Questions were asked in the British Parliament on the 1993 release of Mortal Kombat. Grand Theft Auto (1997), a game in which the player steals cars, runs over lines of Hare Krishnas and shoots cops, was described by the British Police Federation as 'sick, deluded and beneath contempt', and in summer 1999 an MP wrote to the Prime Minister asking if anything could be done to limit sales of the horror-themed game Silent Hill, whose story centres on the disappearance and torture of a young girl.

In the United States, the increasing number of school massacres is leading many to blame videogames directly for childhood violence. In spring 1999, Eric Harris and Dylan Klebold, two Columbine High School teenagers in Littleton, Colorado, shot twelve students and a teacher before committing suicide. The media quickly reported that they were avid players of videogames Doom and Duke Nukem. The previous year, fourteen-year-old Michael Carneal had killed three students and injured five others at his school in West Paducah, Kentucky. After the Littleton incident, the parents of those three murdered children filed a $130 million lawsuit against twenty-four videogame and Internet companies. The plaintiffs claimed that Doom, apparently one of Carneal's favourite games, 'trained Carneal to point and shoot a gun in a fashion making him an ... effective killer without teaching him any of the constraints or responsibilities needed to inhibit such a killing capacity'. The suit was summarily dismissed in May 2000 by a federal court judge, but the scapegoating of videogames continues.

Now it is true that videogames have had a worryingly close relationship with the technologies of killing. Remember the glowing neoplatonism of Battlezone? It was a thing of beauty, but it also became quite grimly implicated in real-life destruction. Atari was commissioned to build an enhanced version of Battlezone for the American Defense Department's Advanced Research Project Agency, as a simulator for real tank drivers. This was only the start of a growing symbiotic relationship between videogames and the military. American warplane company Lockheed-Martin invested in the technology of arcade videogames, thus accelerating their development. The US marines have made their recruits practise Doom, as the game's co-designer Jon Romero acknowledged: 'Soldiers played Doom to feel like they were in a war situation, where you have one-shot kills.' The US Navy now uses a custom hack of Microsoft's Flight Simulator to help pilots learn to fly a T-34C Turbo Mentor, the aircraft used for primary flight training.

But what does it mean to say that a videogame can *train* you to kill? I think it means rather less than critics want it to. When I was at school, my favourite sport was fencing. I was trained to wield my preferred weapon, a sabre, with great speed and precision. The swords we used were blunted, and we all wore protective clothing and face-masks. But I was perfectly equipped, if I so chose, to sharpen my blade and use it to hack limbs off my classmates with a few swashbuckling moves. There is no doubt that my potential capability to kill was enhanced by my fencing activities. But that had no causal, motivational effect of the type that is implied by the idea of 'training'.

Similarly with videogames. In Time Crisis, for instance, the player wields a plastic gun which responds very accurately to light – you aim the gun at the screen and shoot the enemy. A person who is very good at Time Crisis will probably be a good shot with a real gun. But no convincing explanation is available as to why such an otherwise well-balanced individual would want to make the move from play to murder. The soldiers who practise teamwork with Doom are not motivated to kill by their experience of playing that game; they are ordered to do so by their superiors.

Fencing, of course, is a sport whose kinetic form is derived from a long, bloodthirsty history of actual swordfighting, combat and duels. But we class it as a morally neutral sport because its content is non-violent: the risk of injury is very low (far lower than with boxing), and the intent of the fencer is not to kill or maim but simply to win. The same is true of videogames. When I am playing Time Crisis 2 or Perfect Dark, my intent is not to kill. For there is nothing *to* kill; there are only patterns of light on the screen. Similarly, the consequences of my actions have no moral content either, because no one dies.

So to blame videogames directly for childhood violence is absurd, unless one is prepared also to legislate against laser-tag, paintball, martial arts and even body-building – in fact, every type of recreation that could theoretically increase one's ability to kill another human being but has no direct causal connection with murderous activity.

On the other hand, videogames may be one of a complex of causal factors, any one of which in isolation does not produce a killer but which in combination become lethal. Clearly, for instance, videogames might be said to have an influence on real-life violence in the same way that films or any other media do – by having a particular style that may be imitated. The Columbine murderers are thought to have dressed in black trenchcoats in emulation of Keanu Reeves in *The Matrix*. It is possible that Michael Carneal killed his schoolmates deliberately in the manner of a Doom deathmatch. But it would be wrong to conclude that those teenagers would not have killed if they hadn't seen that film or played that game. It seems far more likely that they would simply have picked another wardrobe statement off the rack from television or the cinema.

Modern media, including videogames, offer a vast library of imagery. But the intent to commit violence in the first place is not caused by that imagery; most of the time, stylistic imitation is safely indulged in a play form, such as when children of past generations pretended to re-enact scenes from Saturday-morning Westerns. Anthony Burgess's *A Clockwork Orange* does not argue that Beethoven and bowler hats *cause* murder; they merely provide a convenient style to wrap around Alex's sadistic fantasies. Famously, Stanley Kubrick withdrew his film of that novel after reports of 'copycat' crimes. But if you are going to kill, you can find stylistic inspiration anywhere: in a detective novel, a film, a painting by Hieronymus Bosch, a heavy-metal album or a videogame. They won't, however, implant the murderous desire in the first place.

A videogame can even be seen as positively valuable if it enables the formal imitation of dangerous or criminal activities in a safe and consequence-free environment. Sam Houser, president of Rockstar Games who published Grand Theft Auto 2 in 1999, quotes the New York Police Department as happily approving of the joy-riding and cop-killing in his notorious product: 'We'd rather they did it in your game than on the street.'

And yet, precisely because of their huge commercial and cultural successes, videogames cannot be immune from ethical considerations. We have, after all, been discussing them as art.* So let's return to one of our primary themes: our old friend, the reality of the unreal world.

Genesis

In a dance of fire are new worlds born. At British videogame developers Core Design, they have a special, home-grown software tool designed exactly for the purpose of building new worlds: it's called, not inappropriately, Worldbuild II. After the artists have drawn hundreds of pencil sketches of imaginary landscapes, the topographical features of each area are fed directly into the computer. Acetate plans go up on the walls. Now begins the process of making it an explorable environment.

As in many things, ontogeny (the development of an individual) recapitulates or mirrors phylogeny (the evolution of a type). At its early stages, the human foetus bears certain physiological resemblances to our fishy ancestors. And in the early stages of gestation of a modern virtual world, it resembles the cutting-edge arcade games of two decades ago: the pure, abstract geometry of Battlezone. The digitally created 'land' is a wireframe model made up of hundreds or thousands of polygons; the worldbuilder simply has to drag individual bits up or down with the mouse to create the shapes of what will become molehills, mountains, valleys and rivulets. Block by block, the ground is raised and lowered; edges are smoothed off.

Only then, when the landscape is shaped in three dimen-

---

* 'Ethics and aesthetics are one and the same.' Wittgenstein, *Tractatus Logico-Philosophicus*.

sions, do the artists start to colour it in, choosing from a palette of colours and textures (endless pages of sun-bleached grass, clover patches, subtly different shades of rock) that are simply painted on to the wireframe model. Meanwhile, other artists have been fashioning animals out of their digital version of the Promethean clay. A cow is fashioned from a geometrical skeleton, painstakingly animated through hundreds of frames, and then 'skinned' – not flayed, but given a skin, a colourful cartoon cowhide that is wrapped over the wireframe model. Now the worldbuilder simply chooses the incantatory menu option 'Place Object': the cow is sucked out of its virtual womb, fully formed, and dropped into the field. With no apparent signs of confusion or disorientation, the bovine simply starts padding around the grass, enjoying a nonexistent sun. Inside the game: life, of a sort.

A world can't be built in isolation. Every facet of the videogame development process is organically interrelated with the requirements of the others. For this game, an artist explains, 'The early levels are all meadows and open spaces to get the player comfortable with the character.' The terrain is designed expressly to optimise gameplay.

One theory of how the universe came to exist is a provocative idea called the Strong Anthropic Principle, which suggests that the universe is designed exactly the way it is, with the forces of nature and relative charges of fundamental particles balanced exactly this way, for the sole purpose of allowing intelligent lifeforms such as ourselves to observe it. We are the whole point of creation. In videogames, the Strong Anthropic Principle is not speculation but fact. As Lara Croft's creator has explained: 'The whole Tomb Raider world is utterly dependent on Lara's size and animations. The distance she can jump, reach, run forward and fall are set variables. In this way, her world is designed for her to exist in.'

How strangely comforting. We are everywhere alienated from nature in the real world, but for a time we can feel oddly at home in this unreal universe, where our strengths can always overcome our difficulties. We prefer the fantasy because it is *fair*.

The final frontier

This is a particular kind of utopianist terraforming, where a person's capabilities are never insufficient. But what about the purely visual imagination of videogame worlds? Whereas the Battlezone universe was in its day shockingly new, today's environments are much more instantly recognisable. They draw on only a few basic templates. There is the blasted, neon-lit *Blade Runner* cityscape; the dank metal corridors with exposed piping, steam vents and unpredictable lighting are straight from *Alien*; steel catwalks and pools of orange molten metal ring that *Terminator* bell. Cute, unthreatening worlds in primary colours come straight from animated cartoons – hardly surprising, then, that there is an exodus of talent from traditional animation into the videogame industry.

There is a certain amount of interbreeding among these types, of course. Just as we saw earlier that many games opt for interfaces of a deliberately techno-nostalgic design, so the very environments in games like Quake III, Turok: Rage Wars, Tomb Raider III or Unreal mix hi-tech steel and electric light with architecture of a deliberately archaic grandeur: vaulted stone archways and sweeping staircases. In this way they aim for an effect of vertiginous scale such as that created so masterfully by Giovanni Battista Piranesi's etchings of nightmare dungeons in his *Carceri d'Invenzione* (see fig. 21), which had an enormous influence on the aesthetics of Romanticism and, later, Surrealism.

In this way, such videogames are part of a long tradition of imaginary architecture. But they are still some way behind in inventiveness. Because part of Piranesi's visualised nightmare is that the fabric of space itself is warped: the perspective is deliberately ambiguous, worryingly off-key. As Ernst Gombrich asks in *Art and Illusion*: 'The rope hanging from the pulley – where does it lead? How is the drawbridge tied up? What is the angle of the bannister near the lower edge?' The artist used his illusionistic craft to create a gnawing sense of unease in the viewer. In videogames so far, on the other hand, everything is fanatically, obsessively 'true' in three dimensions. There is no room for interesting fuzziness or spatial ambiguity.

Fig. 21. Piranesi's *Carceri d'Invenzione*: a dungeon master's perspective on the unreal (Rosenwald Collection; photograph © 1999 Board of Trustees, National Gallery of Art, Washington)

The spatial aesthetics of videogames are still stuck in the conservative line of the eighteenth century, because geometrically, it seems, truth is easier than interesting fiction. Yet why should a game not let the player wander round Piranesi's own dungeons? Of course, such skewed spaces would initially be very confusing to the gameplayer, but by building in a sufficient degree of intuitive predictability in other aspects – the way, say, that inertia or gravity works – then the game could still present an enjoyable challenge without becoming thoroughly alienating. It would anyway be impossible to build a world that was thoroughly different in *every* way from the real one.*

Or why should a videogame not let us move through Escherian space, with its baffling perspectival contradictions? Escher's prints depend for their power on a single point of view, deliberately chosen to maximise the illusion. With a moving point of view such as a videogame provides, designers would need to write very clever algorithms to adjust the illusion according to every movement of the player so that the house of cards did not fall.

This wouldn't be easy. But designers ought to have the courage to play with the very fabric of their unreality, to create ever newer kinds of space rather than settling permanently on scientific perspective – itself, as we have seen, a tissue of illusionistic distortions.

In an ideal world

But a good illusion must be cogent. The fabulous, unreal world that we are given to play with must seem to be perfectly real on its own terms. A strange new world is a thing of awe, but of course there is also a certain pleasure to be had from playing in recognisable environments. Tomb Raider II famously included a 'Venice' level, in which Lara pilots a speedboat and spectacularly crashes through the windows of an arched walkway above the water – although it wasn't modelled on a real part of Venice. TOCA 2, however, lets you drive two-litre saloons around accurate models of British racing circuits like Brands Hatch or Silverstone. Metropolis Street Racer (2000),

---

* 'It is obvious that an imagined world, however different it may be from the real one, must have *something* – a form – in common with it.' Wittgenstein, *Tractatus Logico-Philosophicus*.

following the lead set by Driver but exploiting the greater graphical muscle of the Dreamcast system, goes even further by synthesising information from streetmaps, thousands of photographs and hundreds of hours of video in order to let the player drive around faithful recreations of one-and-a-half-square-mile sections of actual cities: the Shibuya district of Tokyo, central San Francisco, and tourist London. If you played this game a lot, and then went for a spin in the real Shibuya, you'd know your way around. It's that good.

Such videogames at the moment, however, fall squarely into the high-velocity driving genre, and for a good reason. Because games as yet have only made a few faltering steps towards a necessary goal of the future: the fully interactive environment. If you were walking a character around that virtual Shibuya, it would soon become apparent that all the complex parts of a building – shop doors, drainpipes, windows – are not real objects modelled by the program. They have no symbolic function: they are simply pictures thrown on to a flat surface. You could not go into a shop or shin up the drainpipe.

Providing a fully functional rendering of such a hugely complex environment as a real city is still beyond current videogame abilities. Even at its blisteringly high speed, Metropolis Street Racer cannot give the player total freedom to drive around: there is a set circuit, with many streets cordoned off by invisible barriers. But it will happen eventually, even in complex exploration games. The problem as things stand is that certain arbitrary simplifications have to be made. All right, say the London levels of Tomb Raider III, you can open *that* door, but this other door's just a dummy, just painted on for atmosphere. But that's our old enemy, functional incoherence. Anything that looks like a door, I should be able to open unless it's locked, or break it down if it's made of rotting wood; if its hinges are visible I should be able to blow them off with a shotgun. Anything that looks like a window, I should be able to smash, with my bare fists if necessary. Conversely, give me a spade, and I should be able to dig ditches or plant flowers if I'm feeling particularly green-fingered.

Let's see no more spatial incoherence either. If I can climb this wall, I should be able to climb up that tree. If I can see a small hole, I should be able to curl up and squeeze through it instead of banging my head on the rocky outcrop. And forget about causal incoherence, too. If you're going to give me mass-ive weaponry to fight mutant dinosaurs in Turok 2, then it should be open to me to shoot the angelic children I am sup-posed to save. Even if that leads to drastic punishment, it should logically be an option.

Because if I can't do any of these things, it doesn't *feel* real. It becomes sinkingly clear that this is an environment with artificial, illogical restrictions on my actions. This is the prob-lem that game designers will have to solve in future: the more behavioural options that are given to the player, and the more gadgetry on offer, the harder it will be to make sure that the videogame environment as a whole is perfectly coherent.

If this cannot be accomplished at the moment for recreations of large 'real' environments like Tokyo, owing to the data inten-siveness problem, that in itself should be a good reason for videogames to develop their architectural imagination in much more creative ways. Even when it is possible to recreate a real environment, we still don't want it to be *too* real. Sam Houser describes the design process of skateboarding game Thrasher: Skate and Destroy (1999) in this way: 'All the levels in the game are based on real-world locations. The testers saw one level and said, "Wow, that's China Banks!" – which is a big place in San Francisco which is now banned, but it's one of the world-famous meccas that any skateboarder knows about.' But even so, the virtual China Banks was deliberately *not* made completely accurate, because then the gameplay would have been boring. 'It's quite hard to take a real-world location that in skateboarding may be good for one rail that everyone rides, but you've got to make the whole level fun,' Houser explains. So the digital China Banks features a host of invented extra curves and ramps. It's even better than the real thing.

Even games that do not try to build a recognisable, real-world place are still rather repetitively reliant on the same hoary old visual references. Littered around Core's studios during the development of Tomb Raider: The Last Revelation, for instance, are photographic and illustrative source books such as *An Introduction to Egyptology*, from which the artists are

Fig. 22. Tomb Raider: The Last Revelation: Egyptian architecture reimagined (© and ™ 1999 Core Design Limited; all rights reserved)

liberally stealing and fusing visual ideas both for the architecture of the tombs and for Lara's assailants, such as a huge golden dog. The resulting environments are at once familiar and strange (see fig. 22). There is a great deal of visual and spatial invention in this game, but it consists of clever combination, not of imagining a world anew from the ground up.

Videogames should try more often to break free of such recognisable templates, the clichés of the torchlit stone tomb, the fairy dungeon, the biomechanoid spaceship interior, the sunny meadow, the *Dune*-derived hi-tech desert metropolis. The abstract, voidal spaces of early videogames were in some senses far more interesting than the third-hand patchwork worlds of the majority of current exploration games. But there, modernist abstraction was a happy by-product, born of technological necessity. As a free choice, it's obviously much harder to make. Some of the most original environments so far in modern gaming have been seen, ironically, in some of the worst products, those triumphs of virtual tourism over symbolic richness Myst and Riven, whose pleasurably organic topography extrapolates inventively from the real, natural world.

Another straightforward conclusion: videogames need to play to their strengths. Shigeru Miyamoto said exactly the same thing in September 1999: 'The beauty of interactive media is it is different from other types of media, so we need to concentrate on those differences.' In this instance, that means recognising that whereas cinema – at least naturalistic, 'live-action' cinema – is tied down to real spaces, the special virtue of videogames is precisely their limitless plasticity. And only when that virtue is exploited more fully will videogames become a truly unprecedented art – when their level of world-building competence is matched with a comparable level of pure invention. We want to be shocked by novelty. We want to lose ourselves in a space that is utterly different. We want environments that have never been seen, never been imagined before.

Virtual justice

Terry Pratchett, the videogame-loving author of the Discworld novels (whose universe, like that of a good videogame, is bizarre but consistent), explained to me just why he enjoys games in these terms: 'For me, it's the fun of exploration, and new challenges. I like the big-screen feel of the Tomb Raider series and, for example, Half-Life ... I like hidden areas, secret rooms, non-player characters who can help you. This gives you a real sense of involvement. What impressed me about Tomb Raider was the breadth of the scenery, and the ... claustrophobia, the sense that you were really there.' And what does he want from the videogames of the future? Simple, really. 'Give me the speargun, the revolver and the shotgun, and turn me loose on an unknown world.' But it's much better when there are plenty more things to do in a videogame than just spraying bullets around. Pratchett agrees: 'That's what I liked about Tomb Raider – it wasn't *defined* by shooting.'

Yet particularly in first-person games, there is still room for massive symbolic improvement. Interesting steps have been made recently by games such as Rainbow Six or Hidden and

Dangerous, where the player's ability to switch control between several soldiers with different mission duties enhances the demands of strategic timing and also, since the environment may be seen from several different viewpoints in rapid succession, increases the sense of that environment's solid existence. Games such as Omikron: The Nomad Soul or Eden, meanwhile, create ever more stunning *Blade Runner* and *Judge Dredd*-style cityscapes whose furniture and surfaces are increasingly interactive in new symbolic ways.

Currently, the third-person game – for instance Tomb Raider, Metal Gear Solid or Zelda 64 – has the edge over the first-person game such as Quake III, which shows a perspectival viewpoint as if you were actually *in* the digital environment. Although it might initially look as if the latter genre should be the more involving, since the illusion is that you are really there, it is almost always less symbolically rich. This limitation derives directly, in fact, from the artificially narrow view angle in such games, and also from the observation that without stereoscopic vision (our two eyes receiving slightly different images in real life) it is much harder to judge depth. Therefore, symbolic interoperation through space is severely limited.

The fun of Turok: Dinosaur Hunter was thus compromised by passages which required the player to make precise jumps, platform-style – yet in a game where you can't see your own feet, such jumps are impossible to judge properly. Equally, however, there are problems in the other direction: third-person games present the rather chancy challenge of aiming weapons in three-dimensional space without giving the player true line-of-sight. Tomb Raider relies on an alienating auto-aiming system, where you just stand there hoping to hit the enemy, while Zelda 64 enables you perhaps too easily to 'lock on' to a monster, and swings the camera right behind the player's character. These examples confirm that gameplay requirements must *always* take account of the particular virtues and limitations of the chosen spatial style and representation.

The example of precision-jumping in Turok partakes of another formal phenomenon which needs to be seriously questioned: unfair challenge. By this I mean either a procedure that, as in Turok, is maddeningly hard to perform simply because the player is not given enough (visual and spatial) information, or more generally a difficulty that is not organically related to and coherent with the rest of the virtual world.

One good example of this, again, is in the Resident Evil games: the quite arbitrary restriction on inventory that we saw in Chapter 3. How much stuff you can carry is illogically determined – a herb takes up as much space as a shotgun – and you can only drop items in special chests. This rule results in incredibly tedious item-swapping and back-tracking between item boxes – a task of absolutely no symbolic interest. It's like filing, or stacking supermarket shelves. Such unfair challenges are purely the result of laziness and lack of imagination: it's a very *easy* way to make the game harder. Similarly, many levels in Tomb Raider II were made arbitrarily more difficult simply by dropping in more guys with machine guns to take a pop at Lara. Making the game harder by thinking up new and interesting gameplay challenges is clearly a more demanding job, but it's going to be far more rewarding to the player.

A more widespread example is the knotty issue of saving games. Most modern videogames that are not predicated upon pure adrenalin-fuelled action require a total of between twenty and sixty hours' play to be completed. Sensibly, the player is not expected to do this all in one go; the current position in the game may be saved to disk, or to a 'memory card'. But often, the process of saving is made into another thoroughly arbitrary hurdle. Tomb Raider III, for example, only allows the player to save when he or she has collected the appropriate power-up, a blue save-crystal, and they are frustratingly few and far between.

Again, it's an easy (for the designers) but incoherent way to make the game more challenging. Saving a videogame should be just like pausing a videotape. The save-crystal (or, in Resident Evil, the typewriter ribbon) is also an unwarranted extra rip in the fabric of the game universe. For this power-up doesn't mean anything in the fictional gameworld. The fact that I have to stop playing now because I'm going out has nothing whatsoever to do with Lara's universe. After all, Lara doesn't know who I am – she doesn't even acknowledge my existence. That is precisely why, for some, she is inexhaustibly desirable.

The moral maze

Desire and fear: our twin primal responses to fire, from the moment Prometheus first unveiled his spark to humans' dumbstruck eyes. Fires burn in hell, yet also in purgatory and in heaven;* heretics are burned at the stake, yet a bonfire is a means of celebration. Many ancient cultures, such as the Zoroastrians or Assyrians, worshipped fire as a god. Fire is the perfect representative of the Romantic sublime: at once beautiful and terrifying.

Videogames so far have not moved far beyond the twin poles of attraction and repulsion – these reptilian emotions, age-old reflexes buried deep in the brain. But this too might change. In the future, for example, videogames should be cleverly designed so as to make you live with the consequences of your actions. Take Goldeneye. The game's mission structure is rather artificially limited: if you accidentally (or deliberately) allow your Russian hacker-babe sidekick Natalya to be fatally shot, you are forced to play that mission again and again until she emerges unscathed to join you in the next operation. It would surely be much more interesting, however, if the game just continued anyway no matter what you had done, so that you had cause to bewail your failure to protect her ever more strongly as you struggled to reprogram the satellite yourself (this would then be a difficult, but not impossible, task). The old-style scrolling shooter Metal Slug already has a rudimentary version of such a 'consequences' system: if your plane is shot down, the game doesn't instantly stop; instead, you get captured and have to fight your way out of prison.

This idea could eventually induce a gnawing sense of personal guilt that is not evoked by novels or films, where we pity or regret the fates of characters who remain distinctly 'other people'. Outcast, as we saw, has made some steps towards this system of moral causation, yet it simply requires the player to

---

* For example, Milton's 'Heav'nly fires' in *Paradise Lost* xii.256; Shakespeare's 'the fires of heaven' in *Coriolanus* I.iv.39.

rebuild his or her reputation after an act of foolish violence, so mistakes can in effect be erased.

Enriching this idea, if attempted, will not be a trivial design task. It would only come to work properly if the paradigm of replayability were abandoned, for as Alain and Frédéric Le Diberder argue, if you are able to wind back to a stage before your error, you have not made a moral decision but simply explored a branch of a system. So videogame creators interested in a new moral architecture would need to somehow create a template for action that doesn't stop, yet still offers the adrenalin thrill of physical danger or swordplay and fire-fights. One way to do this has been suggested by the fascinating though flawed Soul Reaver (1999). The player's character is a vampire called Raziel. When he dies, you do not start again from the last safe point; instead, you shift into the 'spectral realm', the same environments with a twisted, Boschian air, where you continue playing and find previously inexistent pathways to new areas.

In order to increase the player's possible emotional involvement, moreover, non-player characters who may be wounded or killed will need to be more fully characterised (dynamically and iconically), so that the player comes to care about them as ends in themselves, rather than just selfishly regretting their demise because it spoils the game. The Final Fantasy series of role-playing games, while not to everyone's taste, is certainly at the forefront of this sort of approach, yet its major scenes of emotional drama are still prescribed – presented simply for the player to watch. The inevitability of the prescribed FMV fatally draws the sting of the emotional event, for the player knows it could not possibly have happened otherwise. Which in principle prevents basic guilt from blossoming into the more refined emotion of regret. We may be guilty about things which we simply couldn't help, but we only regret things which could have happened differently.

In videogames, regret is an easily vanquishable phantom; it operates merely as a fleeting wound that may be quickly salved. If I had timed that jump correctly, Lara wouldn't have been impaled on the spikes. So I will do it again, properly this time. In 1983, in *Mind at Play*, Geoffrey and Elizabeth Loftus wrote the following about classic arcade games: 'Computer games provide the ultimate chance to eliminate regret; all alternative worlds are available.' This is still true for the I-died-so-I'll-try-again paradigm, while the new story-based games don't even evoke true regret in the first place.

More emotionally involving is the brilliantly manipulative Metal Gear Solid, which slyly made me feel guilty for killing a woman sniper by playing a rather well-written dying scene for her and her opponent. But notice that it makes no sense to wish that you hadn't killed Sniper Wolf – that is, properly to regret your actions – because it is a task that the game demands be fulfilled before you can progress. This videogame balances adroitly on the twin horns of the emotional dilemma by having the main character, Solid Snake, bitterly decry the violent means he is forced to deploy – which, however, are exactly the symbolic gadgets (plastic explosive, grenades, machine guns, guided missiles) that one so enjoys playing with.

Metal Gear Solid, then, toys with the player's emotions in largely non-interactive ways, as a film does. The future challenge is this: if videogames choose to try to expand their nuances of emotional impact interactively, they will need to become irreversible; yet that means having a game system that is able to create an interesting and evocative story even out of really dumb decisions by the player, a huge and perhaps insurmountable challenge.

To begin to guess how videogames might become more sophisticated in the future, remember what they are already really good at. Games will never be as good as films at telling stories visually. They'll never be as good as books at weaving cerebral tapestries of ideas and human lives. But videogames are already extremely good at providing an exhilarating blast of the animal emotions. Fear and triumph – that is why you play a videogame at the moment. Jeremy Smith of Core Design points out that these fundamental pleasures can be traced right back to the beginning of the form. 'Why did we all play that stupid tennis game that used to burn lines on our screens?' he asks, chuckling. 'Because it was actually just good fun to try to beat your opponent or beat the computer at flicking this ball back.' Modern games, vastly more visually thrilling though they are, must still answer the same need. 'We play videogames because they're fun to play. You're not playing it to further your education, you're playing it as a means of leisure,' Smith emphasises.

'And the games business now over the last six or seven years has gone from being a geeky, sad anorak-person in their bedsit playing games, to being a completely accepted culture of life. You can watch videos, listen to music or play a videogame – and at the moment I think playing videogames is top of the list.'

Ashes to ashes

The jewel in the crown of what videogames offer is the aesthetic emotion of wonder.

A beautifully designed videogame invokes wonder as the fine arts do, only in a uniquely kinetic way. Because the videogame *must* move, it cannot offer the lapidary balance of composition that we value in painting; on the other hand, because it *can* move, it is a way to experience architecture, and more than that to create it, in a way with which photographs or drawings can never compete. If architecture is frozen music, then a videogame is liquid architecture. Indeed, the United Nations has funded the development of a 'virtual tour' of Notre Dame cathedral, which uses the engine (the computer code which draws 3D environments) from the first-person videogame shooter Unreal. And new technology pushes this virtue further: the PlayStation2 game Dark Cloud (2000) actually allows the player to build his or her own world, and then to explore it by walking among the constructions. This revolutionary type of videogame certainly provokes and feeds the imagination.

Meanwhile, of course, we may still wonder at the spaces designed by others. Personally, I have found some of the breathtaking environments in Tomb Raider's worlds – particularly in the second game, featuring the huge rusted ship sunk into a vaulted cavern at the bottom of the sea – to be moving in the aesthetic as well as dynamic sense. (Notice, by the way, that this sort of pleasure also depends on the game enjoying a properly designed tempo – you can only look round and smell the flowers, as it were, when there is no immediate threat in the game.)

Such videogames at their best build awe-inspiring spaces from immaterial light. They are cathedrals of fire. Now, it is true that the great cathedrals of Europe, at Rome, Chartres or Köln, purposively evoke wonder not as a purely aesthetic end in itself, but as a means to lead the spectator to humble contemplation of his or her impotence in the face of the grandeur of God. Videogames, on the other hand, represent the latest stage in the secularisation of wonder that has been abroad since the fine arts were divorced from religion and aesthetics was invented. Some people deplore this development;* others argue intriguingly that wonder has always been equally a secular instinct, providing the motivation for empirical scientific investigation.†

Wonder has always been a spur to action, whether creative or pious. Our wonder at the alien potency of fire once led us to invent a beautiful story about a renegade god whose gift to men brought him tortuous retribution. In a later age, wonder at the fiery vault of the heavens led us to refine and systematise the science of astronomy. There is no reason in principle why the wonder induced by videogames should not enjoy a similar motivational power. Early videogame designers were inspired by imagery from comics, films and paintings. Now that videogames enjoy a general popularity and pervasiveness easily comparable to those media, we should be prepared to discover that, just as Percy Bysshe Shelley was moved by wonder to write odes to the forces of nature, so future videogames might plant seeds of inspiration in people who then become painters, architects, animators or videogame designers themselves.

That is the good news, the utopian possible future. But here is the bad news, the embryonic dystopia: how videogames might

---

* See the baleful jeremiads of Roger Scruton's *An Intelligent Person's Guide to Modern Culture* (London, 1998).
† This is the argument of Robert Fisher's fascinating *Wonder, the Rainbow, and the Aesthetics of Rare Experiences* (Boston, 1999).

darken our inner lives. As an industry, videogames will have to choose which side they're on. Because videogames' powerful creative potential incurs a weighty responsibility too. To illustrate this, let me tell you one last little story about the difference between reality and simulation. It is a theme that we've seen in many different contexts: physics, artistic perspective, Japanese fishing games; it has been at the heart of some of the major arguments. But it is not just a nice intellectual puzzle.

Earlier, I described the way in which a videogame such as Time Crisis enables you to simulate the form of killing while being happily dissociated from the morality of the acts represented, because there is no actual killing going on. This in itself is an innocent phenomenon with respectable sporting forebears. But in the specific military context, it becomes a real danger. For modern hi-tech wars are increasingly fought and seen through videogame-type graphical systems. One only has to think of the disturbingly gleeful American generals of Desert Storm showing off their smart-missile videotapes, or of the television commentators on the bombing of Belgrade cooing over grainy film images of tracer-bullets and explosions – for all the world as if they were watching fireworks and no one was actually dying.

Military aircraft and tanks used by Nato now have weapons of such range that it is not at all usual to make direct visual identification of a target; instead, icons are tracked on computerised displays and weapons are locked automatically. Since attacks in Desert Storm and Serbia were fought at the greatest distance possible in order to minimise American casualties, these procedures directly caused numerous widely reported instances of friendly fire: Allied tanks were incinerated from afar; hospitals were bombed. Relying on pixels rather than eyes is perilous, because computers can malfunction, and pixels can lie.

Moreover, if the modern pilot has been trained on souped-up videogame systems, we should not be surprised if, when he is performing exactly the same actions in exactly the same computerised context but in a real war zone, he fails utterly to realise that his actions now have a very real moral content.

Behind the clean glowing lines of his computerised head-up display is an ugly mess of fire and blood. But he's just playing a game.

This constitutes a lethal failure of imagination. And it is in this way that I do think videogames must have a type of moral responsibility. Of course, we cannot blame videogames for the deaths of Serbian civilians, yet videogame-seeded technologies have contributed to the potentially alienating culture of simulation that allowed them to be killed so easily, so cleanly. I think the duty of videogames, therefore, is an imaginative one – an *aesthetic* one.

The situation at present is not thoroughly black. The future is in the balance. Some videogames, for instance, have woken up to the favours they have exchanged with war technology, and are blushing. Metal Gear Solid is an anti-war wargame that features a plot about treacherous goings-on in DARPA itself – the very defence agency that commissioned a version of Battlezone for its tank gunners all those years ago. Metal Gear Solid is also remarkable for its imaginative emphasis on stealth, and at the game's end the player is actually awarded a higher grading the fewer guards he or she has had to kill. Carmageddon, by contrast, which has the player driving around city streets mowing down pedestrians in showers of gore, is a very dull game. And in each of these cases, the aesthetic judgement is also an ethical one.

All this is not to say that we can't still want destructive fun, to blow things asunder in beautiful showers of light. But videogames have irrevocably lost their innocence. Gone, thankfully, are the days of the early 1980s when a game like Custer's Revenge could be released for the Atari VCS console. The player controlled a pixellated, tumescent Custer, and the aim was to dodge arrows and rape an Indian woman by repeatedly pressing the fire button.

A relative maturity of the type which Metal Gear Solid displays is becoming more pervasive, evident in watered-down form even in very simple high-speed arcade shooting games such as Silent Scope or Time Crisis 2. The player in such games is always cast, not as a violent gun-toting maniac, but as a law-enforcing agent of national security. The fictional calculus of letting innocent hostages die versus killing terrorists thus in some small way palliates the violent form.

Meanwhile, the arcade racing game Thrill Drive displays a message to the player warning that in 'real life' he or she should drive carefully and respect other road-users. Interestingly, the game that tries so hard to be a 'realistic' simulation of careering down packed motorways at 200 mph feels the need to remind the player that it is only a digital fantasy – it's not real, after all. Videogames will become more interesting artistically if they abandon thoughts of recreating something that looks like the 'real' world and try instead to invent utterly novel ones that work in amazing but consistent ways – because, as we have seen throughout this book, a 'realistic' simulation is always built on a foundation of compromise anyway. And this will also be an ethical improvement, for one can revel unashamed in the joy of destruction all the more if what is being incinerated could never possibly exist.

A hint of what might be the ruling approach in the future is provided by the fact that the central processing chip in Sony's PlayStation2 console is called an 'Emotion Engine'. This is more than just a good marketing coinage; it also implies a more thoughtful approach – not towards something like an interactive novel, of course, but certainly towards videogame software that will take more chances to make the player stop and think. Videogames' loss of innocence can only be a good thing, aesthetically, as developers increasingly try to create new ways of seeing and playing in their imaginary worlds.

Prometheus gave man the tools of creation. In an alternative version of the Prometheus myth, Zeus takes his revenge on the god by persuading Hephaestus to fashion a woman, Pandora, who lets fly the world's evils out of a jar. From then on, men decide to turn their gifts against each other, by waging war. But one thing is left in Pandora's receptacle: hope.

Whether our digital fire is turned to destructive or creative purposes is still up to us. Let's say to videogame designers: don't bore us, don't alienate us; feed our sense of wonder. Videogames etch memorable, high-speed imagery on to millions of retinas in the industrialised nations. They are rewiring our minds. This is both an opportunity and a danger. If videogames continue to plough clichéd visual and formal ruts, they will furnish the anomic mental landscape of an impoverished and unimaginative future generation, not only of artists but of people in general.

Which is why it is so important for videogames to continue aiming at creative revolution, in any number of wonderful and strange directions. The story of the inner life of videogames is not just a disinterested analysis; it's a challenge, a gauntlet. For it is an inevitable consequence of their extraordinary success that videogames will shape the worlds that we all inhabit tomorrow.

ACHNOWLEDGEMENTS

Eat pixels, sucker: this book grew out of an orphaned article to which Stuart Jeffries kindly gave a home. I am grateful to everyone who agreed to be interviewed: Paul Topping, Richard Darling, Jeremy Smith, Olivier Masclef, Nolan Bushnell, Terry Pratchett and Sam Houser.

David Palfrey saved crucial passages of the manuscript from themselves. Jason Thompson phlegmatically suffered innumerable defeats at Tekken 3 and Gran Turismo, but turned the tables in Bushido Blade. He and Kate Barker also made constructive comments on the text. Thanks are also due to Chris Arrowsmith and Rev. Stuart Campbell for expert debugging.

Dr Mark Griffiths and Maugan Lloyd generously provided psychology material, Gavin Rees was a most hospitable guide to Tokyo, and I enjoyed useful conversations with Caspar Field, Mike Goldsmith, André Tabrizifar and Teresa Grant. My agent, Zoe Waldie, has been an oasis of profound calm and encouragement.

Trigger Happy owes its subtitle and much else besides to the incisive attentions of its editor, Andy Miller: *il miglior fabbro*.

Any infelicities or errors that remain I acknowledge mine. Readers are invited to email comments for future editions to: trighap@hotmail.com

S. P., *London*
November 1999

BIBLIOGRAPHY

In addition to the works cited below I have found useful several non-bylined articles and reviews in the excellent monthly videogame magazine *Edge. Arcade* and *MCV* magazines have also been useful sources of industry reporting.

Adorno, Theodor & Benjamin, Walter, *The Complete Correspondence 1928–1940*, ed. Henri Lonitz, tr. Nicholas Walker (Oxford: 1999)

Amis, Martin, *Invasion of the Space Invaders* (London: 1982)

Aono, Teruichi, 'Shogi as Culture', at http://www.shogi.or.jp/english/aono/sasc1.htm

Avedon, Elliott M. & Sutton-Smith, Brian, *The Study of Games* (New York: 1971)

Benedikt, Michael (ed.), *Cyberspace: First Steps* (1991; Cambridge, Mass.: 1994)

Benjamin, Walter, 'The work of art in the age of mechanical reproduction' (1935), in Mast, Cohen & Braudy (eds), *Film Theory and Criticism* (Oxford: 1992)

Cassell, Justine & Jenkins, Henry (eds), *From Barbie to Mortal Kombat: Gender and Computer Games* (Cambridge, Mass.: 1998)

Crawford, Chris, *The Art of Computer Game Design* (Berkeley: 1984)

Csikszentmihalyi, Mihaly, *Flow: the Psychology of Optimal Experience* (1990; New York: 1991)

Faber, Liz, *Re:play: Ultimate Games Graphics* (London: 1998)

Bibliography

Foucault, Michel, 'Des espaces autres', in *Architecture-Mouvement-Continuité* (Paris: October 1984)

Gibson, William, *Neuromancer* (1984; London: 1995)

Gombrich, E. H., *Art and Illusion: a Study in the Psychology of Pictorial Representation* (1960; London: 1996)

——, *The Story of Art* (1950; London: 1983)

Greenfield, Patricia, *Media and the Mind of the Child: from Print to Television, Video Games and Computers* (Harvard: 1984)

Griffiths, Mark, 'Video games and children's behaviour', in *Elusive Links* (1997)

Hamilton, Robert, 'Virtual idols and digital girls: artifice and sexuality in anime, kisekae and Kyoko Date', in *Bad Subjects* 35 (1997), at http://english-www.hss.cmu.edu/BS/35/hamilton.html

Heidegger, Martin, 'The question concerning technology', in Lovitt, William (ed. & tr.), *The Question Concerning Technology and Other Essays* (New York: 1977)

Herman, Leonard, *Phoenix: the Fall and Rise of Videogames* (Union: 1998)

Herz, J. C., *Joystick Nation* (1996; London: 1997)

Huizinga, Johann, *Homo Ludens: a Study of the Play-Element in Culture* (1944; London: 1980)

Hume, Nancy G., *Japanese Aesthetics and Culture* (New York: 1995)

Kinder, Marsha, *Playing with Power in Movies, Television, and Video Games from Muppet Babies to Teenage Mutant Ninja Turtles* (Berkeley: 1991)

Krauss, Lawrence M., *The Physics of Star Trek* (1995; London: 1996)

Le Diberder, Alain & Frédéric, *L'Univers des Jeux Vidéo* (Paris: 1998)

Lloyd, Maugan, 'Screen violence and aggressive behaviour: an

Bibliography

illustration of the difficulty in statistical verification of a possible causal link' (unpublished thesis, Edinburgh University: 1998)

Loftus, Geoffrey R. & Elizabeth F., *Mind at Play: the Psychology of Video Games* (New York: 1983)

Martinez, D. P. (ed.), *The Worlds of Japanese Popular Culture* (Cambridge: 1998)

Parlett, David, *The Oxford History of Board Games* (Oxford: 1999)

Peirce, C. S., *The Essential Peirce: Selected Philosophical Writings, Volume 1 (1867–1893)*, eds Houser & Kloesel (Indianapolis: 1992)

——, *The Essential Peirce: Selected Philosophical Writings, Volume 2 (1893–1913)*, ed. Peirce Edition Project (Indianapolis: 1998)

Plato, *Timaeus*, ed. & tr. Desmond Lee (Harmondsworth: 1977)

——, *Laws*, ed. & tr. Thomas L. Pangle (Chicago: 1998)

Propp, Vladimir, *Morphology of the Folktale* (1928; London: 1968)

Sale, Kirkpatrick, *Rebels Against the Future: Lessons for the Computer Age* (1995; London: 1996)

Satô, Ikuya, *Kamikaze Biker: Parody and Anomy in Affluent Japan* (Chicago: 1991)

Schwarz, Frederic D., 'The patriarch of Pong', in *Invention and Technology* (autumn 1990), and at http: //www.fas.org/cp/pong–fas.htm

Sheff, David, *Game Over: Nintendo's Battle to Dominate Videogames* (London: 1993)

Tabrizifar, André, *The Transparent Head* (Cambridge: 1991)

Wittgenstein, Ludwig, *Tractatus Logico-Philosophicus* (1921; London: 1992)

Zielinski, Siegfried, *Audiovisions: Cinema and Television as Entr'actes in History* (Amsterdam: 1999)

AFTERWORD

So what happened next? No great revolution in fact occurred in the videogame industry during the year 2000. It was largely a year of waiting: the current generation of consoles drew near to the end of their useful lives, the share prices of hotly tipped publishers such as Eidos tumbled, and the gaming population waited for a new generation of hardware to fulfil companies' grandiose promises.

Sony's PlayStation2 launched in Japan in February, shifting an astonishing 980,000 units on its first weekend. This was not just the biggest ever launch of a videogame console; it was the biggest launch of any consumer electronics device in history. Soon, however, it became apparent that the games available were not getting anyone very excited; most consumers were buying the PlayStation2 for its DVD movie-playback facilities instead. This, of course, would not have worried the company that wants to 'own the living room'. PlayStation2 was acting perfectly as a silicon Trojan horse, inveigling itself into the home under false pretences in order eventually to bring videogaming to the unsuspecting masses. And yet by the time that PlayStation2 launched in Britain in November, its line-up of launch software was no more exciting: a few tarted-up old PlayStation games with prettier graphics, another WipEout game, a decent, though hardly earth-shattering, first-person shooter.

PlayStation2 certainly did not represent the big bang that some were expecting, and it only served to demonstrate the point that an increase in processing power does not instantly entail better gameplay. So that while other companies lined up to announce their own next-generation hardware – Microsoft's

X-Box console, which ought eventually to sound the death-knell for PC gaming, and Nintendo's GameCube – the most successful videogame phenomenon of the year was running on hardware by now nearly 12 years old: the Game Boy.

This phenomenon was Pokémon, the game of nurturing and training pocket monsters that became an extraordinary worldwide success. Over six days in August, the Pokémon Yellow game sold a million copies across Europe. A survey of British teenagers found that they were more likely to recognise Pikachu, the cute yellow mascot of the Pokémon franchise, than Tony Blair, the cute pink mascot of the Labour government. Worldwide, Pokémon grossed $15 billion over the year, and Nintendo continued to manufacture 2,000 Game Boys every hour. With their crude, two-dimensional graphics, the Poké-mon games none the less managed to fascinate an enormous number of people in a way that any number of cutting-edge 3D engines failed to do. This can be attributed entirely to two of our virtues of good games: a sophisticated engine of semiotic play, and a collection of well-designed and likeable characters.

One of the few left-field successes of the year was a game that, essentially, rendered the Pokémon concept in a more humor-ous, adult and pseudo-'realistic' style. The Sims, the new work from Will Wright, the author of SimCity, requires the player to manage a household full of gorgeously animated people who seem to have their own autonomous wills. They flirt, fight, clean up, or sulk all by themselves as the player watches. Your job is to change their environment to their advantage and help them succeed in the careers you choose for them; but you can also set up deliberately fraught love triangles and chuckle over fights in the chintzy living room.

The Sims, by genre a God game, computerises exactly the kind of voyeuristic fascination that led to the television pro-gramme *Big Brother* becoming such a huge success on both sides of the Atlantic, with the added attraction that you can meddle directly with the environment. As an open-ended pro-cess toy that attempts to simulate complex social interactions and affords the player great freedom in her actions, it also became very popular among women: numerous testimonials on the internet and in weekend newspapers described how women who had always previously been bored by videogames found themselves thoroughly addicted to the management of their Sims household.

The Sims also, however, exemplifies the rule that any attempted 'recreation' of the social world inside a videogame is predicated upon a set of moral and political assumptions. In this game, consumerism is the preferred religion: much of the gameplay centres on buying new things for the Sims' house in order to increase its inhabitants' happiness (such as a large mirror, which will boost their charisma, or a new cooker, which will help them cook meals for their housemates and so become more popular), and in helping them climb the slippery pole of a career as a politician or scientist. More money makes a Sim happier; social dissidents are not allowed. Once more, we reach a stratum in videogame design where certain gameplay possibilities have been ruled out by the assumptions buried deep in its structure.

This will, for the foreseeable future, continue to be the case. Even in the very ambitious Republic, a forthcoming game that promises to simulate revolutionary politics in a life-sized eastern European city, there is a fundamental assumption, according to one of the designers at London's Elixir Studios, that everyone is cynically self-interested and power-hungry. That still represents a certain angle, a necessarily partial explanation of how the world works, although it seems a more potentially fruitful and provocative starting point than the Sims philosophy. Simplification in videogame design, as we have seen, is not only inevitable but desirable. But you must choose your simplifications carefully.

Though true 'artificial intelligence' is still very much in its computational infancy, it remains one of the key buzzwords of the videogame industry. Every bog-standard driving game or first-person shooter that comes along claims to have revolutionary AI in its computer-controlled opponents. What this still means, though, is quite the opposite: the computerised opponents are dressed up in a kind of artificial stupidity. Given that a silicon chip can perform precise calculations far faster than a human can, it ought always to beat a human player in games requiring quick, accurate responses. So its skills have to be ramped down in order to simulate typically human failings, rather than ramped up in order to simulate human cleverness.

The best videogame AI to date appears in the keenly anticipated Black and White, a God game that allows you to nurture and teach a creature who evolves uniquely according to your style of play: his behaviour and physical appearance come to mirror the balance of your moral decisions through the game. One of very few products that seeks to push the envelope of videogame concepts, Black and White nevertheless still comes up against the inherent problem of reversible systems. Although your moral decisions have global effects in the gameworld – let your worshippers drown, or destroy them with fireballs, and the remaining population worships you ever more fervently out of fear, while the environment changes to reflect your evildoing – they are, in the end, reversible. Start being nice, and everything will eventually be all right again. Some people argue, indeed, that the designers have failed to make being an evil god sufficiently interesting – you'll eventually choose the path of good after toying with wickedness. That also testifies, however, to the excellent iconic and dynamic design of the little people who worship you: like lemmings, they are so cute that it hurts to see them suffer.

Black and White's amiable, soft-spoken creator, Peter Molyneux, claimed bullishly to me that his creature AI was 'the best in the world, anywhere' – including the university research labs that he is regularly invited to visit. While it is still light-years from the simulation of a communicative consciousness inside a machine, it represents a major step on the path to providing a more dramatically interesting, and even emotionally involving, virtual world.

Another innovative aspect of Black and White is in its cybernetics: every aspect of play is controlled with the mouse, using a highly intuitive 'gestural system'. With this, you can stroke your creature, teach him how to play with balls, or smack him if he takes an unhealthy interest in his own excrement.

Systems of control are, of course, crucial to the success of videogames, and such imaginative new control engines can open up novel gameplay possibilities. There was a certain disappointment, then, as Nintendo unveiled the controllers for its forthcoming GameCube system – they feature nothing more than a now-standard set of buttons plus two analogue sticks. More cybernetically creative was a concept display by Sony at the September 2000 ECTS trade fair, which featured an ordinary web-cam plugged into a PlayStation2. Thanks to internal processing of the web-cam's visual image, the player could wield a big foam sword or other object and have its movements accurately mirrored in real time by the object's onscreen sibling.

While such cybernetic innovations hold out tantalising possibilities for the future, one aspect of videogaming that drew ever greater interest during 2000 was networked multiplayer action, either over wired systems or online. Full-time gamers, such as Britain's Sujoy Roy, can now earn £200,000 a year by travelling the world playing Quake III in organised tournaments. Japanese videogame giant Sega sought to reposition itself as an online gaming company, after its Dreamcast console was almost suffocated by a lack of top-class software support.

So far, Dreamcast is still the only home console that comes internet-ready, but networked videogaming is already huge among the PC-owning population. Professional gamers' leagues are in place in Britain and America, as well as much of Asia, and the BBC launched a television gameshow, *Bleeding Thumbs*, that featured teams competing in bouts of Unreal Tournament. Far-sighted individuals such as Edward Watson, manager of The Playing Fields videogame bar in London, see no reason why in future such videogames should not be officially recognised as sports in their own right. 'Take away what's physically happening,' Watson told me, waving his arm around the neon-lit basement den of The Playing Fields, 'and you couldn't tell the difference between what's going on here and a professional sports tournament. The tactics that can be employed in a videogame are as varied as those that can be employed in any game.' Indeed, action videogames of this type might eventually come to represent a revolutionary democratisation of the nature of sport. Laurels are no longer determined simply by the tyranny of genes. Women and men, able-bodied and otherwise, can compete on a level playing field, a digital city of play where all are equal before the games begin.

This book was written from the assumption that it makes sense to talk about videogames in artistic terms – not in order to argue that games already constitute a fully fledged artform, but in order to point out the potential for such an eventual blossoming. But videogames are still struggling to emerge from their arrested adolescence.

Over the last year there have been ever more examples of this aesthetic stasis: the incoherent behaviour of complex systems in driving or exploration games; the simplistic and eventually tedious semiotics of shooting or platform-jumping, and the slavish plagiarism of the same old cinema aesthetics – slimy biomechanoid spaceship interiors, moodily lit warehouses, rocky dungeons and sandy dunes. Moreover, games still try to tell cinematic stories, though in principle they cannot; and a bad story bolted on to a game is often worse than none at all.

One of the most eagerly awaited videogames of 2000 had been Perfect Dark, an espionage-themed first-person shooter by the same company that made Goldeneye. But this supposed 'spiritual sequel' to the superb Bond adaptation failed to live up to its hype: it was compromised as a single-player game by numerous faults identified throughout this book. Play was bookended by a panoply of badly written and nastily animated narrative cut-scenes; the lazy sci-fi fetishism of its character design, in PVC-clad heroine Joanna Dark, was a blatant and doomed attempt to steal the thunder of Lara Croft; incoherencies of function and space abounded; and the game's inadequate temporal resolution – owing to a wrongheaded choice to privilege visual detail over frame-rate – made it unplayable at higher difficulty levels.

A revolution isn't made in a day. With the advent of the next generation of hardware, videogame designers do have a broader canvas to work on. But they could easily continue to paint the same old compromised clichés in prettier colours; and, as in any cultural form, most of them probably will. The innovators and artists, however, need to follow a different path. And so this book's challenge remains the same. Videogames

can only continue to thrive and evolve as long as they concentrate on what they do best: build us ever more realistic
constructions of ever more aesthetically wondrous worlds.

S. P., London
September 2000

INDEX

Index

Index

Index

Index

Index

PHANTOMS IN THE BRAIN
Human Nature and the Architecture of the Mind

V. S. Ramachandran & Sandra Blakeslee

A combination of gripping stories and cutting edge science that reveals many of the big questions concerning our consciousness.

'One of the most original and accessible neurology books of our generation.' Oliver Sacks

'*Phantoms in the Brain* is one of the funniest and most original books on neurology ever written.' *Guardian*

1 85702 895 3   £8.99

THE CODE BOOK
The Secret History of Codes & Code-breaking

Simon Singh

Since humans began writing they have also been communicating in code. In *The Code Book*, Simon Singh reveals, through thrilling stories of espionage, intrigue, intellectual brilliance and military cunning, the gripping history of cryptography.

'It is hard to imagine a more enthralling book.'
Independent

1 85702 889 9   £7.99

THE MAN WHO LOVED ONLY NUMBERS
Paul Hoffman

The extraordinary life of Paul Erdos, a man obsessed by mathematics from an early age. For six decades he had no job, no hobbies, no wife, no home. Travelling until his death at 83, he raced across four continents to prove as many theorems as possible, fuelled by a diet of espresso and amphetamines, earning himself a reputation for being one of the most prolific and eccentric mathematicians in history.

'Hoffman's vibrant biography is full of warmth and enthusiasm, displaying Erdos's genius, curious singlemindedness, humanity and humour.'
Scotsman

1 85702 829 5   £7.99

MY TINY LIFE
Julian Dibbell

Crime and passion in a virtual world – *My Tiny Life* is an utterly compelling journey into a virtual Garden of Good and Evil, into a perfect, miniature universe, at the moment when it is irreversibly doomed.

'A gnostic parable of a fall from nirvana.' *i-D*

1 84115 057 6   £6.99

HARE BRAIN, TORTOISE MIND
Guy Claxton

There are two ways of thinking: the crisp, clear, business-like thought of the hare brain and the contemplative tortoise mind. Claxton argues that we should learn to trust the tortoise. It can't fail to win when it has intuition and inspiration at its command.

'Claxton, a well-read experimental psychologist, backs up anecdotal studies of creativity with up-to-date information about the latest research into brain function. The result is a fascinating book which told me many things I ought to know but didn't. I am hugely grateful to him.'
Times Educational Supplement

1 85702 709 4   £7.99

BRING HOME THE REVOLUTION
Jonathan Freedland

A radical reassessment of modern America that looks beyond the tired clichés of a nation riddled by race and crime and argues that the dreams of many contemporary British reformers are reality in America. Now is the moment to apply them at home in the UK.

'Freedland is developing into the Orwell of our times: a humane revolutionary who can change the world through his pen.' Will Hutton

1 84115 021 5   £6.99

NEW RULES FOR THE NEW ECONOMY
Kevin Kelly

A mould-breaking look at the future of business economics from the executive editor of *Wired*, in which he argues that the digital revolution has created a new networked economy that spurns the traditional business wisdoms and craves innovation, imagination and originality.

'It sounds absurd, defying the laws of capital and conventional economics. But Kevin Kelly has just published a compelling guide to just such a world.'
The Times

1 85702 892 9 £7.99

FERMAT'S LAST THEOREM
Simon Singh

The extraordinary story of a riddle that confounded the world's greatest minds for 358 years, and how an Englishman, after years of secret toil, finally solved mathematic's most challenging problem.

'A magnificent story, one told with infectious enthusiasm. If you enjoyed *Longitude* you will enjoy this.'
Evening Standard

'Singh judges to perfection the level of detail needed to grasp the magnitude of Wiles's achievement – the fascination of pure mathematics has never been more effectively conveyed to the general readership.'
Daily Telegraph

1 85702 669 1 £6.99

GENOME
The Autobiography of a Species in 23 Chapters
Matt Ridley

By picking one newly discovered gene from each of the 23 pairs of human chromosomes and telling its story, Matt Ridley recounts the history of our species and its ancestors from the dawn of life to the brink of future medicine.

'What better way to tell the story of what it means to be human than through the story of these 23 pairs of tiny molecules? It's a brilliant idea and, as with all of Ridley's books, it is wonderfully executed.'
Evening Standard

1 85702 835 X   £8.99

DRAGONFLY
Bryan Burrough

On 12 February 1997, two Russian cosmonauts joined an American astronaut for a routine test mission on board the only permanent manned outpost in space, the dilapidated, eleven-year-old Mir space station. Within two weeks they were fighting the worst fire in the history of space travel – an epic, six-month misadventure that would climax in the most harrowing accident in space since Apollo 13.

'The most definitive account of the mistakes and mismanagement that consistently jeopardised the world's only working space station . . . utterly compelling.'
Observer

1 84115 088 6   £7.99

All Fourth Estate books are available from your local bookshop,
or can be ordered direct from:

Fourth Estate, Book Service By Post, PO Box 29,
Douglas, I-O-M, IM99 1BQ

Credit cards accepted.

Tel: 01642 675137   Fax: 01624 670923
Internet: http://www.bookpost.co.uk
e-mail: bookshop@enterprise.net

Visit the Fourth Estate website at:
www.4thestate.co.uk

Please state when ordering if you do **not** *wish to receive further
information about Fourth Estate titles.*